P9-AOG-749

POWER AND RESTRAINT

POWER

—— AND ——

RESTRAINT

A SHARED VISION FOR THE
U.S.–CHINA RELATIONSHIP

RICHARD ROSECRANCE AND
GU GUOLIANG, EDITORS

PUBLICAFFAIRS
New York

Copyright © 2009 Collection by Richard Rosecrance and Gu Guoliang, editors.

Published in the United States by PublicAffairs™,
a member of the Perseus Books Group.

All rights reserved.
Printed in the United States of America.

No part of this book may be reproduced in any manner whatsoever without written permission except in the case of brief quotations embodied in critical articles and reviews. For information, address PublicAffairs, 250 West 57th Street, Suite 1321, New York, NY 10107. PublicAffairs books are available at special discounts for bulk purchases in the U.S. by corporations, institutions, and other organizations. For more information, please contact the Special Markets Department at the Perseus Books Group, 2300 Chestnut Street, Suite 200, Philadelphia, PA 19103, call (800) 810-4145 ext. 5000, or e-mail special.markets @perseusbooks.com.

Book Design by Trish Wilkinson
Set in 11 point Adobe Garamond

Library of Congress Cataloging-in-Publication Data
    Power and restraint : a shared vision for the U.S.-China relationship / Richard Rosecrance and Gu Guoliang, editors — 1st ed.
p.   cm.
    Includes bibliographical references and index.
    ISBN 978-1-58648-742-3 (hardcover)
    1. United States—Relations—China. 2. China—Relations—United States.
I. Rosecrance, Richard N. II. Guoliang, Gu.
JZ1480.A57C67 2009
303.48'273051—dc22   2008043623

First Edition

10 9 8 7 6 5 4 3 2 1

CONTENTS

Foreword • C. H. Tung
    A U.S.-Chinese Perspective   *vii*

Introduction • Graham Allison
    Keeping China and the United States Together   *xi*

PART ONE: GENERAL PERSPECTIVES

CHAPTER ONE • *Ernest R. May and Zhou Hong*
    A Power Transition and Its Effects   3

CHAPTER TWO • *Joseph S. Nye and Wang Jisi*
    The Rise of China's Soft Power and Its
    Implications for the United States   23

CHAPTER THREE • *Lawrence Lau, Mingchun Sun, Victor Fung,*
David K. Richards, and Richard Rosecrance
    U.S.-China Economic Interactions: Trade, Finance,
    and Economic Modernization   35

CHAPTER FOUR • *Chen Zhiya and Ashton B. Carter*
    Shaping China-U.S. Military Relations   45
    Comments on Chen Zhiya's "Shaping China-U.S.
    Military Relations"   61

CHAPTER FIVE • *Etel Solingen*
    Economic and Political Liberalization in China:
    Implications for U.S.-China Relations   67

CHAPTER SIX • *Tony Saich*
China and the United States as Interacting Societies 79

CHAPTER SEVEN • *Yu Keping*
Strengthening the Strategic Dialogue between China and the
United States on Core Political Values 95

PART TWO: PROBLEM AREAS

CHAPTER EIGHT • *Xu Shiquan and Ezra F. Vogel*
Dampening the Taiwanese Flash Point 107

CHAPTER NINE • *Pan Jiahua and Kelly Sims Gallagher*
Global Warming: The Road to Restraint 119

CHAPTER TEN • *Yang Jiemian and Graham Allison*
Avoiding Crisis between the Two Great Powers 137
Comments on Yang Jiemian's "From Crisis Management to
Strategic Cooperation" 153

CHAPTER ELEVEN • *Gu Guoliang and Steven E. Miller*
Arms Control and the Spread of Weapons of
Mass Destruction 163

CHAPTER TWELVE • *Zhang Yunling and Alan S. Alexandroff*
Cooperation in Governance: The Regional Dimension
in a U.S.-China Shared Vision for the Future 179

CHAPTER THIRTEEN • *Jia Qingguo and Richard Rosecrance*
U.S.-Chinese Interactions over Time 197

Conclusions • *Richard Rosecrance and Wang Jisi*
The United States and China Together? 207
Notes 213
About the Contributors 233
Index 241

A U.S.-CHINESE PERSPECTIVE

C. H. Tung

If the twentieth century was shaped by the conflicts of great powers, the twenty-first century will be shaped by how we, the human race, can successfully take on the challenges of energy security, climate change, food security, and scarcity of natural resources, all of which are issues crucial to sustainable development and economic growth in the new century. Beyond the aforementioned challenges, the world continues to face the threat of nuclear weapons proliferation, transnational terrorism, and localized conflicts. It is also urgent to improve global efforts to prevent epidemimcs and the drug trade. Finally, there is a need to push for further globalization of the world economy and to create an international financial system. There is also an urgency to improve global efforts on epidemic prevention and drug trade eradication. Today, the world yearns for peace, stability, and sustainable development, but never has the world been faced with so many transnational challenges coming together all at the same time. To successfully overcome these challenges, multilateral cooperation by the international community, particularly by its major powers, is critical.

The United States is the most developed and strongest nation in the world. China is the largest and fastest developing nation. In the multilateral effort to overcome these challenges, a good and productive relationship between the United States and China is essential. Indeed, no bilateral relationship among major powers today would be more crucial in shaping global order and agenda than the one between China and the United States.

Although there is general consensus among scholars and political commentators on the importance of the China-United States relationship, it remains controversial as to whether the relationship will become more congruent or more conflictual in the coming years.

The recent rise of China's power and influence in global affairs has ignited heated discussions in the United States. There are those in the United States who propose a "hedging strategy" aimed at preparing for conflict with China as well as engaging it for cooperation. The idea of hedging against China, however, runs an enormous risk of fostering a negative Chinese reaction, which would in turn affect U.S. interests. Meanwhile, other American and Chinese observers see more opportunities for the two great nations to broaden the scope of cooperation, although they do not necessarily underestimate the difficulties in avoiding confrontation.

Motivated by a strong desire to more clearly identify the common interests—and possibly shared values—of China and the United States, and intrigued by the intellectual challenges in doing so, a group of some of the most distinguished Chinese and American scholars, each an expert in his or her own respective field, has conducted a major research project that dates back to the fall of 2006. Coming from such diverse scholarly areas as politics, economics, international security, international relations, and environmental studies, they gathered together in three plenary sessions, held respectively in Hong Kong in March 2007, in Beijing in December 2007, and at Harvard University in Cambridge, Massachusetts, in February 2008.

This volume is a product of this fruitful collaboration that involved not only conferences and writings but also informal communications, candid exchange of ideas, and, where possible, consensus building. Some of the chapters are the result of joint efforts between Chinese and American scholars. In cases where joint articles were not deemed practical, authors express their views individually. Whether working in collaboration or separately, all of the authors called for better mutual understanding between China and the United States so as to allow both nations to better cope with common challenges.

Never before in my long business and political career have I been involved with such serious and stimulating academic debates on issues of such political significance. As an enthusiastic participant in and staunch supporter of this project, I feel more optimistic about China-United States relations today than during the time prior to this initiative. My optimism is not simply due to the fact that the process has helped to narrow the perception gap between the Chinese and American participants but because of the friendly and productive spirit in which the discussions were conducted. In truth, it was an inspiring process. The more opportunities we have in holding such dialogues, and the more widely the strategic visions reflected in this volume are shared, the higher hopes we can hold for a healthier China-United States relationship in the future. Indeed, never before has the world needed a strong China-United States relationship as much as it does today.

Needless to say, I congratulate all the contributors in this book for their achievements, but our acknowledgements should be extended to a much longer list of institutions and individuals who made the project possible and successful. Special thanks go to Victor Fung, vice chair of the China-United States Exchange Foundation and chair of the Asia Center Advisory Board of Harvard University, who instrumentally initiated this project and enthusiastically supported it every step of the way. We also thank Harvard University's Kennedy School of Government, in particular its dean, David Ellwood, and Lawrence Summers; the Chinese Academy of Social Sciences, particularly its Institute of American Studies, headed by Huang Ping; Peking University's School of International Studies, and Yuan Ming, as well as many others.

KEEPING CHINA AND THE UNITED STATES TOGETHER

Graham Allison

Two Great Powers usually have a difficult relationship. Each seeks more power or economic strength than the other. If one power is rising and the other is already ascendant, their relations are typically tense or hostile. Very rarely has the rising power surpassed the established leader without conflict, and usually it has involved military confrontation. We all know that the United States surpassed Great Britain after 1890 without fighting a war (see Chapter 1). But the tension between Britain and a rising German empire grew and finally led to war in 1914. In the 1930s, Soviet economic growth and the emergence of Nazi Germany pitted two rising powers against one another. They fought a devastating war from 1941 to 1945, killing over 30 million men and women. The United States and the Soviet Union waged a cold war from 1945 to 1991 driven by military, economic, and ideological competition. Though it did not lead to direct war, the superpowers came close to conflict on more than one occasion. When Japanese growth rates exceeded those of the United States in the 1980s, many expected Japan to become "number 1"; some experts forecast that the strains would worsen and even end in conflict.[1]

In the twenty-first century, the United States and China are destined to be the largest and strongest powers in the international system. China's rise has been proclaimed to be "peaceful," but in a prior century the American rise was scarcely pacific. The United States threatened war with Canada and Britain and actually fought against Mexico, annexing nearly half of that country in 1848. China was also vigilant and quick to react in its neighborhood. As U.S. forces neared the Yalu River in October 1950, China intervened in the Korean War, even though the United States possessed nuclear weapons and Beijing did not. Neither state has been relaxed in the presence of challenging neighbors.

Nonetheless, it is possible—and perhaps likely—that the rise of China can be accommodated by the United States and that the two countries can have peaceful and even cooperative relationships in the next generation. This can be achieved, however, only if two conditions are met: (1) the United States and China must share vital interests, and (2) both governments (aided by their societies) must act positively to create a cooperative relationship. Merely relying on "business as usual" in economic or military interactions will not suffice to produce this outcome.

U.S.-Chinese relations are much deeper and more multifarious than were U.S.-Soviet ones. U.S.-Soviet connections were governmental and military; they were not social. There was no pattern of economic interdependence. The meetings of the United Nations Security Council—and its permanent members (P5)—represented a veto-ridden failure, and there were no other forums where the Great Powers could meet free from the glare of world publicity. Bilateral attempts to improve relations failed. Nikita Khrushchev made an unsuccessful visit to the United States in 1958, and the May 1960 Paris summit was cancelled after a U.S. spy plane was shot down over Soviet Russia. Khrushchev's risk-taking in Berlin and Cuba further sharpened tensions. He believed firmly that the "correlation of forces" was turning in Soviet favor.[2] When one gambit failed, he was emboldened to double the stakes and roll the dice.

In contrast, both Chinese and American leaders have been careful and respectful of one another in recent years. The United States needed Chinese help against its Cold War enemy, the Soviet Union. China and the United States developed a fragile consensus on Taiwan, elaborated in both 1972 and 1978. According to their agreement, both sides of the Taiwan Strait concur that there is but one China, and the United States does not disagree. The United States believes that force should not be used to reunify Taiwan with the mainland, and it is committed to assisting Taiwan in its defense unless Taipei unilaterally declares independence. Beijing has not foresworn the right to use force if Taiwan declares "independence" or if reunification is indefinitely delayed. The United States has favored a peaceful resolution of the conflict, but it has not actively encouraged the parties to find a solution, nor has it proposed a solution of its own. Perhaps it is time for the United States to encourage a solution, especially if discussions can be held between the two parties with few or no preconditions, as seems possible with the election of a new Pan Blue leadership in Taipei.

More important, economic relations between China and the United States are becoming so deep and interdependent that a form of "economic deterrence" may be emerging. Robert McNamara described the nuclear balance between the United States and the Soviet Union as "mutual assured destruction." It was impossible for one country to attack the other without triggering massive nuclear retaliation. Even after a first strike, the other could always strike back. This concept may have an economic analogue. Over time, the progressive interdependence of the United States and the Chinese economies could reach the point where official capital flight or trade embargoes would be so damaging that they would no longer be realistic options. In this situation, MADE (mutual assured destruction of the economy) could take its place in the lexicon of acronyms alongside MAD (mutual assured destruction of the society). In fact, MADE could be attained before MAD (China would have to greatly increase its nuclear arsenal to threaten massive retaliation). To what extent MADE exists now is a subject for further analysis.

Another significant question is the degree and process of internal reform in China. In the past, U.S. presidents have pressed for the "democratization" of the developing countries. In the Chinese case, as Etel Solingen's chapter argues, "liberalization" may be a more appropriate near term objective than "democratization," given the nationalist reactions that might be unleashed by an attempt to achieve a premature and possibly illiberal democracy.[3] Unless property rights, the rule of law, a fully developed and independent court system, an incipient group or party system, and an expanded middle class were achieved in advance, choosing a government by holding national elections could be counterproductive. It could even lead to nationalist extremism and military expansion (as occurred in the early stages of Japanese and German "democratization" in the late nineteenth century and in the 1930s). Further "liberalization" would involve completing economic reforms, dismantling state-owned enterprises (SOEs), adopting a freely fluctuating exchange rate, and establishing a pension and welfare system. Greater protection of retired workers would also reduce the need for savings and increase consumption, thereby stimulating imports.

The military relationships between China and the United States are also very important. Though the Chinese defense budget is much smaller than the U.S. budget, it has been increasing very rapidly in recent years. How much a prudent U.S. should hedge depends on Chinese intentions, which have been opaque. The United States has not sought to deny China minimum deterrent capabilities, but it has expressed concerns about China's growing threat to American mastery of the sea lanes, including the waters around Taiwan. It has also voiced concerns about Chinese measures that could endanger U.S. and GPS satellites in space. Military-to-military contacts can limit misperceptions and misunderstandings. But China faces difficult choices in developing its military arsenal without directly challenging the United States.

On the environment, China and the United States are the greatest contributors to worldwide pollution and greenhouse gases. China's installation of one new coal-fired power plant per week will worsen the situation unless carbon capture and sequestration technologies are developed and applied. In recent years China has added new generation capacity almost equal to the entire Indian power grid each year. A pragmatic response on both sides would be to form a partnership to develop new ideas and low-carbon technologies for public and private use. Catastrophic climate change may still be avoidable, but only if China and the United States both act to reduce their emissions. This would require each side to overcome the temptation to pollute while the other is reducing greenhouse gases.

The prospect of agreement on this and other issues depends on the two Great Powers concurring on (1) common objectives, and (2) common fears. The common objectives are economic growth and international stability. The common fears are global warming, international terrorism, and the spread of nuclear weapons. The potential or actual spread of nuclear weapons to Iran and North Korea must be prevented or reversed, hopefully without military intervention. China's role in the Six-Party Talks on North Korea has been critical to persuading Pyongyang to halt production of fissile material. China should join the international community in pressuring Tehran to achieve a similar result in Iran.

In the longer term, the most significant fact is that China has grown *because* of existing international institutions and values, and not despite them. China's stunning advancement has not depended upon overturning present-day realities. Unlike the recent cases of Soviet Russia and Nazi Germany, where the rationale for one dictatorial regime required overthrow of the existing system, China has so far been prepared to sustain the current system and gain further and more equal inclusion within it rather than displace it. If this remains true, there must be new informal arrangements in which Chinese and U.S. elites and their rising successors can exchange ideas and discuss means of achieving such results.

No previous Great Powers rose with the consent of their predecessors. British and German elites seriously discussed the possibility of cooperation in the 1890s, but these talks ended because of the Anglo-German naval rivalry. The United States and the Soviet Union held meetings on many subjects, but rarely did decision-makers or their associates develop social as well as political ties. Whereas Britain and the United States benefited from shared ideological, political, and cultural backgrounds, China and the United States speak different languages and exist in regions remote from one another. Their historical development has differed, though the history of both was stunted by the practice of European imperialism. Yet, perhaps surprisingly, the goals of American and Chinese citizens are remarkably similar: to pursue happiness, to provide for their families, to benefit their societies, and to enrich life for future generations.

The essential means of achieving these objectives has been different in the two cases. In the one case, the driver was economic liberalization; in the other, it was democratization as well as a market economy. It is therefore all the more important that officials, students, and rising elites meet regularly to exchange views on the state of the world, endeavoring to find common understandings of developments and perhaps even shared visions about what should be done. As was noted earlier, similarities of interest are not enough to unite two otherwise disparate societies. One has to stretch beyond routine interactions to deepen and intensify the range of common ideas and practices. We hope that the meetings, observations, and suggestions of the authors of the chapters in this volume can make some contribution to this cause.

PART ONE

GENERAL PERSPECTIVES

CHAPTER ONE

A POWER TRANSITION AND ITS EFFECTS

Ernest R. May and Zhou Hong

Bases of Relations

Historically, China has engaged American emotions more than any foreign country except Britain and Israel. Since the early nineteenth century Americans have presumed a special relationship with China.[1] Unlike other relationships, this one obviously does not stem from a common language or culture or from shared experience. It is not even based on knowledge or evident understanding. China has nonetheless kept a larger presence in the minds of Americans than have nearer nations, such as Canada or Mexico, or sometime adversaries, sometime partners, such as France, Germany, Russia, or Japan. This continuing sense of closeness despite distance and ignorance is the first point to keep in mind when trying to place in historical context the question of where U.S.-Chinese relations may be heading.

A second, closely related point is that China has often tested to its limits the ability of the U.S. government to develop and pursue a coherent foreign policy. The United States never has been the nation-state of Western political philosophers, whether Machiavelli or Hobbes or the "neo-realists" of today. The United States began as a loose alliance among former British colonists who previously had little to do with one another. It evolved into a republic that could sometimes act as a unit— and act with vigor. Within it, however, sovereignty continued to be shared between state governments and a national government, and in the national government authority lay—and lies—with an executive and a legislature independent of one another and more or less continuously in conflict. With regard to relations with other nations, as the legal scholar Edward Corwin writes, the U.S. Constitution represents an open "invitation to struggle."[2] Because of the strength of public feeling in various parts of the union and in the separate parts of the national government, the struggle has at times concerned relations with China.

A third point has to do with the better-known special relationship between the United States and Britain, not because it can serve as a parallel or model but because episodes in that relationship illustrate how interaction between a dominant power and emerging competitors can result in either conflict or accommodation. Between roughly 1890 and 1910, while the British relationship with Germany went from cooperation to antagonism, the British relationship with the United States went from friction to friendship. Between 1920 and 1930, with the United States now dominant, conditions that seemed made for rivalry and conflict were subdued by negotiations in which the two nations and others sought to maximize common interests rather than individual national interests. To ask why this happened in these two cases suggests some possible questions about alternative patterns that might play out in U.S.-Chinese relationships.

Americans became interested in China in the mid-eighteenth century. Benjamin Franklin was the young nation's first eminent Sinophile. He described China as "the most ancient, and from long Experience the wisest of Nations." He thought it a better model for America than any European nation, including Britain, largely because he saw its mandarins as an aristocracy of merit rather than of birth. He also thought that China's silk industry might exemplify how farmers could be individual entrepreneurs while at the same time boosting productivity through division of labor.[3]

In the nineteenth century, American opinion about China was divided. Admiration and awe for China persisted—witness the proliferation of American Christian missions and schools in China and the many sermons given in churches across the land in order to raise money and recruit volunteers for these efforts. Witness, too, the romantic recollections of the clipper-ship era's China trade, on which Franklin Roosevelt frequently dwelt, reminiscing about his seafaring Delano ancestors. But Americans who heard or read about China could not fail to see how rapidly China was being outstripped by the industrializing economies of the West. American workers protested the inflow of low-wage Chinese laborers. Chinese became targets of rioters and lynch mobs. Prejudice was so strong that Chinese in the U.S. received little protection from the legal system. A "Chinaman's chance" became a synonym for no justice at all.

By and large, American elites condemned discrimination against Chinese. Many remained supportive of and optimistic about the continually expanding Christian missionary endeavors. Others saw China as a vast potential market for the products of its own rapidly expanding industries. During the deep slump of the 1890s, when American textile mills were often idle, the argument was heard that if only the Chinese would lengthen their shirts by one inch, those mills would hum for generations.[4]

Though anti-Chinese agitation eventually died down, the rest of the mix persisted—and persists. America developed a small corps of "China hands." Some worked for the government; some for American companies; many for newspapers or magazines. A significant number were teachers and scholars.[5] Many nonexperts felt China's allure. One example is Henry Kissinger. In his memoirs, extravagant praise goes to Zhou Enlai: "Urbane, infinitely patient, extraordinarily intelligent, subtle," Kissinger writes, "he moved through our discussions with an easy grace that penetrated to our new relationship as if there were no sensible alternative."[6] Zhou is the other hero of Kissinger's memoirs (Kissinger being the first).

Despite all that he was told about the corruption and ineffectuality of the Chinese Nationalist government, Franklin Roosevelt died believing that China would grow to be a powerful democracy and "policeman" for its region. After 1949, American rhetoric often portrayed China as temporarily under foreign rule—a "Slavic Manchukuo," in the phrase of 1960s Secretary of State Dean Rusk.[7] Even unrelenting critics of Mao's regime, such as William F. Knowland of California (often called "the Senator from Formosa"), seemed to presume that ordinary Chinese admired America and aspired to have political and economic institutions like those of the United States. After the events of 1989, American after American predicted that China would follow the examples set in Eastern Europe.

But fascination with China sometimes held a touch of fear. The Chinese had once been rich and powerful. They might become so again. Their elite retained the reputation for sagacity that had so impressed Benjamin Franklin. When anti-Chinese rioting was near its worst in California, the California writer Bret Harte produced his verse on "the heathen Chinee"—Ah Sin, who outwitted competitors at the card table. From the 1920s to the 1940s, one of the best-known characters in American popular fiction was the Chinese-American detective Charlie Chan. And there were so many Chinese. In the 1980s the American political scientist James Q. Wilson came back from a visit to China, saying to his friends, "Can you imagine a billion Israelis?"

The mixture—awe at China's antiquity, culture, and size; uneasiness about its future; and discomfort over the roles of Americans there—should be recognizable to anyone who keeps up with current American commentary on China. Charles Kindleberger's maxim, *"plus ça change, plus c'est la même chose*—sometimes," evokes the uncertainty.

Politically most important has not been this widespread ambivalence but rather the intensity of feeling among Americans interested in China. Passion gives groups influence almost independent of their numbers. Witness Zionists, Cuban refugees, even friends of Syngman Rhee or Ngo Dinh Diem or Ahmad Chalabi.

For some Americans, especially from missionary backgrounds, it was unacceptable for China to have turned to Marxism-Leninism for its creed. They insisted that the United States treat this "Slavic Manchukuo" as a pariah, denying it diplomatic recognition or a seat at the United Nations. This self-styled Committee of One Million helped to push the U.S. government into such a stance and to keep it there for two decades.[8]

This recollection calls us to the second point—about the difficulty of formulating China policy, given that Americans who are passionate about China influence policy choices within a constitutional system where sovereignty and authority are both fractionated. In the nineteenth century, merchants, cotton growers, and churchgoers in the eastern United States worked through the executive branch to promote trade and missionary activity in China. Groups in the western United States worked through municipalities, state governments, and Congress to vent anger against "cheap Chinese labor." At a time when U.S. consuls were trying to charm Chinese viceroys on behalf of American shippers and evangelists, Congress passed a law forbidding any Chinese to become U.S. citizens. This was the first blanket immigration restriction in American history.[9]

Jockeying across and between governments and branches continued. The Open Door notes of 1899 and 1900 signaled continued executive branch support for trade and investment. Populists and Progressives in the states and in Congress continually deplored what President William Howard Taft maladroitly labeled "dollar diplomacy." Woodrow Wilson's turn toward an emphasis on promoting democracy in China partly reflected such sentiment.[10] In the 1920s and 1930s, the executive branch and Congress were frequently at odds about China.

After the Communist victory in the civil war, Congress seemed to become dominant. Republicans charged the Democratic administration of Harry Truman with having "lost China." Truman's secretary of state, Dean Acheson, tried to appease these critics by removing or reassigning "China hands" known to have been critical of the Chinese Nationalist regime. In the Republican administration of Dwight D. Eisenhower, Acheson's successor, John Foster Dulles, tried to advertise that he was purging these "China hands," but actually Acheson had left him little to do.[11] Until the 1960s, when signs of the Sino-Soviet split began to become clear, only persons in the good graces of Nationalist China's supporters in Congress could hold senior posts in the Department of State relating to East Asia.[12]

Since the U.S. relationship with the People's Republic began to mend in the 1970s, divergence between the executive branch and Congress has been often manifest.[13] When President Jimmy Carter surprised Congress by announcing normalization of relations with Beijing, Congress responded with a Taiwan Relations Act that contradicted nearly everything Carter said. Ever since, the actual U.S. position has been so ambiguous as to exasperate not only Chinese officials but also many Americans trying to deal with them. Though they have received much less front-page attention, tensions between the executive and legislative arms—as well as within both branches—have made the U.S. position with regard to Tibet equally ambiguous.

Nevertheless, despite having a political system that makes the Ottoman and Byzantine empires seem comparatively simple, the United States has from time to time succeeded in working out genuine policies.

Here, a digression is needed on the meaning of the word *policy.* The 2005 edition of the *Oxford English Dictionary* gives thirteen definitions, mostly archaic. The "chief living sense," it says, is a "course of action adopted and pursued by a government" or "any course of action adopted as advantageous or expedient." The two parts of this definition are at odds. The first implies a settled purpose and some degree of predictability. The second seems to apply more to maneuvers or stratagems chosen along the way. To some extent, the two parts of the definition overlap with *strategy* and *tactics,* though, strictly speaking, these are military terms, used metaphorically when applied to politics or business or games, and all too often used in government without adequate regard to General George Marshall's caution that if political problems are discussed in military terms, they are likely to become military problems. In any case, it is useful to keep in mind the two meanings because *policy* in its first sense—a course of action pursued over a significant period of time—inherently requires concurrence across the branches of the national government and across party lines, with broad underlying support among interested citizens. The particular expedients used to pursue a policy seem in their nature to be matters for executive discretion, though, in practice, the legislature or lobbies outside can restrict this discretion.

But it is policy in the first sense that the system has at times produced. One example is the support given China against Japan from the Manchurian Incident of 1931 to the end of the Pacific War. During those years, the United States did more business with Japan than with China. "Realists" such as the young George Kennan saw support for China as moralistic sentimentality. This was a theme of the then-authoritative history *The Far Eastern Policy of the United States,* by Yale president A. Whitney Griswold. But with backing from citizens influenced by missionaries; readers of Pearl Buck's 1931 novel, *The Good Earth*; viewers of the movie version; fans of Charlie Chan; and the like, Franklin Roosevelt and a few of his aides and congressional leaders cooperated in step-by-step assistance to China and in intensifying pressure on Japan to give up its war of conquest. They agreed that, in the long term, Americans would be better off with a strong and independent China.[14]

Another example is the U.S. policy of not intervening in the Nationalist-Communist civil war.[15] The Luce publications (e.g., *Time* magazine), U.S. Representative Walter Judd, and others argued vehemently for active aid to the Nationalists. General Albert Wedemeyer, formerly the commander of U.S. forces in the China theater, prepared a formal report saying that the Nationalists could win the civil war if only the United States would provide arms and logistical support and put a few thousand advisors alongside Nationalist field commanders.

General Marshall, who had previously been Wedemeyer's boss and patron, was then secretary of state. Behind closed doors, Marshall explained to congressional leaders why he opposed Wedemeyer's recommendation. It would, he said, involve "obligations and responsibilities on the part of this Government which I am convinced the American people would never knowingly accept. . . . It would involve this Government in a continuing commitment from which it would be practically impossible to withdraw . . . and which I cannot recommend as a course of action."[16]

Most of the congressional leaders found themselves in agreement with Marshall. As a sop to the strong supporters of the Nationalists, they voted money for aid, but there were to be no U.S. advisors on or near a battlefield. Privately, the Republican Senate leader, Arthur Vandenberg of Michigan, described the aid package as little more than "three cheers for Chiang."

This joint executive-legislative policy of course was in the background of the later "loss of China" furor. It nevertheless seems in retrospect to have been a wise and prudent course of action. The aftermath owed something to the fact that Marshall's successor, Acheson, did not get along well with—indeed usually looked down upon—anyone who stooped to running for office. Marshall, having headed the army, understood better the qualities as well as the powers of elected officials on Capitol Hill.

A third example is the "opening to China" that occurred during the Nixon administration.[17] The story, particularly in the memoirs of the principals, is one of a cleverly contrived surprise, astonishing everyone, especially the Soviet leadership and the U.S. secretary of state. And that story is not untrue. But the background included years of quiet discussion involving Presidents Lyndon Johnson and Richard Nixon and their aides on one side, and congressional leaders on the other. The Senate Foreign Relations Committee held extended public hearings, fostering debate on the question of whether it was wise for the United States to continue having no formal relationship with the People's Republic. Senate Majority Leader Mike Mansfield worked both openly and behind the scenes, seeking a new opening to China. The surprise trips to China of Kissinger and then Nixon were preceded by many conversations between Nixon and members of the House and Senate, including partisans of the Nationalists, such as Judd.[18] Congress was surprised by the way in which Kissinger and Nixon effected the opening but not by the policy they pursued.

Since the set-to between Carter and the Congress, the possibility of a coherent U.S. China policy has often been called into question. Journalists and scholars alike have decried a pattern of incoherence. From Ronald Reagan onward, candidates for the presidency have promised a tougher stance on economic and security issues. Once in office, they have slowly settled into stances rather similar to those of their predecessors. One reason has been recognition that the issues are more complicated and delicate than they seemed from the outside. President Bill Clinton said publicly in 1996 that he had probably been mistaken to have begun his presidency by pressing the Chinese, before all else, to improve their record on human rights.[19] Another reason is the slow dawn of understanding that even popular presidents don't make policy all by themselves. But a glance backward at least to the period between the early 1930s and the early 1970s suggests that effort invested in bringing together the two branches and a substantial segment of the interested citizenry can lead to coherent policy.

The British-German-American Example

The final bits of background offered here concern international realignments at the end of the nineteenth century and in the 1920s.[20] No piece of history is ever quite like another. Mark Twain is credited with saying that, though history never repeats itself, it sometimes rhymes. In these particular cases, the differences may be so wide that even rhyme is hard to find. Edwardian Britain never had the resources or internal dynamism that would make it comparable to the present-day United States. China today is like Germany and the United States of a century ago in little more than impressive economic growth. And one has to look very hard at the United States and other nations of the 1920s to detect significant resemblances to nations of today. Nevertheless, experience at the turn of the century and in the 1920s can be instructive in suggesting some of the processes that engender enmity or friendship across national boundaries.

In the 1890s the British statesman Joseph Chamberlain (father of Neville Chamberlain) led a movement for cooperation among the "Teutonic powers," meaning the British Empire, Germany, and the United States. He and others argued that the three were essentially similar in culture, values, and institutions. (Recall that manhood suffrage was more nearly universal in Imperial Germany than in either Edwardian Britain or the segregated United States.) Working together, the argument ran, the three could encourage the whole world toward liberalism, capitalism, peace, order, and representative government.

Why did the next two decades see Britain and Germany instead become enemies? British leaders—Chamberlain among them—did resent and resist Germany's efforts to acquire a larger "place in the sun." But most of the blame has to go to Germany and its willful ruler, Kaiser Wilhelm II. Time after time, Wilhelm chose precisely the move or language most likely to irritate Britons. He designed and advertised his navy as a threat to the Royal Navy. He sought colonies or bases or concessions encroaching on British spheres of control. In 1914 Germany attacked France through neutral Belgium, thus tipping Britain into a war that it might otherwise not have entered.

The central reason for Germany's self-destructive behavior was that the kaiser and his ministers were preoccupied with their own domestic politics. Their chief base of support was the landed aristocracy of Prussia. A very large socialist movement with allies from the middle classes wanted to reduce the power and privileges of this aristocracy. Wilhelm and his ministers found it useful—almost necessary—to have trouble abroad in order to maintain quiet at home, and it seemed much safer to taunt Britain than nearby France or Russia.

Why did Britain and the United States not also become enemies? The Americans goaded the British as much as did the Germans, and for a like reason. Not only in Washington but in many states and cities, it was good politics to attack Britain. In 1895 a conservative Democrat, Grover Cleveland, threatened war if Britain did not submit to arbitration a dispute over the boundary between British Guiana and Venezuela. The indignation in London matched almost any ever stirred up by the kaiser. Chamberlain, then the colonial secretary, advised the cabinet to "place in strong relief the fact that Britain is an American Power with a territorial area greater than the United States themselves, and with a title acquired prior to the independence of the United States."[21]

The American government began even earlier than Germany to build a big navy. As of 1900 the U.S. Navy was second only to the Royal Navy and was regarded in the admiralty as the greatest immediate threat to British supremacy on the seas. The United States moved unilaterally to renounce treaties with Britain so that it could build and completely control a canal across Central America. The U.S. secretary of state, himself an Anglophile, tried to achieve this goal without being needlessly offensive, but the chairman of the Senate Foreign Relations Committee, Henry Cabot Lodge the elder, would not permit it. Lodge insisted on humiliating public demands.

Theodore Roosevelt, elevated to the presidency by the assassination of President William McKinley, imitated Lodge when he negotiated for the surrender of Canadian territory adjacent to Alaska, which would give the United States sole control of access to the newly discovered gold of the Klondike. The British agreed to arbitration by a panel, which was to include an "impartial jurist." Roosevelt notified them gleefully that he had chosen for this post a former U.S. senator who had long demanded annexation of the disputed land. Roosevelt and his successors insisted on total U.S. control of the Caribbean, where Britain had many possessions and a history of naval dominance. Woodrow Wilson commenced his presidency by trying to overthrow a regime in Mexico that had support from both British investors and the British government. Wilson unilaterally pronounced the Mexican regime undemocratic and illegitimate.

Why did Britain not react to America's challenges as to those from Germany? Why did successive British governments repeatedly turn their cheek to the Americans? It was certainly not affection due to a common language or heritage. Though there were social and even marital ties with the American plutocracy, most ministers and most officials in London disdained Americans and bridled at American words and actions. They would have nodded approval if hearing another remark by Georges Clemenceau—that the United States was the only nation to have gone from barbarism to decadence with no intervening period of civilization.

But a chain of British decision-makers calculated coldly that the costs of resisting American pretensions would be too high. Unlike Germany, the United States had no nearby rivals that could be enlisted for balance. Canada was effectively a hostage. Most important of all, America had sympathizers within the British electorate. During the American Civil War, when the British government had wanted to help the Confederacy, churchgoers and Britons who saw the United States as a model of democracy had successfully protested. No influential group of the turn of the century wanted a comparable experience.

Hence, the British government chose to make a virtue of necessity and to yield to the Americans in every dispute with as good grace as was permitted. When a Liberal government came to office in 1906, its new foreign secretary, Sir Edward Grey, declared that the pursuit and maintenance of American friendship was and would be a "cardinal policy" of the United Kingdom.

The example of Imperial Germany clearly warns how dangerous it can be for a rising power to use foreign policy as a means of satisfying domestic political needs. The counterbalancing example of the British-American relationship shows how a great nation can benefit from swallowing its pride and being guided by long-term calculations of interest, both international and domestic.

The second possible rhyme is found in the actual peacemaking that followed the Great War and the disappointing outcome from the treaty negotiations of 1919. After the war, the United States was statistically the greatest power ever. Britain and America's other wartime partners owed large sums to the U.S. government and U.S. banks and were hard put even to meet interest payments. Though the United States had rapidly reverted to peacetime conditions, it had demonstrated awesome ability to mobilize and project military power.

In 1916, before entering the European war, Wilson had called for a U.S. Navy "second to none." Congress had authorized construction of a capital-ship fleet larger than that of Britain. Though shipyards had temporarily turned to building cargo ships, troop transports, and small warships suitable for antisubmarine operations, the program seemed about to resume under the new Republican president, Warren G. Harding. Britain would face a challenge that it probably could not afford to meet. This seemed to make it likely that Britain would tighten its two-decade-old alliance with Japan, for Japan had prospered from the war and had a history of naval and diplomatic rivalry with the United States. Japan had taken over from Germany control of Shandong. As a result of intervening to support anti-Bolshevik forces in Russia, it also held substantial tracts in Siberia. What with past difficulties, American criticism of Japan's imperialism, and discrimination against Japanese in cities and states of the American West, there was worldwide speculation about the possibility of an eventual Pacific war, perhaps pitting Japan *and* Britain against the United States.

In 1921 Harding's new secretary of state, Charles Evans Hughes, convened a nine-nation conference in Washington to discuss issues that might roil U.S. relations with Britain, Japan, and other nations having interests in the Pacific. To the astonishment of all the assembled delegates and of most Americans, with the notable exception of senior Republicans and Democrats from the relevant committees, Hughes offered to abandon the projected shipbuilding program and to scrap some existing construction. Britain's First Sea Lord, who had arrived assuming that the Americans would be stubborn and would hence help him persuade his own government to spend money on new warships, was described by a journalist as looking "like a bulldog, sleeping on a sunny doorstep, who has been poked in the stomach by the impudent foot of an itinerant soap-canvasser."[22]

Eventually, the conferees agreed on a treaty providing for capital ship parity between the United States and Britain. Japan was to be allowed a fleet 60 percent the size of either the American or British—adequate, it was argued, for secure control over Japanese home waters. Other treaties and bilateral and unilateral declarations resulted in ending the Anglo-Japanese alliance; committing all the powers, at least verbally, to an "open door" for trade and investment in China; and ending Japanese occupation of Shandong and Siberia. For the time being, speculation about a possible future Pacific war came practically to an end.

Late in 1922, after the Washington agreements were all complete, Hughes turned to Europe, where peace still seemed far away. He made a cautious offer to have American financiers participate in discussions about how to normalize relations between the former Western allies on the one hand and the Germans on the other. This led in time to arrangements that seemed to bind the former enemies to future cooperation.

The Washington and Locarno systems, of course, had only brief lives. The Great Depression, Japan's turn toward militarism, and the rise of Nazis in Germany ushered in the awful violence of the Second World War. Nonetheless, the 1920s offer another example of a potentially dominant power (the United States) reaching peaceful accommodation with both a declining power (Britain) and a rising power (Japan).

Why did this happen? Why did the United States forsake gaining apparent naval dominance? Why did Japan not only agree to naval inferiority but voluntarily abandon Shandong and Siberia? Why did Britain give up its traditional insistence on naval supremacy? Why did the

United States forego the opportunity to keep down potential rivals and instead promote the economic growth of nations that would be its enemies in the next great war?

For the United States, the answers lie primarily in a combination of ideology and politics. Harding's successor, Calvin Coolidge, would say famously, "The chief business of America is business." Though Progressives and Democrats distanced themselves from Coolidge, they tended in practice to agree with him. The common priority was domestic prosperity, measured by industrial output, corporate profits, bond and share values, and commodity prices. Except for citizens of some coastal cities and their local governments and representatives in Congress, few Americans really yearned for a navy "second to none." Hughes crafted his limitation proposals on a well-founded premise that Congress would probably not continue to pay for such a navy. (It is an instructive marginal point that evidence to this effect went unnoticed by all the other governments participating in the conference, the British government included. Even then, with Wilson's humiliation by the Senate a fresh memory, foreigners tended to forget Congress's power to shape policy.)

Given Britain's economic condition, Hughes's proposals seemed a godsend. For Japan, this was also the case. Japan was suffering a deep postwar recession. A newly formed cabinet, headed for the first time by a commoner, Hara Kei, had priorities like Coolidge's—prosperity for businessmen and farmers above all else. Hara and his colleagues were glad of a chance to escape the burden and expense of occupying Shandong and Siberia and building the warships desired by their naval staff. Within the navy itself, the narrowly dominant faction was led by the admiral who represented Japan in Washington, Kato Tomosaburo. More knowledgeable and realistic than many of the younger officers in his service, Kato reasoned that Japan would gain in the long run if it grew to be economically stronger and enjoyed friendly relations with the potentially all-powerful United States.

The key to what happened at the turn of the century had been Britain's choice of forbearance toward the United States, coupled with Germany's choice to put display of independence and of military and naval power ahead of all else. The key to the global détente of the 1920s was the choice of the United States—the executive branch and Congress, and Republicans, Progressives, and Democrats all in tandem—to forego parading military and naval power and instead to encourage global economic growth for mutual benefit, though of course of particular benefit to Americans.

Could what happened at the turn of the previous century and in the 1920s find some parallel in years ahead? If the answer were to turn out to be "yes," the explanation would probably lie in interaction of domestic economic and political factors in the United States, China, and other nations. American leaders would need to feel concern, as did British leaders of the Edwardian era, about the domestic costs of quarrels—about blocs among the public with personal, emotional, or other stakes in a trouble-free relationship with China. Chinese leaders and leaders elsewhere would need to have equivalent concerns.

The dynamic of the American-Chinese relationship could be tipped in one direction or another, as in the 1920s, by marginal choices on both sides between claims for national security on the one hand, and prosperity and domestic welfare on the other. The Anglo-American rapprochement of the early twentieth century was assisted by Theodore Roosevelt's defense policy. Despite his giving offense to Britain over matters such as the Alaska boundary and Panama, he was careful to avoid the kaiser's mistake of threatening Britain's essential security. While remaining a vocal Mahanite navalist, he held back actual fleet-building to the point that the admiralty ceased to count U.S. naval growth as a cause for alarm.

Could the American-Chinese relationship turn into an antagonism like that of Britain and Imperial Germany? Of course it could. Could the relationship instead become as warm as that between Britain and the United States? Probably not. Cultural and linguistic differences are too great. Nevertheless, for two and a half centuries, there has collected in the United States a reservoir of respect for and interest in China that can provide some cushion against shocks. The effect was evident in the rapid return of good feeling for China after the dissolution of the Chinese-Soviet alliance and again after 1989.[23] Potentially, it gives the executive branch and the Congress some latitude for resisting temptations to take offense against China. How much latitude, time will tell.

Could the U.S. and Chinese governments, along with other global and regional powers, find a way of controlling the most dangerous aspect of their current relationship—their growing competition in military and naval forces? Could anything faintly resembling the Washington system of the 1920s be re-created? The answer is: almost surely not. Today's weaponry is totally different. Practically all missiles, aircraft, and ships in any nation's military establishment look threatening from the standpoint of other nations. And, for the United States, the politics of national defense are also totally different. In the 1920s the U.S. Navy had only scattered local support. With the automobile boom under way, the iron and steel and manufacturing industries did not need to be subsidized by naval construction. Now, however, defense contractors and subcontractors are important elements in the economies of most states and a large number of congressional districts. When defense spending was reduced after the end of the Cold War, the chief reductions were in manpower and in operating and maintenance expenditures, not in research on or procurement of weaponry for what U.S. defense posture statements characterize as "full spectrum dominance." And what is known of Chinese force development suggests that similar dynamics are at work in China.

Nevertheless, the example of the 1920s deserves to be kept in mind along with that of the period 1890–1910. It encourages thinking about making armaments a subject for discussion, if not negotiation, just as a way of getting out in the open the rationales for weapons systems that one side or the other could regard as menacing. Also, recall of the collapse of the Washington and Locarno systems emphasizes the point that a truly dramatic change in world economic conditions—if it occurred—has potential for turning an international system predicated on cooperation into one where snarling national and ideological rivalries could make another era of massive violence suddenly more imaginable than it seems at present.

The United States and China Today

Will it occur? Many in the United States accept the notion that conflict between a rising power and the established hegemon is inevitable. Some argue that China's trajectory in many ways resembles the historical rise of Germany in the late nineteenth century and that the outcomes between the United States and China in future will be like those between Britain and Germany in 1914. However, the world environment, which supports Great Power politics, has changed dramatically over the past century.

Even the "nation" has itself been altered. The nation-state is a relatively recent creation in international history. It established a monopoly of control over its territory and resources only within the past two centuries. According to Karl Polanyi, the nation's newly acquired capacity to mobilize domestic resources has led to increasing battles abroad.[24] Europe's nation-states embarked on arms races and formed alliances to protect their power position, culminating in the First World War. In the interwar period realism continued to serve as the dominant rationale among the Great Powers. After 1945 the balance of power was buttressed by bipolar nuclear capacity, which deterred overt war between the United States and the Soviet Union. Although the realist world continued, a new order began to take shape alongside it. New institutions were created, including the United Nations, the International Monetary Fund (IMF), and the General Agreement on Tariffs and Trade (GATT). In Europe a stable equilibrium was established that permitted the domestic development of welfare states. It enshrined a new customs and currency union and admitted a range of new members to the integrated group, growing initially from six to twenty-seven members. Recently the European Union (EU) has been admitting one new country per year, and no end is in sight.

The mercantilism of the past was modified, and national self-sufficiency is no longer sought. The invention of computers and the popularization of television have facilitated the free flow of information. Large cross-border corporations were established to take advantage of the newest innovations. Trade and investment increased as more economies, such as China's, opened their doors to the international system. The old mercantile way of economic conduct became obsolete as more polities, such as the East Asian "tigers," came to understand that trade can generate domestic income. Economic development is no longer a zero-sum game; the success of a large economy will likely bring prosperity to countries it trades with.

China in recent years has earned the title of "World Factory," and without China the rest of the world would be deprived of a great variety and volume of goods to consume. The economic world is more closely integrated. A stock market crash in the United States immediately affects China's market. The present economic base of the international political system is very different from that of the traditional balance-of-power equipoise.

There has been a de facto "privatization" of the economy, which has in turn altered the role of government. The Chinese government no longer possesses the ability to manage every economic sector on its own. Private and foreign enterprises are becoming increasingly influential, and state enterprises are declining in number and importance.

Moreover, it is becoming increasingly difficult to calculate the power a state possesses outside its borders. Should a state engage in military action, it may find that it will have insufficient resources to gain victory because conflicts cannot easily be settled by force alone. The best strategy for China and the United States in these circumstances is to seek understanding and cooperation, not confrontation.

Both China and the United States seek "power" in some sense. But there is a difference between control over resources (*Macht)* and dominion over others (*Gewalt* or even *Herrschaft*). In the era of globalization, *Gewalt*, physical capacity for domination, is dubious; and *Herrschaft*, or actual domination, is no longer a realistic objective for any nation, at least in its relations with other states possessing measurable *Macht*. The lesson taught by the successful expansion of the EU holds relevance for the United States and China. EU members aim at greater growth and an increase of jobs. EU membership involves more partners and stakeholders in "governance" without "government." In somewhat the same way in which rivals like France and Germany could lay down their cudgels in forming the Coal and Steel Community, the United States and China can settle differences cooperatively. "Subsidiarity"—the European principle that problems should be solved at the lowest appropriate level—could be applied in U.S.-China interchanges to deal with North Korea, environmental, and other challenges. These are, after all, "household" differences.

The need to combat the threat of terrorism, to maintain a balanced world economy, and to reduce greenhouse gases are agreed between the two Great Powers. The two countries have similar domestic economic objectives as China becomes an increasingly middle-class nation.

Conclusions

China's rise will undoubtedly occasion fears in the United States. How can they be dealt with or dispelled? Cultural differences exist and will remain. Taiwan and the Tibetans seem to be manageable subjects of dispute. An opportunity exists to deepen the interpenetration of the two economies. In the period after the Second World War, the nation-state has become a bounded Prometheus. Actions of multinational firms, nonstate actors, and international institutions have made the world more interdependent. The international power constellation has become codetermined by economics. Newly created rules, norms, codes of conduct, and institutions now bind the nation-state. Nonetheless, the long-term future of the United States and China will depend upon a bilateral ability to empathize with another primary party, to avoid pressing one's advantage, or to linger over imagined slights. Self-interest will have to be even more enlightened over the long term to achieve such goals. This will become easier when nations recall the blunders they made in 1914 and earlier.

CHAPTER TWO

THE RISE OF CHINA'S SOFT POWER AND ITS IMPLICATIONS FOR THE UNITED STATES

Joseph S. Nye and Wang Jisi

THE RISE OF CHINESE POWER IS ONE OF THE MOST IMPORTANT aspects of world politics at the beginning of the twenty-first century. In fact, the "rise of China" is a misnomer. "Reemergence" would be more accurate, since by its size and through its history the Middle Kingdom has long been a major power in East Asia. Technically and economically, China was the world's leader (though without global reach) from 500 to 1500. Only in the last half millennium was it overtaken by Europe and the United States. At the beginning of the industrial age, Asia was responsible for an estimated three-fifths of world product. By 1940 this fell to one-fifth, even though the region was home to three-fifths of the world's population. Rapid economic growth has brought that back to two-fifths today, and analysts speculate that Asia could return to its historical levels by 2030 or 2040. The term *Asia,* of course, includes Japan, India, Korea, and other countries, but China may eventually play the largest role. Its high annual growth rates of 8 to 10 percent led to a remarkable increase of its gross national product in the past three decades. This pragmatic economic performance, along with its traditional culture featured by Confucianism, enhanced China's "soft power" in the region and around the world.

Soft Power

Power is the ability to affect others to obtain the outcomes you want. One can affect behavior in three main ways: through threats of coercion ("sticks"), through inducements or payments ("carrots"), or by attraction, which makes others want what you want. A country may obtain the outcomes it wants in world politics because other countries want to follow it, admiring its values, emulating its example, aspiring to its level of prosperity and openness. In this sense, it is also important to set the agenda and attract others in world politics, and not only to force them to change through the threat or use of military or economic weapons. This "soft power"—getting others to want the outcomes that you want—co-opts people rather than coerces them.[1]

Soft power rests on the ability to shape the preferences of others. It is the possession neither of any one country nor only of countries. At the personal level, we all know the power of attraction and seduction. Political leaders have long understood the power that comes from setting the agenda and determining the framework of a debate. Soft power is a staple of daily leadership and politics.[2] The ability to establish preferences tends to be associated with intangible assets such as an attractive personality, culture, political values and institutions, and policies that are seen as legitimate or having moral authority. If I can get you to want to do what I want, then I do not have to force you to do what you do *not* want.

Soft power is not merely the same as influence, though it is one source of influence. Influence can also rest on the hard power of threats or payments. And soft power is more than just persuasion or the ability to move people by argument, though that is an important part of it. It is also the ability to entice and attract. In behavioral terms, soft power is attractive power. In terms of resources, soft power resources are the assets that produce such attraction. Some resources can produce both hard and soft power. For example, a strong economy can produce important carrots for paying others, as well as a model of success that attracts others. Whether a particular asset is a soft power resource that produces attraction can be measured by asking people through polls or focus groups. Whether that attraction in turn produces desired policy outcomes has to be judged in particular cases. But the gap between power measured as resources and power judged as the outcomes of behavior is not unique to soft power. It occurs with all forms of power. Before the fall of France in 1940, for example, Britain and France had more tanks than Germany, but that advantage in military power resources did not accurately predict the outcome of the battle.

In international politics, the resources that produce soft power arise in large part from the values an organization or country expresses in its culture, in the examples it sets by its internal practices and policies, and in the way it handles its relations with others. Governments sometime find it difficult to control and employ soft power, but that does not diminish its importance. It was a former French foreign minister who observed that Americans are powerful because they can "inspire the dreams and desires of others, thanks to the mastery of global images through film and television and because, for these same reasons, large numbers of students from other countries come to the United States to finish their studies."[3] Soft power is an important reality. Neorealists like Kenneth Waltz who focus on the structure of power measured by physical resources and deny the importance of soft power are like people who do not understand the power of seduction. They succumb to the "concrete fallacy" that something is not a power resource unless you can drop it on a city or on your foot.[4] Classical realists like Hans Morgenthau (or, earlier, Nicolo Machiavelli) did not make the mistake of ignoring the power of ideas.

The soft power of a country rests primarily on three resources: its culture (in places where it is attractive to others), its political values (when it lives up to them at home and abroad), and its foreign policies (when they are seen as legitimate and having moral authority). The German editor Josef Joffe once argued that America's soft power was even larger than its economic and military assets. "U.S. culture, low-brow or high, radiates outward with an intensity last seen in the days of the Roman Empire—but with a novel twist. Rome's and Soviet Russia's cultural sway stopped exactly at their military borders. America's soft power, though, rules over an empire on which the sun never sets."[5] But cultural soft power can be undercut by policies that are seen as illegitimate. In recent years, particularly after the invasion of Iraq, American soft power has declined. According to many observers, America's attractive or soft power has been declining while that of China has increased. In a recent

BBC poll of twenty-two countries, nearly half the respondents saw China's influence as positive compared to 38 percent who said the same for the U.S.[6] While polls are snapshots, and it would be a mistake to read too much into such opinions, they do indicate an interesting trend.

China's Soft Power

China has always had an attractive traditional culture, but now it is entering the realm of global popular culture as well. The Chinese film *Crouching Tiger, Hidden Dragon* became the highest grossing non-English film of all time. Yao Ming, the Chinese star of the National Basketball Association's Houston Rockets, could become another Michael Jordan, and China hosted the 2008 Summer Olympics. The enrollment of foreign students in China has tripled from 36,000 to 110,000 over the past decade, growing 20 percent annually.[7] The number of foreign tourists in China has also increased dramatically, with 23 million visiting between January and November 2007.[8] By July 2007, China had created and funded over 170 Confucius Institutes in some fifty countries around the world to teach its language and culture.[9] While the Voice of America was cutting its Chinese broadcasts from nineteen to fourteen hours a day, China Radio International was increasing its broadcasts in English to twenty-four hours a day.[10]

In terms of political values, the era of Mao's revolution is long past. Although China remains a one-party polity, the success of its political economy in tripling gross domestic product over the past three decades has made it attractive to many developing countries. In parts of Asia, Africa, and Latin America, the so-called Beijing Consensus on a tightly controlled political system plus a market economy has become more popular than the previously dominant Washington Consensus of market economics with Western-style democratic government.[11] China has reinforced this attraction by increasing its foreign economic aid and facilitating access to its growing markets.

China has also adjusted its diplomacy. Two decades ago, it had great reservations about multilateral arrangements and was at cross purposes with many of its neighbors. Subsequently it has joined the World Trade Organization, upheld multilateral diplomacy in solving international disputes, contributed more than 9,000 troops to serve in UN peacekeeping operations,[12] become more helpful on nonproliferation diplomacy (including hosting the Six-Party Talks on denuclearization of the Korean Peninsula), settled territorial disputes with neighbors, and joined a variety of regional organizations of which the East Asian Summit is only the latest example. In recent years, rather than playing up its rhetoric against "American hegemonism," Beijing is rigorously promoting the idea of international cooperation for building up a "harmonious world," and trying to reassure the outside world that it is committed to a "peaceful path of development." This new diplomacy helped to alleviate fears and has reduced the likelihood of other countries allying to balance a rising power.[13]

But just as China's economic and military power does not yet match that of the United States, China's soft power still has a long way to go.[14] China does not have cultural industries like Hollywood, and its universities are not yet the equal of America's. Unlike America's soft power, which is largely generated by its civil society, China's soft power depends heavily on its government work. A major part of potentialities in Chinese society, including burgeoning nongovernmental organizations, remains untapped.

Whereas America's image has been damaged since its invasion of Iraq, China's image suffers from its domestic deficiencies, such as official corruption, social inequality, and environmental degradation. The Western world continues to criticize China for a lack of democracy, human rights, and the rule of law. Although the Beijing Consensus may be appealing to some developing countries that reject Western-type democracy, the applicability and sustainability of the Chinese model of development have yet to be tested. On the one hand, China's new diplomacy has enhanced its attractiveness to its neighbors in Asia. On the other hand, its impressive military buildup without much transparency has also aroused security concerns in the region, especially in Japan, which may reduce the effectiveness of Chinese diplomacy. China has not succeeded in persuading the European Union to lift its arms embargo, apparently because of Beijing's "belligerent" stance toward Taiwan. Despite all these problems that China must still overcome, however, its soft power will definitely keep pace with its hard power growth.

The Soft Power Discourse in China

There is no lack of Chinese interest in the idea of "soft power." Since the early 1990s, dozens, or maybe hundreds, of essays and scholarly articles have been published in the People's Republic of China on soft power. And there has even been a new Chinese journal entitled *Soft Power*, with its first issue published in late 2006, although the contents of the journal are mostly related to the business world.[15]

"Soft power" has also entered China's official language. In his keynote speech to the Seventeenth National Congress of the Communist Party of China (CPC) on October 15, 2007, Hu Jintao stated that the CPC must "enhance culture as part of the soft power of our country to better guarantee the people's basic cultural rights and interests." Hu recognized in that speech that "culture has become a more and more important source of national cohesion and creativity and a factor of growing significance in the competition in overall national strength."[16]

There does not seem to be any official effort in China to define the term *soft power*, and Chinese scholars continue to debate its scope, definition, and application. Moreover, they do not agree with one another as to how that phrase in English should be better translated into Chinese, since at least three Chinese words—*shili*, *quanli*, and *liliang*—carry meanings similar to *power*. Different translations thus reflect nuanced interpretations of the term *soft power*.

How Chinese View Their Soft Power

Notably, in recent years there have been numerous Chinese publications on China's own soft power, and their views are divergent. Few observers deny the importance of soft power to China, but some stress that only a rapid growth of hard power can provide China with the bases on which to enhance its soft power, implying that priority should be given to the increase in hard power rather than soft power. Yan Xuetong, a renowned international relations scholar, has criticized Joseph Nye for not dividing soft power into political power and cultural power (though that seems to be a misreading of the concept). Yan contends that the wielding of political power, for example, showing China's credibility and determination in strengthening military power and deterring Taiwan independence by force, is more important than spreading cultural influences.[17]

Most other observers, however, do pay more attention to culture as a necessary ingredient, even a core element, of soft power. Many try to portray China's soft power today by analyzing both its strengths and weaknesses. On the positive side, to many people in the world China's performance is strikingly admirable in sustaining a high rate of economic growth over the past three decades, which has helped some Chinese get out of poverty. The economic and social progress would not have been possible if China's political institutions were not strong and resilient. Whether China's performance has provided a development model (the so-called Beijing Consensus) for other countries to follow is subject to debate, but the accumulated economic power and social capital have certainly boosted China's confidence, pride, and capacity to project its political power and cultural influences abroad.

Chinese analysts tend to attribute China's recent achievements to its cultural merits and traits. They also tend to believe that along with its increased hard power Chinese culture should be more attractive to other peoples. Some also point to ethnic Chinese outside of China as a great asset that can contribute to its soft power. In addition, China's foreign policy has been highly successful, with (arguably in the eyes of others) its high moral principles and increasingly adroit diplomatic skills.

Meanwhile, a number of Chinese publications admit the limits and constraints to China's soft power, especially when they compare it with America's influence in the world. Some subtly point to the lack of transparency in government work and rampant official corruption that damages China's image. Others refer to the "brain drain" China is still suffering from, which reflects insufficiencies in China's educational (and possibly political) system. Still others suggest that the Chinese government should do better in its public relations work internationally.

Soft Power Interactions Between China and the United States

Just as the national interests of China and the United States are partly congruent and partly conflicting, their soft powers are reinforcing each other in some issue areas and contradicting each other in other issue areas. This is not something unique to soft power. In general, power relationships can be zero or positive-sum, depending on the objectives of the actors. For example, if two countries both desire stability, a balance of military power in which neither side fears attack by the other can be a positive-sum relationship.

Undeniably, the polities of these two countries represent different value systems and ideologies. In the eyes of China's political elites, the United States is attempting to remake the whole world in its image, and China, as a socialist country led by the Communist Party, is without any doubt a main obstacle to achieving America's strategic goals. Chinese officials are always sensitive to and alerted by such American schemes as what Condoleezza Rice called "transformational diplomacy" that are aimed at spreading out American influences deeply into other countries' domestic spheres. The Chinese also watched closely and worryingly the "color revolutions" in Eastern Europe and elsewhere, which were seen as staged or encouraged by Americans to undermine existing governments. To this extent, the expansion and wielding of America's soft power as part of a "smart" combination of culture, political values, and foreign policy will not be welcomed by China.

To the American general public and elites alike, China under the Communist Party leadership is a political symbol that they find difficult to accept and comprehend. In general, Americans are favorably impressed with China's great achievements in the past three decades. However, if they were asked whether these achievements have been made "because of" or "despite" the Communist Party leadership in China, most would probably be perplexed. They harbor mixed feelings in seeing China's soft power rise in world affairs, as reflected in a number of American publications, including a recent book entitled *Charm Offensive: How China's Soft Power Is Transforming the World.*[18] Most of these works assume a zero-sum perspective and cast a more negative rather than positive light on China's soft power growth.

In their respective foreign policy pronouncements, Americans and Chinese often have opposite views and goals. While Americans want to maintain their leading position in global affairs, Chinese are opposing "hegemonism," a code word for American ambitions to dominate the world, and promoting "multipolarity," apparently based on a decline in American power. Nonetheless, the seemingly opposite goals belie some very fundamental realities, according to which the soft power interaction between the United States and China is far from a zero-sum game.

First, there is little evidence that the increase in China's soft power is aimed at counterweighing America's soft power, or that the "color revolutions," regardless of their connection to U.S. strategic objectives, are intended against China's influence in the countries where they occurred. The tainted American image in Europe and the Islamic world has little to do with Chinese diplomacy there and would not directly result in any boosting of China's cultural and political influences. Just as Yao Ming is not in America at the expense of Michael Jordan, Hollywood movies and TV series like *Desperate Housewives*, which are easily available in China, would do no harm to the quality of Chinese movies. Although some people in China may blame the popularity of American cultural products for reducing the attractiveness of Chinese products, a counterargument can be made that such competitions are needed and healthy. Similar cases can be found in China-U.S. educational exchanges, in which each side benefits from better students and teachers.

Second, the perception that the Chinese model of combining market economy with one-party rule will challenge the Western model (market, democracy, and rule of law must be together) and values is dubious. More research should be done to illustrate how many, and to what extent, other developing countries are actually able to learn from the Chinese model.

For all we know, Americans would be pleased should North Korea or Burma (Myanmar) now begin to move toward the Chinese-style market economy.

Third, China is using its soft power in diplomacy that may help the United States protect its interests in certain countries and regions. To be sure, China's actions are taken first of all to serve its own interests, but its quiet efforts to persuade the North Koreans to terminate their nuclear weapon programs and to embark on economic reform do facilitate U.S. policy objectives on the Korean Peninsula. Likewise, Beijing's quiet diplomacy to persuade the Burmese government to modify its behavior at home may pave the way for stabilizing the situation in that country. What is more, China has successfully convinced Khartoum to accept a UN presence in Sudan, which was originally rejected under Western pressures.

Fourth, Chinese guardedness against American soft power is essentially defensive, especially in China's domestic affairs. Despite their suspicions of American intentions and their doubts about the relevance of American experiences to China's own path to modernity, Chinese political elites share the basic values of democracy, human rights, and rule of law, as well as market economy. Increasingly, President Hu Jintao and Premier Wen Jiabao, among other Chinese leaders, are emphasizing the necessity of building up democratic institutions in China.[19] Although democracy in China is referred more often to "deliberative democracy" than universal suffrage, elective politics is seriously studied and increasingly practiced at various levels of Chinese government. This trend contrasts sharply with some countries and communities where radical ideas are prevailing. As an American analyst observed a few weeks after the September 11, 2001, terrorist attacks, "We used to emphasize that China and the United States hold different values. But if we compare the gap between American values and the values held by the Taliban and Al-Qaeda, differences between China and the United States are negligible!"[20]

Finally, in reality Chinese are borrowing many skills and practices that construct America's soft power. A great number of Chinese government

officials, military officers, judges, and lawyers, among other profession-
als, have been trained in the United States, and they have made contributions to America's knowledge as well. In the field of foreign policy,
many Chinese think tanks have emerged in the past decade or so, and
the examples they refer to are their counterparts in the United States
rather than those in Japan, Russia, or Germany.

Conclusions

It is not surprising to see Chinese leaders and academics referring explicitly to China's soft power and adopting policies to promote it. In a sense,
this reflects a sophisticated realist strategy for a country with rising hard
power. To the extent it is able to combine its hard power resources with
soft power resources, it is less likely to frighten its neighbors and others
and thus less likely to stimulate balancing coalitions. Successful strategies
often involve a combination of hard and soft power that is called "smart
power." For example, in nineteenth-century Europe, after defeating Den-
mark, Austria, and France with Prussian hard military power, German
chancellor Otto von Bismarck developed a soft-power strategy of making
Berlin the attractive diplomatic capital of Europe. During the Cold War,
the United States used both hard and soft power against the Soviet
Union. Thus it is not surprising to see China following a smart-power
strategy. Whether this will be a problem for other countries depends on
the way the power is used. If China sought to manipulate the politics of
Asia and exclude the United States, its strategy could be counterproductive, but to the extent that China adopts the attitude of a rising
"responsible stakeholder" in international affairs, its combination of hard
and soft power can make a positive contribution. In return, much will depend upon the willingness of the United States to include China as an
important player in the web of formal and informal international institutional arrangements.

China is far from America's or Europe's equal in soft power at this
point, but it would be foolish to ignore the important gains it is making.
Fortunately, these gains can be good for China and also good for the rest

of the world. Soft power is not a zero-sum game in which one country's gain is necessarily another country's loss. If China and the United States, for example, both become more attractive in each other's eyes, the prospects of damaging conflicts will be reduced. If the rise of China's soft power reduces the likelihood of conflict, it can be part of a positive-sum relationship.

CHAPTER THREE

U.S.-CHINA ECONOMIC INTERACTIONS: TRADE, FINANCE, AND ECONOMIC MODERNIZATION

Lawrence Lau, Mingchun Sun, Victor Fung,
David K. Richards, and Richard Rosecrance

PRIOR TO 1750, CHINA AND EUROPEAN STATES WERE ON PARALLEL economic tracks. Each faced a land constraint that required labor-intensive cultivation to produce sufficient food and fuel. Cultivation depended on local labor and could not be farmed out to others or to overseas colonies. Energy sources were not adequate to permit a shift of labor from land to manufacturing and machine industries. Europe, however, solved both these problems, and China did not.

Europe's American colonies permitted extensive cultivation to take place elsewhere. Britain's coal provided the energy needed to power machines and factories. European labor, freed from the land constraint, could then migrate in large numbers to factory cities to serve the Industrial Revolution. No such advantages were available in China. It had no land-abundant colonies; its sources of coal were in the Northwest, and it was in the Yangtze Delta where mechanical operations were performed. Beijing and the delta were not initially linked, and they would not be tied together by railways until after the mid-nineteenth century.[1] But for these differences, an Industrial Revolution might also have begun in China in the late eighteenth century.

China today, however, is certainly catching up. After taking power in 1949, the Communist leadership focused investment and savings on both industry and agriculture. The gains of the Five Year Plans in the 1950s, however, were not matched during the Great Leap Forward and the Cultural Revolution. It took Deng Xiaoping's opening in 1978 to regain momentum, at which point Chinese economic capabilities spurted forward. The three decades since have witnessed perhaps the most revolutionary economic growth recorded by a single nation in the annals of economic history.[2] This growth was initially stimulated by an import-substituting industrialization strategy (fostered by high restrictive tariffs), which was modified in the 1980s to focus on manufacturing production designed for exports. The Special Economic Zones of Fukien, Guangdong, Dalian, and others bounded ahead, sustained by foreign as well as domestic investment. Foreign trade, not consumption, became the engine of this growth, and China's dependence on exports initially resembled that of the first industrial nation, Great Britain, in the 1840s.[3]

Perhaps equally important, the United States and Chinese economies fitted together, hand into glove. High labor costs induced U.S. industry to relocate part of its production functions to Chinese plants. Low labor costs permitted Chinese industry to serve these companies and to begin to move up the value chain.

The U.S.-China relationship is differentiated, however, in that China presently concentrates on manufacturing production whereas the United States focuses on finance, high-tech innovation, and services. Nonetheless, over time the two economies will become more similar. In purely economic terms, the process of equalization will be reflected in the enhanced flow of finance and labor between the two increasingly open countries. As they approach economic parity, however, political relationships will become even more important as soft power (see the previous chapter) increases on both sides. The tenor of those relations will determine the ultimate political outcome between China and the United States.

China and the Globalized World Economy

In the globalized industrial system of today, products are no longer made in one factory or under one roof. Instead, production is increasingly spread across different countries, and components are assembled into a final product only at the very last stage. China has become the world's manufacturing hub, but it represents only the last step in assembly and processing. As a consequence, China has been importing raw materials, components, and semifinished goods from Asian countries while exporting finished goods to the United States and the European Union. In terms of "value-added," however, the Chinese contribution to the total value of the product currently averages about 20.4 percent on exports to the world and only 17.1 percent on exports to the United States. Companies from the United States, Europe, and other countries contribute (and garner) much of the remaining value. Under these circumstances the Chinese trade surplus technically is only proportionate to the "value-added" amount.

It is also important to recognize that the competitors in the world economy today are not uniquely states. Rather, corporations and integrated supply chains are vital players in international competition. Participants in the supply chain now form a new kind of team, and competition therefore occurs not just between companies or countries but between integrated supply chains.[4] Nonnational elements vie with national and territorial ones for precedence in this competition. Their success and failure helps to determine the success of states associated with them.[5]

China participates in forming sophisticated supply chains, and, of course, will not indefinitely remain as the final stage of low-end manufacturing. Best-in-class processes of labor-intensive production might leave China and migrate to areas such as Bangladesh or Vietnam. Ultimately, China's garment industry might be "hollowed out" by emerging nations in Asia, Latin America, Africa, or other parts of the world. As China seeks to move up the ladder, it will try to develop value-added services and information technology industries. This progression in turn will require stronger banking and financial sectors than now exist. Over time, a more proficient university and graduate education will be necessary to create the skills and capabilities needed to fashion new competence and also to create regulatory frameworks as China transitions from state-owned industries to a largely private economy. In the short run China is beginning to exit from plastics, furniture, and textile industries, and it has therefore cut export subsidies in these categories.

Present Imbalances

Good long-term economic relations between China and the United States depend upon remedying existing financial and trade imbalances. These stem at least initially from the fact that the United States focuses on consumption and China on investment. Relative to its ability to pay (over time), the United States slights savings and overstresses consumption. China saves too much, invests too much, and does not consume enough. The current account imbalance is a direct function of these factors.[6] China now exports production that cannot be consumed at home because of excessive savings/investment. Excessive U.S. consumption undermines savings and thus supports purchases that the United States over time cannot afford. The United States has to borrow abroad to finance this consumption. Thus, the United States needs to save more and consume less—otherwise future generations will have to do so— and China needs to save less and consume more. Moves by both countries to correct these conditions would reequilibrate the trade balance.[7] Total savings in the United States are now around 15 percent of gross domestic product (GDP) while in China they are over 40 percent of GDP. Chinese consumption has actually declined in recent years.

The deep recession of 2008 has lowered Chinese stock market indices, but as effervescence resumes, there is a long-term danger that China could follow the Japanese path of the 1980s and build up an asset price bubble that would have to be lanced. When the Bank of Japan raised interest rates in 1989, industries and financial corporations—tied together by mutual investment in each other's shares—suffered a cumulative reverse, leading to a collapse of the Nikkei Index and a decade of negative growth for Japan. This might have been avoided if monetary authorities had previously encouraged "a shift to domestic demand-led growth"[8] by the Japanese people. Then the bubble would not have emerged in the first place.

An increase in Chinese consumption is equally important to sustain growth and achieve equilibrium in international payments. Revaluation of exchange rates will also facilitate a greater degree of balance in the trade account.[9] Facing large surpluses, China has "sterilized" incoming payments for its exports, thereby increasing liquidity. The excess liquidity within China could lead to an asset bubble (as money chases stocks and real estate) or inflation (if money chases goods). In the short term, "sterilization" suppresses inflation because it diverts purchasing power elsewhere. In the long term, however, interest rates are depressed, and domestic prices remain too low. Sterilization perpetuates global trade imbalances, because the exporting power does not allow its surplus to circulate and produce domestic price increases. Fostering low interest rates, sterilization stimulates borrowing on a worldwide scale. Ultimately, excessively low interest rates will generate a Chinese capital exodus to find higher returns elsewhere. This is what happened in South Korea, when the government had to modify its sterilization efforts as a result. If, however, China had pegged its currency but abandoned sterilization, prices and ultimately interest rates would have risen at home, equilibrating the international imbalance. Alternatively, if China had allowed its currency to freely fluctuate, it would have risen on the exchanges and stimulated greater imports while restricting exports. Neither, of course, happened in actual fact.

In the United States if the government had cut its massive fiscal deficit and increased taxes, this would also have rectified the imbalance through the combined effect of reducing private and public consumption. Because of U.S. military expenditures in Iraq and the recession of 2008, however, the United States further cut interest rates and accentuated its deficit spending. In 2008 the Federal Reserve emphasized liquidity rather than restraint and was criticized by Paul Volcker, former chief of the Federal Reserve, for doing so.[10]

The excess liquidity created in China has already led to the migration of capital overseas. Sovereign wealth funds like Chinese Investment Corporation (CIC) have been created to find higher returns abroad, and not in the (low return) U.S. money market. But further appreciation of the renminbi is needed in the long term, conjoined also with a fall in the value of the U.S. dollar, if balance is to be reattained. These shifts will ultimately have to be negotiated in a context that involves other countries, and one should expect a replay of the Plaza and Louvre accords of the 1980s, this time with China as an integral partner.

Prospective Balances?

China is aware of the monetary imbalances and is moving to restructure its maturing economy. New investment vehicles have been set up to allow domestic Chinese to invest outside their country. Without such outlets the Shanghai exchange will suffer persistent "bubbles" of inflationary expectations, perhaps demanding central bank intervention. Qualified Domestic Institutional Investors (QDIIs) have been authorized to invest nearly $50 billion overseas, and the CIC—China's sovereign wealth fund—has been given an initial capital of $200 billion to invest outside China. Because of low interest rates and the decline of the U.S. dollar, however, China has suffered losses in its investment in the U.S. money market in recent years. These reverses could be moderated by buying TIPS (inflation-protected Treasury bonds), but Chinese foreign direct investment (FDI) in the United States is the long-term solution, both in terms of returns and monetary value.

In China, foreign FDI has been even more important. Foreign-invested enterprises (involving large amounts of U.S. and European FDI) have accounted for 57 percent of the national total of China's value of exports and imports in recent years. A similar point cannot be made about Chinese foreign direct investment in U.S. enterprises. These have been limited and restricted, at least until recently.

In 2004 Lenovo acquired IBM's personal computer business. But the failed attempt by CNOOC to buy Unocal in 2005, due to U.S. political sensitivities, slowed but did not derail Chinese FDI into the United States. A new wave occurred in 2007 with major M&As and "Greenfield" FDI deals, including CITIC's preliminary attempts to invest in Bear Stearns and Huawei's joint acquisition of 3Com with Bain Capital (see Table 3.1). Greenfield investments, following the Japanese precedent in investing in the United States, have been particularly important because they not only avoid the political sensitivities of buying established U.S. corporations but also generate political support by bringing employment to new regional

Table 3.1. Major FDI Activities of Chinese Firms in the United States Since 2002

Time	Acquirer/ Investor	Target of M&A or Greenfield FDI	Sector	Details	Amount (US$)
Dec. 2007	CIC	Morgan Stanley	Banking	Convertible bonds	$5 billion
Nov. 2007	China Merchants Bank	Greenfield FDI	Banking	Received U.S. Fed approval to open branches	N.A.
Nov. 2007	Yongor Group	Smart & Xin Ma	Apparel	100 percent stake	$120 million
Oct. 2007	CITIC*	Bear Stearns	Banking	6 percent stake in convertible bonds	$1 billion
Oct. 2007	Minsheng Bank	UCBH Holdings	Banking	9.9 percent stake	$200 million
Sept. 2007	Huawei	3Com	Tech	100 percent stake	$2.2 billion
Aug. 2007	Wanxiang Group	AI	Machinery	30 percent stake	$25 million
July 2007	Chinasoft	Greenfield FDI	Tech	Est. subsidiary— Chinasoft USA	N.A.
July 2007	CIC	Blackstone	Finance	10 percent stake	$3 billion
Dec. 2004	Lenovo	IBM	Tech	Purchased IBM's PC Business	$1.25 billion
Nov. 2003	Xinjiang D'Long Group	Murray	Manu.	100 percent stake	$400 million
Sept. 2002	China Netcom	Asia Global Crossing	Tech	100 percent stake	$80 million

*Proposed but not excecuted.

areas. In established sectors, China needs to know what is and what is not politically sensitive. It may be useful for both governments to compile a list of industries that will be open for "national treatment" and can be freely bought and sold by foreign investors on both sides. This would provide guidance to private sectors in their FDI activities in the other country. Sovereign wealth funds are probably less sensitive than corporate investments, first because they do not take high percentage stakes in most enterprises, and second, because they are surely more conservative than hedge funds (which also have a much greater capitalization—in the tens of trillions of dollars) because of government involvement.

The commercial banking sector is another area of growing interest on both sides. Foreign interest in establishing banks in China has stemmed from the large spread between Chinese lending rates and deposit interest rates maintained by the People's Bank of China (PBOC). This disparity guarantees a profit to the commercial banks, because they can lend at high rates and pay relatively low rates to depositors. As these rates are liberalized over time, however, the guaranteed profit will fall. Interbank lending and borrowing will provide a source of funding to the system even when depositors are given higher rates of return. In the short-to-medium term (prior to the establishment of full liberalization of China's capital account) a listing of auxiliary depository receipts (ADRs) of major Chinese and U.S. firms would allow foreign investors to gain access to their respective equity markets. China particularly needs to find outlets for its excess capital because the Shanghai exchange currently exhibits very high price-earnings ratios, and Chinese investors, fearing excessive speculation in home markets, are itching to go overseas.

The Longer Term—Reciprocity?

Though Maynard Keynes pointed out that "in the long term, we are all dead," it is still useful to think about the relation between the United States and China once Beijing completes its modernization, thirty years from now. This will be a future in which capital will flow freely and tariffs will be low. Mundell-Fleming conditions will then apply. Mundell and Fleming pointed out that central banks could choose only two of three possible policy options: (1) ensure capital mobility; (2) change exchange rates; or (3) change interest rates. If capital mobility is selected, then authorities have to decide between manipulating interest rates or exchange rates. If they hope to control both, they would have to reject capital flows and put on capital controls.

Under conditions of capital mobility—a more likely outcome in modern globalized economies—central banks will have to choose between regulating their interest rates or their exchange rates. If a central bank seeks to lower interest rates while keeping a highly valued exchange rate, money will simply leave, and the currency will be forced downward. If, however, it seeks to lower exchange rates while maintaining domestic interest rates, incoming capital will negate the lower exchange rate. In short, the typical strategies used by developing countries in the past—combining a low-valued currency, capital controls, and tariffs—will no longer be available. Foreign trade surpluses will lead to automatic increases in prices, and the currency will float upward, pressing toward equilibrium with trading partners.

One-sided and continuing surpluses will no longer emerge. Sterilization will be a thing of the past. In response to unemployment, labor—at least in theory—will be able to flow overseas, as it does now in Europe under the terms of the Schenken accords. Equilibrating flows will thereby balance differences in trade accounts, reinforcing openness.

There is already a greater degree of economic openness in China than some international observers might have expected. Focusing on their strengths in labor abundance, Chinese leaders have lowered tariffs on goods with high labor content, confident in their ability to best competitors. In time, however, China's major advantage will reside not in abundant labor but in abundant capital. The United States will also have capital abundance, but its edge will shift more to human capital than to financial or manufacturing capital. Under these circumstances, both sides can maintain economic openness. It is important to remember, however, that with higher interest rates, populations will have to accept adjustments and even temporary unemployment when imbalances emerge. Such adjustments can be tolerated between two countries if they have already established strong economic links sustained by large amounts of foreign direct investment (patterns of ownership) in each other's economy. Then investors can make money when either country prospers and do not have to be upset when their domain of residence suffers a short-term setback. And residences may shift, at least temporarily. As things proceed, more and more Americans will seek to "top off" their education with study in China, and a large number of Chinese will continue to pursue degrees in the United States.

Conclusions

Countries that have been close economically nevertheless have gone to war. As a result of high levels of trade, the equalization of factor prices between Germany, Britain, and France was in 1913 similar to the equalization observed between the Atlanta, San Francisco, and New York regional markets in the United States.[11] Britain and Germany invested in each other's industry, though a far greater amount was sent to colonies and developing countries overseas. In 1913 Great Britain had placed over 11 billion pounds sterling in foreign investments, more than twice that of any competitor. In no case, however, did this amount to a significant share of another Great Power's national income. Despite FDI overseas, liquid foreign equities accounted for the vast preponderance of foreign investments.

In the future it is possible to imagine two nations—for example, China and the United States—owning large proportions of real estate, companies, and financial instruments within each other's country. This might not prevent conflict, but it would raise "economic deterrence" stakes against war to an unprecedented height. Norman Angell was wrong to think that economic interdependence among the Great Powers would prevent war in 1913. But nations in 1914 did not own vast shares of each other's companies and real estate as they are commencing to do now. Great Britain did not lose huge amounts from its quick sales of German stocks in August 1914. But as countries, sovereign wealth funds, and multinational hedge funds invest abroad, their exposure becomes unprecedented, and the devastating effects of major war are thus compounded.

CHAPTER FOUR

SHAPING CHINA-U.S. MILITARY RELATIONS

Chen Zhiya

The Importance of the Sino-American Military Relationship

The relationship between China, the largest developing country in the world, and the United States, the largest developed country, is the most important bilateral relationship in the world. As military relations between China and the United States constitute a key component of bilateral relations, the Sino-American military relationship directly bears on overall bilateral relations between the two nations. Regional security and prosperity, with implications for both East Asian security and its development, are dependent on the strength of this relationship.

The military relationship between the two nations has affected the resolution of global security issues and has the potential to impact on the future global security situation.

Both countries possess substantial military power. There is no need to repeatedly point to the formidable military strength enjoyed by the United States, though it is worth noting that increasingly the United States is viewed by other countries as posing a security threat rather than providing a security guarantee to other nations. And although some American government and academic institutions regularly exaggerate China's military capability, there is no denying the fact that China has huge military potential.

In 2006 the United Nations used 6 billion U.S. dollars and 100,000 peacekeepers from over 100 countries to support eighteen peacekeeping missions on four continents.[1] These missions conformed to the UN Charter, reflected international consensus, and answered to the desire of people of different racial, religious, and cultural backgrounds in the relevant regions to end conflict and create peace. China and the United States have both made contribution to such UN peacekeeping missions. However, compared with their strength or potential, they should actually have done more. China and the United States, alone or in collaboration, have the capability to redefine peacekeeping within the framework of the UN Charter. When strategists of the two countries consider their respective defense strategies and bilateral military relations, this should be a common framework for further thought and action. China-U.S. military relations have major global significance.

It takes great foresight and elimination of bias to manage China-U.S. military relations. U.S. and China analysts do not expect to redress all prejudices and bias in bilateral military relations through one inquiry or one workshop. However, it is indeed my hope to eliminate the biases of the past and open up a process of reshaping bilateral military relations with foresight through common sense and empathy.

Returning to Common Sense

I support considering China-U.S. military relations on the basis of common sense, for the following reasons:

China Uses Force Only in Self-Defense

Western scholars tend to find New China under the leadership of Mao Zedong "bellicose." Yet China is not a bellicose country. The first military commandment in the long tradition of the art of war in China advises against unchecked aggression. True, during the Cold War, China fought wars with the other four permanent members of the UN Security Council and at all four directions of its boundaries (the Korean War in 1950–1953, the Taiwan Strait crises in 1954 and 1956, the Border War between China and India in 1962, and border conflict between

China and Russia in 1969). However, an in-depth analysis of each and every case reveals that China's use of force with other countries has always been war in self-defense, in which the extent of the use of force has been appropriate. In other words, China does not use force unless it is under extreme provocation, unless there is no other choice, and unless the other country fires the first shot.

Self-Preservation Is a Right of All Nations

China has the right to self-preservation. The Chinese military has always had the mission of safeguarding territorial integrity and sovereignty. It has not been easy for the Chinese people to "stand up" (in 1949, Chairman Mao Zedong declared that Chinese people had stood up). And the Chinese people who have stood up can absolutely not allow any foreign invasion into our country. This is the fundamental purpose behind creation of the armed forces. Chinese scholars describe the evolution of the Chinese people's ideology in the previous century as one of national salvation or security overwhelming enlightenment. This is indeed a very profound view given the weight of national salvation in Chinese souls.[2] Calls for transparency for the Chinese military are comprehensible only in theory and perplexing in reality. China develops its military forces on the basis of defending its homeland, and the military preparations conducted to prevent Taiwan secessionist forces are a part of homeland defense. Military preparedness against secession of Taiwan is an extension of this tradition and a continuation of the mind-set of striving for national survival. So long as the possibility of secessionist moves such as the holding of a UN membership plebiscite (for Taiwan) exists, China and the Chinese people will not be able to shake off the memory and mind-set of national salvation, and strategic transparency will not be necessary or possible.

Even so, considering concerns of the United States and some surrounding countries, China has participated in the UN arms transparency mechanism. The choice has not been made easily. It is actually a rather risky decision given the current collective psychological background of the Chinese people.

China Honors Its Commitments

China has always been a country that honors its commitment and promises. *The General Code of Civil Law of the PRC* provides that "if any international treaty concluded or acceded to by the People's Republic of China contains provisions differing from those in the civil laws of the People's Republic of China, the provisions of the international treaty shall apply, unless the provisions are ones on which the People's Republic of China has announced reservations."[3] In other words, if the Chinese government signs a piece of international law, it supersedes Chinese national law. The record of China implementing international treaties is there for all to see. This is adequate to prove that China is different from the United States. China does not take freedom of action as a strategic purpose. It hopes and stands ready to handle international relations on the basis of fair and rational international contract rather than might.

Westerners sometimes believe that "nobody, including Chinese leaders, knows where destiny will bring China, the military power."[4] In fact, Chinese principles of action are well known:

- Safeguard state sovereignty and territorial integrity
- Resolve international disputes by peaceful means
- Not engage in hegemony, expansion, or arms races
- Not be the first to use nuclear weapons, not use nuclear weapons against non-nuclear-weapon states or nuclear weapon-free zones, complete prohibition and thorough destruction of nuclear weapons
- Conclude international convention on the nonweaponization of outer space, and peaceful use of outer space
- Maintain the central role of the UN Charter and the UN Security Council in maintaining world peace; international use of force has to conform to the UN Charter and be authorized by the UN Security Council
- Oppose nuclear proliferation, stand for global arms control

Furthermore, with the concerted efforts of China, Russia, Kazakhstan, Tadzhikistan, and the Kyrghyz Republic, disputes over a boundary longer than 3,000 kilometers (1,860 miles) between China and the former Soviet Union were properly and fundamentally resolved within six years, which is rare in modern international relations.[5] This forcefully proves that increased strength has not changed China's external behavior mode.

China-U.S. Military Relations as Viewed by Others

The Sino-American military relationship is a component of U.S. military relations with the world. It is, of course, also a component of China's military relations with the world. However, given the different natures of the two countries' military influence over the whole world, we will now look at China-U.S. military relations from the perspective of U.S. military relations with others.

- Since the end of World War II, a consistent strategic goal of the U.S. armed forces has been freedom of action. In the words of President George W. Bush, "the U.S. does not need approval of the UN or anyone to take action." This is the biggest difference in military policy between the U.S. and almost all other countries. Freedom of action is the central principle of the U.S. national security strategy, defense strategy, military strategy, and space policy. In reality, *freedom of action* means to formulate rules and the "power to set global agenda."[6]
- The United States seeks overwhelming military advantage and has never been satisfied with maintaining military balance of power with any country. Currently it is seeking to redefine war with American rules.
- Since the end of World War II, the United States has frequently used force with other countries. In an overwhelming majority of occasions, the world has found the United States to be a threat rather than a force for greater security.[7]
- The record of the United States implementing international arms control treaties suggests that the United States has become the greatest uncertain factor in global arms control.

- The driving force of arms buildup in the United States is mostly internal, from the military-industrial complex, rather than being responsive to external threats.
- The net result is that *uncertainty* brought by the United States to the world exceeds the *security* that the United States brings to the world. For example, who can guarantee that neoconservatives will not again dominate U.S. foreign policy in ten or twenty years' time? What does this uncertainty mean to future world security and military buildups in other countries?

The preceding points are supported by literature and facts. U.S. scholar Walter McDougall points out that "the Soviet threat is an element in U.S. military build-up but is not the most important one in any sense"; "in other words, the U.S. military build-up follows its own logic."[8] Another U.S. scholar, Gordon Mitchell, notes that "the driving force of U.S.-Soviet arms races comes from an arms race inside the U.S. military."[9] In this regard it is quite understandable why the French scholar Emmanual Todd has suggested that the U.S. strategic objective seems to maintain world non-peace rather than peace.[10]

The U.S. military policy toward China, as part of U.S. national strategy and power in East Asia, is inevitably influenced by its overall military policy. Incidents in China-U.S. military relations can be better explained against this backdrop.

- The United States took the initiative or had choices whereas China had to respond or had no choice. The Yinhehao incident, the 1996 Taiwan Straits crisis, the bombing of the Chinese embassy, the military aircraft collision—there is no exception to the pattern of U.S. initiation. Although there was also room for improvement in crisis management by China, these incidents first of all should not have happened. It was the United States who created them or created the environment for them to occur.
- Since the 1990s, China has gradually become the central element in strategic planning for the U.S. military, and war with China has almost become the standard scenario of U.S. military transforma-

tion.[11] Admittedly there is some objectivity in the concern by the U.S. strategic circle over the "rise of China" or "Chinese military development." However, more importantly, "having enemies is a precondition for the revolution in military affairs to succeed. Terrorism, no matter how, does not have such a weight. China with its rapid economic growth provides a convenient excuse."[12]

U.S. conjecture and precaution over long-term Chinese military development is a projection of the U.S. strategic mind-set, a strategic inertia driven internally, and represents U.S. thinking aloud in most cases. Only when the discussants are aware of such self-projection and strategic inertia can the discussion about what China does and does not do become meaningful.

Understanding with Empathy

Common sense and empathy are like the two legs of a human being: a step forward by any one leg will bring the other one step forward, propelling him forward into a broader space.

Empathy is the most important basis for countries to coexist peacefully. If we cannot understand the perspectives of others, allow for their difficulties and expectations, or regard them as people with dreams and weaknesses just as we ourselves have, we will unavoidably exaggerate our own strengths and the others' weaknesses.[13] Understanding with empathy is an irreplaceable psychological virtue in handling international relations. It is intangible but brings tangible results.

Empathy may bring about self-discipline in big countries. If you expect others to respect rules and undertake responsibility, it goes without saying that you yourself must respect rules and undertake responsibility first. Reciprocity is the precondition of empathy. "Responsible" international behaviors are mutual. Because every country cares about its own core national interest, a decent distance should be maintained from the others' core national interests. Such is the strategic self-discipline of large or powerful countries.

Empathy might have only been a choice during the Cold War, but nowadays it is a must. First, for too long, some countries regarded empathy as an optional approach. The lesson of the Cold War is that strategies of powers constitute action and reaction. The arms race was an irrational action and reaction created by a rational logic. The result has been the disintegration of the Soviet Union and the spread of the deadly weapons left behind. These weapons have now become the most dangerous threat to the United States.

Second, since the Cold War's demise, the U.S. military has become the only superstrong military with global war-fighting capability, and its strength has continued growing in the so-called transformation of military affairs. However, U.S. national security has not improved accordingly. On the contrary, the establishment of the Department of Homeland Security seems to suggest that the United States has become more insecure in some respects.

Third, humankind has moved into a new era: civilization is now as fragile as glass balls in the turbulence of scientific revolution. American scholars have tried to determine how many revolutions in military affairs have taken place throughout history. No matter what the conclusion is, such linear thinking is no longer useful in observing and understanding the revolution in military affairs today. Driven by the scientific and technological revolution, the age of the revolution in military affairs (RMA) has arrived. War and human security are at the threshold of an unpredictable revolution. This is an epoch-making challenge to all countries:

- Weapons of mass destruction (nuclear, chemical, and biological) continue to exist, and humankind still lives under the nuclear shadow.
- Weapons of mass disruption (information) are on the rise. The process of informationalization and networking is also a process of expanding and deepening vulnerability of the whole society.
- Weapons of mass uncertainty (gene, nanometer, and nonkinetic energy) have the potential of creating devastating threats that are difficult to defend against. War may become "micro" and strange. For centuries, science has helped us to understand nature. In recent years, life science and biotechnology have changed the character of nature or even defeated it. This is a revolution that is qualitative

and directional. If humankind uses this capability in war, the revolution in military affairs will be transformational.

- With a notable imbalance in international military power and a loss of monopoly by states over violence, nonstate entities will greatly increase the complexity of global security affairs, and they may increase the suddenness of crisis and the strategic significance of its consequences.[14] In this sense, human civilization is at the crossroads of survival or disaster.

- For all countries, developing new destructive powers is more a question of will rather than ability whereas developing effective defense is becoming increasingly difficult. It is just because of the enormous difficulty of defense that a preemptive strategic strike will become more attractive in theory. The United States will be more advanced than other countries in many areas of RMA by one or even a few steps, but it will not monopolize the effects of RMA. The advanced status of the United States may not mitigate the American security dilemma but will certainly increase global security risks.

- If human civilization is not able to put an end to a strategy dominated by prejudice, bias, and inertia, the strategy will ultimately terminate human civilization. The various strategic propositions that have appeared since the end of the Cold War either fail to fully *explain* the world, due to subjective limitations, or fail to fully *change* the world, due to objective limitations. The framework of realism can no longer hold the rapidly changing world. In other words, the world of strategies dominated by prejudice and stereotyping veiled by rationality is inevitably distorted.

What is needed is a return to common sense and empathy. We can start by asking the right questions and identifying the right direction. As Albert Einstein said, "You can't possibly resolve problems along the line of thinking that has created them."

In order to avoid the mistakes of the early years of nuclear revolution, the new revolution in military affairs has to be strategically controlled. The international community must as soon as possible make laws on information security and prohibition of weaponization of outer space;

spell out explicit restrictions on the military applications of genes, nano weapons, and nonkinetic technologies; and act more resolutely to oppose first use of nuclear weapons, manufacture of new nuclear weapons, or nuclear proliferation, and to promote nuclear disarmament, thereby putting war and the revolution of science and technology under control before their power grows beyond human capability to control. War and new destructive capabilities—rather than countries themselves—are the common potential threat to all countries. Effective strategic control of RMA requires a change of mind-set and new global cooperation.

The precondition for strategies to exist is a recognition of their limitations and fallibility. Empathy helps us to be aware that we ourselves have limitations and are fallible. Such a recognition or awareness is useful for nations such as the United States and China as they conscientiously seek strategic self-discipline.

China-U.S. Military Relations Can Be Shaped

For many years, the China Foundation for International and Strategic Studies (CFISS) has persisted in observing China-U.S. military relations with common sense and empathic understanding. It maintains contact with relevant institutions of the United States during both good and bad times of China-U.S. relations. These exchanges give us a firm conviction that China-U.S. relations can be shaped. In international relations, particularly in future China-U.S. relations where possibilities are enormous, conviction is as important as rationality—perhaps even more important.

Various "realist" strategies are no longer in contact with reality. We need to move beyond the "power first" concept. Common sense tells us that problems created by power obsessions have exceeded what the theory can resolve. It is a prescription worse than the disease it is intended to cure. To shape China-U.S. military relations, we need to set our eyes on the interests of future generations, on shared interest of the world and on maximization of common interests and minimization of diverging interests. Common sense, more empathic understanding, more courage, and more imagination must take precedence over power and strategizing.

At the 2006 China-U.S. Track II Dialogue, former defense secretary William Perry and former assistant defense secretary Ashton B. Carter raised the point that the United States should pursue a responsible hedging of China.[15] Their use of the word "responsible" is a positive sign. It indicates that the responsibility of the United States is also recognized, and it demonstrates the hope that military interaction between the two countries will be more coordinated. President Richard Haass of the U.S. Council on Foreign Relations put forward the idea that U.S. policy toward China should focus on opportunities to integrate China into existing international systems.[16] American scholar Thomas Barnett bravely opposed the Pentagon when he argued for a China-U.S. military alliance.[17] These views are encouraging steps taken by the U.S. strategic circle toward the elimination of prejudice, bias, and inertia in the China-U.S. relationship. Moreover, these statements have been made during an environment of prevailing animosity against China within the U.S. Department of Defense. They demonstrate not only wisdom but also courage and conviction.

At the same 2006 workshop, the point was made that a new thinking should be adopted to observe and handle China-U.S. military relations. That is, the two sides should focus on common interests, jointly form ideas or plans that are beneficial to explore, consolidate and expand their common interests, and use these ideas and plans to promote strategic mutual trust and cooperation and create a mutually beneficial future. In order for such a new approach to be accepted by both sides and become a strategic common understanding, we should always bear in mind the following points:

First, China-U.S. military relations per se are very important. In other words, even in the absence of a common strategic enemy, it is still important to maintain a normal or even close relationship, which serves the fundamental interests of both China and the United States, promotes peace in East Asia and the world at large, fundamentally increases national security of both countries, and improves the quality of global security. In contrast, abnormal or even adversarial military relations between China and the United States not only constitute a burden on both sides but also exacerbate imbalances of objectives, capabilities, and resources on both sides; lead to major risk and danger; pose potential threat to bilateral relations and regional security; and even become an obstacle to future globalization processes.

Second, China-U.S. military relations are the weakest link in overall bilateral relations and do not reflect the reality and prospect of the two countries moving toward interdependence. The history of bilateral military relations shows that when overall relations experience disturbance, the military exchanges are the first to be affected, and when the overall relations turn for the better, military ties are the last to get repaired. We can hardly say that the current military-to-military relations have moved out of the old historical track. Such a situation certainly neither serves the strategic interest of either country nor is conducive to peace and stability in East Asia.

Third, the Taiwan-related military policies of the United States act like a master switch that decisively affects the direction and nature of military relations between China and the United States, thus influencing the quality and process of military-to-military interaction. There are various questions in China-U.S. military relations such as transparency, code of conduct, reciprocity, and so on. However, the key is absence of solid strategic mutual trust, the root cause of which is the Taiwan question.

As is known to all, preventing the secession of Taiwan is China's strategic bottom line. This line has to be defended against any adversaries and at all costs. Also known to all is the fact that given the U.S. arms sale and military assistance to Taiwan and possible U.S. reaction at a time of crisis, the Chinese military has to make military preparations on the basis of the most difficult and most complicated scenarios. It is an overwhelming mission. In such an environment and facing such a future, it is fairly unrealistic to expect the Chinese military to be substantively transparent to the United States on its core combat capabilities.

China-U.S. military relations are in inverse proportion to U.S.-Taiwan military relations: the closer the latter, the further away the former. U.S.-Taiwan military relations have turned and continue turning nonissues in China-U.S. military relations into issues, minor issues into big problems, and big problems into tough questions that are hard to resolve. A necessary precondition for interaction between the two militaries is respect by the United States of China's core national interest.

Although the situation across the Taiwan Strait has recently relaxed somewhat, the nature of U.S.-Taiwan military relations has not changed. Taiwan-related military policies of the United States are closely linked to its strategic misgivings and hedging against China. They are even reciprocally reinforcing each other.

There is a view in the United States that how China treats Taiwan will be how China treats other countries in Asia. This is completely wrong. Taiwan is a matter of internal affairs. China's relations with its Asian neighbors are external affairs. There are fundamental differences between internal and external affairs. To be frank, such an opinion plagues the ones who hold it. We can only oppose any policy choices made under the influence of such an opinion.

There is another view in the United States that there is uncertainty in China's future military policy and in the future of China-U.S. relations and that, in this connection, the United States should shift its strategic focus to East Asia, strengthening military transformation and maintaining its military advantage. Uncertainty in overall and military relations does exist. However, how can we cope with such uncertainty? Are we leaving for our future generations a war-fighting mind-set and new weapon platforms, or a habit and tradition of mutual trust and cooperation? The two sides need to sit down and have in-depth discussions of questions like this. Nonetheless, it has to be pointed out that if the Taiwan factor were somehow linked to this type of question the discussion would hardly produce any result.

Elsewhere, Ashton B. Carter writes that you cannot expect the Chinese military to fight its enemies with bows and arrows. Those days are long gone. The military strength of China will certainly develop together with the country's increasing economic, scientific, and technological power. Whether the development of Chinese military power should follow certain rules and what type of strategic understanding should be reached with its neighbors and the United States can be explored by the relevant parties. Except for strategic transparency, it is not completely impossible for China to provide necessary tactical and technical transparency since, after all, there is nothing ulterior in China's motives. However, the existence of the Taiwan factor prevents us from substantive discussion of these matters.

Fourth, in order to establish a sound interaction between the two militaries, the United States needs to limit its "worst-case scenario" and "precautionary" strategies appropriately. In Chinese proverbs about the art of war, "where there is precaution, there is no danger" and "count[ing] on one's own strength rather than others' kindness" is considered realistic. Nonetheless, to "take every conceivable precaution" points to the harm of worst-case analysis. The two strategic planning tools have certain rationality. However, the history of the Cold War and arms race between the two superpowers shows that the possible benefits of worst-case analysis are far less than the costs and accompanying risks. It was because Deng Xiaoping moved in his strategic thinking out of the worst-case scenario of an early large-scale nuclear war that China was able to begin its reform and open up, developing itself and promoting world prosperity at the same time. It is only by thinking beyond worst-case scenarios that we can prevent vicious cycles and bid farewell to strategic confrontation between powers in favor of an age of peace and development.

Fifth, we need to shift from crisis management to opportunity management. The China Foundation for International and Strategic Studies has in recent years participated in a joint research project with the Carnegie Endowment for International Peace on crisis management. In that process both parties realized that for too long China and the United States have looked at bilateral relations from the perspective of how bad their relations may become even though the objective is better bilateral relations. We seek to reverse that situation. By identifying the positive potential of our relations, we can create conditions for the realization of the best scenarios. This is opportunity management.

As aforementioned, this is not a choice but a must.

Jointly Opening Up New Future Frontiers with Great Foresight

A number of scholars from China and the United States believe that it is impossible for China-U.S. relations to be too good or too bad. Although this reflects reality to a certain extent, I have never been satisfied with it. On the contrary, I believe that China-U.S. relations have developed to a point where the two sides must work together to open up new frontiers with foresight.

From the Wild West to the Pacific Coast and later in outer space, the United States has defined a new identity. Will the rise of China close or limit such American frontiers? This line of thinking will almost automatically produce a series of confrontational games and preventive measures in U.S. strategic planning.

This chapter has presented the other direction—that is, China and the United States jointly opening up new frontiers in the future. I believe that so long as the American strategic planning system is willing to take up this question it will also produce a series of answers that might in the end bring change to the strategic planning of the U.S. military itself: from planning for war to planning for global peace.

Here I would like to propose that the two sides explore how to establish and deepen a relationship of constructive cooperation in the military and security fields. This is my vision of China-U.S. military relations. To this end, China and the United States should reach the following strategic common understanding in the security and military fields:

- China and the United States are not enemies now, and they will not be enemies in the future. China does not and will not have any intention to challenge the United States militarily.
- Any problem or difficulty that might arise between the Chinese and U.S. militaries over Taiwan is in the nature of crisis management rather than strategic confrontation.
- China and the United States should discuss how to establish a relationship of constructive cooperation in the security field.

If China and the United States become "partners in constructive cooperation," they will not make trouble for each other but provide help and take actions together. Providing help and taking joint actions are preconditioned. For China, a basic precondition in international affairs is the UN Charter. Within the framework of the UN Charter, the United States has the power and the experience to play a leading role, and China may render its support and take part in relevant actions. However, China will not take part in or support unilateral American actions such as the Iraq War. Once China decides to give support and take part in joint actions in international security affairs, the Chinese action will be substantive and complete in the sense of covering the whole period of action. China will not pay just "lip service" or let the work taper off once it gets started. China honors its commitment and obligations as a partner.

In the areas of antiterrorism, nonproliferation, hostage rescue, and evacuation of overseas nationals, China and the United States give each other substantive assistance when legitimate and reasonable right of self-defense is exercised. China and the United States should explore ways and mechanisms to improve strategic common understanding. The two nations have important common strategic interests such as peace, stability, and nuclear nonproliferation in extensive areas in the world. What on earth is preventing us from taking joint action? If China and the United States reach a long-overdue common understanding on the question of Taiwan, they will have overcome the biggest psychological barrier between them. After that, it only takes imagination.

World War II was decisive for the fate of China. During that period, the United States was a friend of China. Reform and opening up are also determining the fate of China. The negative policies and actions of the United States toward China in the past thirty years have not produced strategically irreversible results. On the whole, the United States can still be regarded as an amicable country. This is a sentiment both China and the United States should retain.

At present, China has arrived at a new history and epoch-making starting point. The future road of China will be like a new long march leading to strength and prosperity and to a society based on green consumption. It is a way of life that is measured by level of comfort rather than speed and by quality of life rather than power. The transformation of China to such a society and strategic collaboration between China and the United States will inject huge power into globalization and open up new common frontiers for the two countries. Whether or not such an epoch-making transformation takes place in China, general China-U.S. relations and their military relations—in particular, a reassuring situation across the Taiwan Strait—are extremely important.

COMMENTS ON CHEN ZHIYA'S "SHAPING CHINA-U.S. MILITARY RELATIONS"

Ashton B. Carter

IN HIS CHAPTER FOR THIS VOLUME, DR. CHEN ZHIYA ASTUTELY points out the need to shape U.S.-China military relations, writing that "U.S.-China military relations are the weakest link in the overall bilateral relations and do not reflect the reality and prospect of the two countries moving toward interdependence."[18] Chen's analysis parallels one conducted by Dr. William J. Perry and this author for the Harvard-Stanford Preventive Defense Project,[19] in which we sought to answer a question frequently asked in the U.S., in China, and indeed around the world: "Will the United States and China be friends or foes in twenty years?"

Chen concludes his analysis by recommending a three-part "strategic common understanding" between the U.S. and China. All three proposed common understandings are sound advice to the governments and militaries of both countries, and this paper elaborates on each.

Prudent Hedging

Chen's first proposed common understanding is "China and the U.S. are not enemies now, and they will not be enemies in the future."[20] The first part of Chen's sentence is certainly true, and the second part is very likely to be true. A strategic competition, or worse, conflict between China and the United States would be mutual assured destruction. It would demolish an economic relationship that is vital to both. It would destabilize the Asia-Pacific region where, despite enduring animosities dating back to

World War II and before, prosperity and political development have proceeded at an astonishing pace for decades—first in Japan and Taiwan, then South Korea, and now South and Southeast Asia and China itself. A U.S.-China cold war would be wasteful for both militaries, which face other pressing threats from terrorism, proliferation, and a host of regional and transnational problems around the world. A hot war would involve a catastrophic clash between two of the planet's largest military machines and possibly even escalate to nuclear conflict. For two governments to bring themselves to this point would be contrary to their individual and common interests. The overwhelming evidence of recent trends across the board suggest that the path of conflict is, indeed, very unlikely.

Yet senseless conflicts have too often scarred history. Therefore, the second part of Chen's proposal might usefully be amended to read that China and the U.S. *should* not be enemies in the future. Both sides should recognize that a sensible future is not automatically guaranteed. Both need to work toward it actively—*shaping* the relationship, to use Chen's apt word.

Many in the U.S. frame the issue of China's strategic destiny in terms of China's "true intentions." But what matters are not the intentions of China's current leaders but of its future leaders. These will be shaped by the attitudes of a younger Chinese generation, by the possibility of U.S.-Chinese strife over such hot spots as Taiwan, by the ability of Chinese society to manage its breathtaking social and political transformation, and—importantly but not deterministically—by U.S. behavior. No one, including China's current leaders, knows what the future Chinese leadership's "intentions" will be. As Perry and I wrote, "China's future intentions are not a *secret* they are keeping from us, they are a *mystery* to both sides."[21]

In this strategic circumstance, the U.S. has no choice but to adopt a two-pronged defense policy toward China. The first prong is engagement, encouraging China to become what Robert Zoellick called "a responsible stakeholder." The second prong is to adopt a prudent hedge against the unlikely but possible circumstance of strategic competition. It is critical that hedging be done prudently, meaning with restraint and openness. History is also littered with examples of imprudent hedging, leading witlessly to conflicts that can and should have been avoided. China's military leaders doubtless conduct the same analysis as U.S. strategists and have a hedge of their own. Hedging is contagious. It can get out of control because one side's hedging can appear to the other to be the leading indicator of the very change in intentions against which it is hedging.

Perry and I suggested some "dos" and "don'ts" of prudent hedging for the U.S. side.[22] The most important "dos" were to continue to do what the United States has been doing for decades in Asia: maintain stability for the benefit of all through relationships with long-standing allies like Japan, South Korea, and Australia, and new partners like India. Other important "dos" were to modernize U.S. naval and aerospace forces to make sure regional and global balances are not upset, and to monitor Chinese military activity so the U.S. can measure its responses to potentially destabilizing developments. One of the very important "dos" was to encourage U.S.-Chinese military-to-military contacts and, where possible, joint activities.

Perry and I also stated some "don'ts"—types of U.S. hedging that would not be prudent. For example, the U.S. should not attempt to transform its security relationships in Asia into an encircling anti-China alliance. It should not change its long-standing policy regarding Taiwan (see below). It should not pursue a self-defeating attempt to neutralize China's nuclear deterrent through counterforce or missile defense. And it should not attempt to deny China access to oil or other resources that are pursued fairly through market mechanisms.

Taiwan

Chen's second "strategic common understanding" reads: "Any problem or difficulty that might arise between the Chinese and U.S. militaries over Taiwan is in the nature of crisis management rather than strategic confrontation." Once again, this sound proposition must be made a reality by hard work on both sides.

China has a long-standing policy of not renouncing the use of force against Taiwan. The United States has a long-standing policy of opposing both the use of force by China and the pursuit of independence by Taiwan. This policy standoff is widely recognized to be a tense one, but no one has discovered a way to improve upon it unless and until the situation on both sides of the Strait evolves in a fundamental way. So all three parties appear, to date, to avoid challenging the status quo.

But the status quo brings with it an odd but unavoidable consequence for the militaries of both the U.S. and China. The U.S. is obliged (in fact, this is written into law, the Taiwan Relations Act) to be prepared to resist the use of force by China. It is quite obvious from Chinese military moves—notably the deployment of a large missile force opposite Taiwan and the testing of an antisatellite interceptor—that the People's Liberation Army (PLA) is under instructions to be prepared to use force to intimidate Taiwan and to attempt to neutralize U.S. defenders. And so the world is treated to the spectacle of the militaries of two countries, that are otherwise pursuing mostly friendly relations, planning and deploying forces against each other on a daily basis. For the U.S. military in particular, the Taiwan situation means investing in its own forces to prevent Chinese improvements in counter-air, counter-carrier, counter-information, counter-space, and other capabilities from upsetting the balance in the Strait.

It would be unwise to ignore the dangers of this miniature and localized but very real "arms race." But there is no reason why—through dialogue, openness, and restraint on all sides—this situation cannot, to use Chen's words, remain "in the nature of crisis management rather than strategic confrontation."

Cooperation

Chen's most important injunction to the two militaries is his last: "China and the United States should discuss how to establish a relationship of constructive cooperation in the security field." Avoiding imprudent hedging and crises over Taiwan are necessary to avoid the potential strategic downside of U.S.-China relations, but it is much more important to capitalize on the potential upside. To this third recommendation

I would add that the two sides should not only discuss, but *act to en-hance*, constructive cooperation.

The world presents many common dangers and challenges to the global order upon which both China and the U.S. depend. In Chen's elegant phrase, "Humankind has moved into a new era: civilization is now as fragile as glass balls in the turbulence of scientific revolution." Terrorism, for example, is exemplified at the current time most conspicuously by Islamist fundamentalist extremism. But the march of science creates two trends that will make terrorism a danger to nations that are responsible stakeholders—as both the U.S. and China aspire to be—as far into the future as one can see, and long after today's dangerous ideologies have spent themselves. The first trend is the ability of smaller and smaller substate groups to obtain the destructive power formerly reserved to governments. The second is the growing interconnectedness and resulting fragility of modern society. It will long be the task of national security establishments, including in the U.S. and China, to protect the global order from these scientific trends. To "terrorism" can be added weapons of mass destruction, chaos and genocide in failed states, transnational crime, and natural disasters as areas where the militaries of the U.S. and China can usefully cooperate without in any way compromising their "prudent hedging." Joint action can take the form of combined planning, exercising, and actual conduct of operations. Indeed, cooperation against common dangers can ultimately contribute to the trust in each other's long-term evolution that would make hedging unnecessary.

Conclusions

The development of the overall U.S.-China relationship is outpacing the development of the military-to-military relationship, and the latter must catch up. Greater "transparency" in general is a good goal, but the defense relationship could usefully expand its agenda in three directions. First, candor about the mutually perceived need for prudent hedging in general and for the "Taiwan contingency" in particular might result in a set of "dos" and "don'ts" for both sides. Second, military-to-military dialogue should move to action in the many fields that are not sensitive but where mutual benefit will result. Third, over time the content of the relationship should evolve from containing the dangers of the U.S.-China strategic relationship to capitalizing on its upside. In Chen's words, "We need to shift from crisis management to opportunity management."

CHAPTER FIVE

ECONOMIC AND POLITICAL LIBERALIZATION IN CHINA: IMPLICATIONS FOR U.S.-CHINA RELATIONS

*Etel Solingen**

TWO APPROACHES IN INTERNATIONAL RELATIONS ASSESS THE RISE of China in starkly different ways. The first stems from a general theory that Great Powers are bound to challenge each other, often by force. There are many variants of this approach, but most share a view of a world in which there is no recognized ultimate authority and where states strive for survival in zero-sum fashion. This competitive approach predicts that Great Powers will take advantage of each other's vulnerabilities and abstain from making more concessions than needed.[1] Applied to China, this view predicts its rise will lead to a "power transition" with the United States. It posits an aggressive Chinese hegemonic state, vastly militarized, and espousing a version of a Monroe Doctrine, seeking to eject the United States from the region. In this view, a U.S. policy of engagement only whets China's appetite for power.[2] Yet empirical research has dealt a significant blow to theories focusing purely on relative capabilities and expansionist tendencies of Great Powers.[3] Indeed, as applied to China, the most aggressive era (under Mao) coincided with China's weakest relative power position. Today a far more powerful contemporary

*I would like to acknowledge useful suggestions from the editors, participants at the two conferences on The Future of U.S. China Cooperation, cosponsored by Harvard University's John F. Kennedy School and the Chinese Academy of Social Sciences (Beijing, December 15–16, 2007, and Cambridge, February 20–21, 2008), and Jack Snyder.

China shows restraint and pragmatic accommodation, thus far. These and many other anomalies and departures from mechanistic power-based theories do not bode well for many of their predictions, yet these theories are likely to linger for decades to come.[4] Furthermore, as international relations experts on cognitive processes have pointed out, these theories sometimes have a way of *creating* realities on the ground, making sure the worst happens by perennially preparing for it. Security dilemmas find fertile ground in mutual mistrust and lack of transparency.[5]

A second approach builds on elements of the liberal tradition adapted to the conditions of an emerging global economy. Richard Rosecrance's seminal study of "trading states" portrays an interdependent world where incentives to avoid war overwhelm incentives to fight.[6] The search for absolute gains—in which everybody can benefit from cooperation—thus helps states transcend atavistic territorial ambitions. Rejecting rigid structural power theories, Rosecrance sees globalization as replacing the old foundations of state power—territorial size and stockpiles of classical factors of production—with new ones, embedded in the flows of goods, capital, and labor and in managerial, financial, and creative capabilities. Whereas territorial states aimed at conquest, the vocation of trading and virtual states resides in international commerce and the mastery of ideas, knowledge, creativity, capital, and information. Clearly there are many differences between this view emphasizing productive and trading energies and the previous one, which focused purely on military capabilities. Crucially, instead of inescapable systemic processes leading inexorably to wholesome competition, the trading state approach offers the important insight that, in the real world, the *choice* between presumed atavistic tendencies and interdependent alternatives *does* exist. But who makes that choice?

For starters, domestic groups with different preferences regarding a globalizing trading system make different choices. Ruling coalitions and constituencies favoring further "internationalization" create conditions for cooperation, whereas their "backlash" counterparts thrive under military competition and economic autarchy.[7] On the ashes of earlier autarchic models, Deng Xiaoping and his internationalizing successors have made that choice, moving China away from the widespread hunger and turmoil of a previous era into a budding modernized state.[8] Just as expected from a trading state standpoint, the post-1979 model required a peaceful rise or "peaceful development," a new matrix of regional relations, a "charm offensive" vis-à-vis the Association of South East Asian Nations (ASEAN), a set of more mature economic and political relations with North East Asian neighbors (including Japan), and a new openness to multilateral cooperation and regional institutional arrangements. From the perspective of the architects of this new model, regional and global instability are anathema to efforts to lure foreign investment, natural resources, and broad international acceptability, without which continued economic growth and domestic political stability would be threatened. An internationalizing China and a stable regional environment pave the road to *xiaokang shehui*, a "well-off" society endowed with a majoritarian middle class.[9]

The grand strategy of integration into the global economy has served China well, helping it attract an estimated $450 billion in foreign direct investment (FDI) by 2003, capturing about 20 percent of all FDI going to the industrializing world today, and rendering China the world's third-largest exporter. China's foreign trade increased from 10 percent of gross domestic product in 1978 to about 44 percent in 2001.[10] Foreign reserves are over $1.4 trillion. And yet one should not minimize the serious political challenges to the model, including rural reform and urbanization, tensions between central and local interests, rising unemployment, an aging population, corruption, high dependence on foreign investment for continued growth, and various other potential bottlenecks on the road to sustainable development.[11] Given where we are today, what are some of the outstanding challenges and opportunities for cooperation between the United States and China?

Relations between the two Great Powers—as in any set of relations—include areas that can be categorized as benign, difficult, and potentially intolerable. The benign entails a lot of common ground, the ability to converge on focal points with minimal or moderate effort (e.g., increased cultural exchange, counterterrorism, health, avoiding/minimizing global economic downturns). The difficult requires far more work than the benign and entails potentially higher costs of adjustment on all sides (e.g., exchange rates, trade balances, energy resources, climate change, nuclear policies on North Korea and Iran, and relations with leaders involved in gross violations of human rights or destabilizing policies in Sudan, Myanmar, Venezuela, North Korea, Iran, and elsewhere). Yet, on the whole, the difficult if tolerable issues may not be as bad as they appear. By contrast, the potentially intolerable ones lodged between China and the United States could derail cooperation in the previous two categories. They cry out for solution. Taiwan, military modernization, and democracy and human rights within China are in this category.[12] This chapter concentrates on one issue in the third category that has been the focus of much academic and policy debate: does democratization matter for sustained cooperation? Is economic liberalization sufficient in itself for sustaining good relations?

Internationalization and the Democratic Peace

There is reason to believe that internationalizing ruling coalitions beget regional cooperation that is both intensive (in depth) and extensive (in scope), creating robust conditions for the emergence of zones of stable peace.[13] How are these conditions affected by the presence or absence of democracy? The proposition that mature democracies do not fight wars *against each other* has become the closest claim to a law of international politics, the so-called democratic peace theory. There is an understandable intellectual and policy excitement offered by the possibility that the global reach of democratization might not only solve the internal security dilemma of citizens but also remedy interstate security dilemmas. However, several findings on the connections between internationalization, democracy, and international behavior must be considered before reaching any definitive conclusions.

First, democracy is a sufficient—but not a necessary—condition for the absence of war. States may diverge with respect to regime type, and they may yet avoid war. Furthermore, states with different regime types can blend mixed purposes (values) into broad cooperative frameworks. Mixed and nondemocratic dyads and clusters in East and Southeast Asia, for instance, have developed patterns of cooperation on the ashes of earlier brutal conflicts. The period of confrontation in the mid-1960s has now been wholly overcome. The eventual transition to democracy in some of these states may have improved the quality of cooperation among democratic dyads but was arguably not necessary for the emergence of cooperation. Elsewhere, the absence of war in South America for nearly a century—with few exceptions—coexisted with decades of authoritarianism and preceded the wide dispersion of democracy throughout the continent in the 1990s. Furthermore, deeper cooperation (denuclearization of the Southern Cone and the establishment of the Mercosur preferential trade bloc) followed a broader shift toward integration in the global economy as a whole. It reinforced internationalizing strategies and helped create and sustain cooperation. Even in the realm of nuclear policy one finds an international arrangement (the nonproliferation treaty, or NPT) widely subscribed to by different types of regimes.[14] Furthermore, nuclear-weapons-free-zones have been established in regional domains where democracies were sometimes a minority (e.g., Latin America, the South Pacific, Africa, and Southeast Asia). Nondemocratic regimes made commitments to denuclearize in Argentina, Brazil, Egypt, Kazakhstan, Belarus, Ukraine, South Korea, Taiwan, and many other places. The vast majority of both democracies and nondemocracies have abided by their NPT commitments (although most *known* NPT violators have been nondemocratic, including Iraq, North Korea, Libya, and arguably Iran). Both democracies and nondemocracies have acquired nuclear weapons, and both have failed to fully abide by Article VI.

Second, in theory the confluence of democracy and internationalization makes the relationship between internationalizing coalitions and cooperative behavior more robust, particularly where internationalizing coalitions are strong domestically and throughout a region. Strong internationalizing coalitions with wide support for their economic outlook can afford to reinvent themselves through the democratic process, as various East Asian cases suggest.

Third, even if democracies may not go to war against each other, inward-looking democratic dyads and regional clusters arguably lead to more shallow cooperation than internationalizing ones. Finally, the conjuncture of inward-looking *and* nondemocratic dyads and clusters are likely to yield the most conflictive regional orders of all, combining the pernicious effects of both.

Transitions to Markets and Democracy

What do we know about temporal sequences regarding the onset of democracy and economic liberalization (internationalization) respectively? Figure 5.1 summarizes some general trends in recent decades. The vertical axis depicts regime type (democracy/nondemocracy), and the horizontal axis depicts the nature of ruling coalitions (internationalizing/inward-looking), yielding four possible ideal-types.

Figure 5.1. Regime Type and Domestic Coalitions

Ruling Coalitions	Regime Type	
	Democracy	Nondemocracy
Inward-looking	A: Inward-looking Democracy	B: Inward-looking Nondemocracy
Internationalizing	C: Internationalizing Democracy	D: Internationalizing Nondemocracy

Cell A denotes a democratic state ruled by an inward-looking coalition (India for many years, until the 1990s). Cell B points to a nondemocratic state ruled by an inward-looking coalition (many industrializing states in the post-1945 era; some contemporary Middle East states, among others). Cell C indicates an internationalizing ruling coalition steering a democratic state (Costa Rica, many European states). Cell D represents a nondemocratic state ruled by an internationalizing coalition (Singapore is a classical example, and so is China). Cells A and C (democratic) were rather unpopulated throughout much of the Cold War whereas cell B was crowded. Cell D became populated by Asian tigers in the 1960s, fueling the theory of "authoritarian advantage."[15] This theory suggested that nondemocratic regimes were better equipped to carry out painful reforms. However, as Adam Przeworski et al. concluded,[16] the theory built on success cases only, relying on best practices rather than average ones.

Many authoritarians may have tried to internationalize, but, in the long run, only a minority succeeded.

In the post-Cold War era there were massive transitions from cells A, B, and D into cell C. The *Peace and Conflict 2008* study by the Center for International Development and Conflict Management points to the significant rise in democratic and transitional regimes and the decline in nondemocratic ones in the past two decades.[17] Some transitions entailed moves along one axis only (A to C, for instance, with formerly inward-looking democracies embracing internationalization, as in India; or D to C, with internationalizers moving from nondemocratic to democratic systems, as in Chile). Other cases entailed twin transitions (from B to C), following either of two stylized paths away from inward-looking authoritarianism. In the first path, democracy took hold before a turn to internationalization, in a two-step sequence (from cell B to A, then to C), as in various South American countries (but not Chile). This path conformed to the "democratic efficiency" theory, suggesting that democratization—even at a slow rate—makes internationalization more palatable because of its greater legitimacy and informational advantages.[18] From this standpoint, democracy makes internationalization more sustainable. In the second path, internationalizing coalitions first steered states into the global economy (cell D) and only later into the democratic/internationalizing cell C. Many Asian tigers fit this model.

Some scholars regard economic crisis as the prelude to democratization, as far back as Martin Lipset in 1959.[19] Others view rising expectations during rapid economic growth—not crisis—as triggering democratic transitions.[20] Mary Gallagher found that China exceptionally defies both of these models for two reasons.[21] First, Chinese FDI liberalization preceded the privatization of state industry and the development of a national private sector, unlike the transition in other socialist countries. Second, FDI has been the dominant source of external capital, unlike in most other East Asian states. In this view, "reform and openness" (*gaige kaifang*) weakened civil society (particularly labor) and strengthened the state, accounting for regime stability and delayed democratization. Others trace this stability to gradualism in economic reform (no shock therapy and no losers from reform), and to the clothing of reform in nationalist rhetoric. However, the assumption that there have been no losers, no demands for political change, and that nationalism can always deflate domestic criticism is questionable.[22] Further, democratization can lead to aggressive foreign policy behavior.

Domestic Transitions and External Behavior

While acknowledging the fact that mature democracies do not go to war with each other, Edward Mansfield and Jack Snyder[23] show that *transitions* to democracy are laden with problems. Relying on both quantitative and qualitative evidence from the French Revolution onward, they find leaders in transitional societies are prone to use nationalism instrumentally. The links between transitions to democracy, intense nationalism, and war–they argue–are particularly strong in democratizing Great Powers. More specifically, Mansfield and Snyder suggest that their study validates the following hypotheses:

- Countries undergoing incomplete democratization with weak institutions are more likely than others to *become involved* in war.
- Countries undergoing incomplete democratization are more likely than others to *initiate* war.
- Incomplete democratization with weak institutions is especially likely to lead to war when powerful elites feel threatened by the prospect of a democratic transition.
- Countries undergoing complete democratization have a moderately higher risk of involvement in war shortly after the transition, but no elevated risk once democracy is consolidated. The increased risk of war for countries undergoing complete democratization applies mainly to states already involved in enduring rivalries whose nationalist and militarist institutions and ideologies were forged in earlier phases of democratization.

Mansfield and Snyder believe China is still far away from the kind of sustained and balanced economic development that can lead smoothly to democratic consolidation. To be sure, they consider the diffusion of democracy not only inexorable but also a positive development for global peace and stability in the long term. At the same time, they warn of the need to get the sequence right, namely to consolidate central legal and economic institutions before proceeding to fully fledged political parties and electoral competition.[24] This is consistent with promoting the rule of law and independent courts; guaranteeing property rights; developing a rational, impartial, and efficient administration; and allowing a professional and balanced mass media. The consolidation of these democratic institutions can act as a barrier against leaders who may be tempted to secure their domestic political survival through parochial nationalism. Without the prior consolidation of institutions, they argue, leaders have incentives to use nationalism and violence to draw attention away from domestic cleavages and to shore up their own legitimacy. War then becomes the by-product of nationalist provocations. The mobilization of nationalist support as a rallying theme is invariably a double-edged sword—in democracies and nondemocracies alike. In premature democracies, the overlap between prodemocracy, nationalist, and economic protectionist forces is a source of concern. The sustainability of an internationalizing strategy is thus critical.

How does this apply to China? China's internationalizing coalition has thus far prevailed over domestic forces favoring a return to closure, but some argue that democratization could empower farmers, the hinterland, the unemployed, and those segments of the military, state enterprises, and the Communist Party that have been adversely affected by economic openness to express themselves against internationalization.[25] An economic downturn could multiply the power of inward-looking forces, in a similar fashion to economic inequality, local corruption, environmental threats, and inadequate social safety nets. In earlier eras, internationalizing coalitions faced a dramatically different global economic, political, institutional, and strategic context than they do now. Today the uncertainties regarding the long-term effects of globalization render its political future opaque. Internationalization could still be reversible.

Notwithstanding the dangers of democratic transitions and perhaps illiberal democratization, one should consider the significant advantages of mature democracy in producing democratic peace.[26] Democracies are found to be more prone to join international institutions, particularly democratic "clubs" such as the Organization for Economic Cooperation and Development (OECD); to prevail in wars they do fight; to abide by their international commitments; to enter more preferential trading arrangements than their counterparts; to reduce civil war tensions; and to be more likely to choose their wars wisely and win them at lower costs (although one could not have guessed that from the U.S. adventure in Iraq).[27] Democracies may not be the most reliable allies, but their publics think they are.[28] Perceptions matter. Studies have also found nondemocratic leaders to be more prone to "gamble for resurrection" by going to war, to lengthen wars, and to tolerate higher war costs. Other work found transitional (mixed) regimes to be of particular concern because they are far more susceptible than either full democracies or autocracies to political instability, armed conflict, terrorist attacks, and international crises.[29]

Conclusions

Although the bulk of this chapter discussed recent findings of relevance to the debate over whether democratization affects the possibility of continued cooperation, I also pointed to the perils of pure balance-of-power thinking. The United States and China seem to have avoided this trap thus far.[30] However, closure, isolationism, and nationalism—on both sides—can revive these dangerous self-fulfilling modes of thinking. Democratization could arguably heighten nationalism. Ideally, fully consolidated internationalization can enhance the viability of national elections.

Along the range of issues stretching from benign, to difficult, to potentially intolerable in U.S.-China relations, the question of a nuclear North Korea was traditionally deemed to fall under the intolerable category. In days past, China strongly objected to any insinuations of "regime change" on the part of the United States, and America resented what it perceived as China's relaxed approach to North Korea's progressive nuclearization. These perceptions have been changing, particularly after China's support for UN Security Council resolutions on North Korea following the latter's 2006 nuclear test. The February 2007 breakthrough in the Six-Party Talks was a major step in the direction of implementing the September 19, 2005, Joint Statement, even if problems and hard negotiations remain. China's leverage over North Korea and its commitment to enforce the latter's compliance in successive phases of implementation will test the possibilities for further cooperation in this area. This issue-area has great potential to move into the "difficult" category, but crucial steps remain to be taken. The February 2007 agreement in the Six-Party Talks established a working group on a Northeast Asia Peace and Security Mechanism, which could provide the foundations for a stable, cooperative Northeast Asia.

There are important precedents for China's commitment to multilateral frameworks. China's "charm offensive" has already led to an understanding that a peaceful and prosperous Southeast Asia could guarantee continued overseas and regional investments, a sustained flow of natural resources required for China's own economic growth and political stability, and a smooth operation of crucial sea lanes in the Strait of Malacca—through which 80 percent of China's oil shipments transit. In 1999 China signed the Southeast Asia Nuclear Weapons Free Zone Treaty, and in 2002 it agreed to the Declaration on the Conduct of Parties in the South China Sea. In 2003 China and ASEAN signed the Joint Declaration on Strategic Partnership for Peace and Prosperity to coordinate foreign and security policy, and China acceded to ASEAN's Treaty of Amity and Cooperation, ahead of any other superpower. In 2004 China and ASEAN agreed to resolve quarrels concerning disputes in the South China Sea without the threat or use of force and approved a Plan of Action to Implement the Declaration on the Strategic Partnership for Peace and Prosperity, designed to deepen cooperation in economics and security. China has clearly supported ASEAN's institution-building efforts in East Asia, including the ASEAN Regional Forum and the ASEAN+3 processes.[31] Despite the different array of partners in Northeast Asia, including councils—like the Six-Party Talks—that included some historical rivals, China has entered a multilateral institutional arrangement that can help sustain a shared internationalizing strategy among four major global powers and two regional ones. These developments notwithstanding, differences between China and the United States regarding the nature of East Asian regional institutions remain.

Clearly, nobody can be certain of the tenor of U.S.-China relations twenty years down the road. We know that decisions in international relations are largely based on imperfect information. Yet we can try to avoid mistakes others have made. One can legitimately quarrel about what issues are most important or most dangerous in U.S.-China relations. First, skillful efforts on both sides can resolve to mutual satisfaction even those issues that fall under the potentially intolerable category. Second, an important task for the future will be to think through appropriate sequences and trade-offs across issues in the three categories identified earlier in this chapter. Some Chinese experts perceive we exist in a "period of strategic opportunity." Many Americans agree. It is up to those who share such convictions on both sides to make sure the opportunity is not wasted.

CHAPTER SIX

CHINA AND THE UNITED STATES AS INTERACTING SOCIETIES

Tony Saich

THOUGH THE SOCIETIES OF BOTH CHINA AND THE UNITED STATES will continue to evolve over the next twenty years, it is China that will experience the greatest changes. How China's social and political systems evolve will have a profound impact on the nature of U.S.-China relations. The magnitude of these changes will present both opportunities and challenges for the government, the people of China, and foreign nations. We know that Chinese society will age rapidly, with a significant gender imbalance and a growing middle class living in a more urban environment. We are less certain about what the consequences of these multiple transformations might be. Of course, over time the rate of economic growth will slow, but China's leaders are hoping that growth will last long enough and be robust enough to ensure that the country will grow rich before it grows old, an unlikely outcome, and mitigate the problems of inequality, un(der)employment, and environmental degradation that are part and parcel of China's development trajectory. What is even less certain is how the leadership will respond to the governance and political challenges of transition. Reforms have produced a burgeoning middle class, and historically middle-class nations have pressed for greater political inclusion and the devolution of more power to society. Can the Chinese Communist Party (CCP) develop a sustainable political model that combines economic liberalization with an authoritarian power structure? The answer to this question will profoundly affect the nature of China's relationship with the United States.

Demographic Trends: Creating New Challenges

By 2030, China's population will be nearing its peak of around 1.52 billion (it will rise to 1.54 billion in 2040 before starting to drop), but it will be seriously skewed in terms of dependency ratios. The aging will have significant consequences on savings rates, which will lower dependency ratios, and on the need to increase spending on medical care.[1] Overall, China will age 13.8 years during the first half of this century, as opposed to the United States, which will age 3.6 years.[2] It is unlikely that China can become rich before it grows old, even if it can maintain current growth rates. This takes us into uncharted waters; no society has grown old before it has grown rich. This will increase the pressure on maintaining high-quality growth and developing effective policies for urbanization.

At the end of the twentieth century, China officially entered the aging stage in terms of the internationally recognized criterion, with 10 percent of its population over sixty years of age. By the end of 2006, there were 149 million people over age sixty, accounting for 11.3 percent of the population.[3] With the elderly growing at 3.2 percent per annum, five times the total population growth, the number of those over sixty will be 248 million by 2020 and 437 million by 2050—over one-quarter of the population. According to the United Nations, the number of the oldest old (those over eighty years of age) in China will also increase, from 11.5 million in the year 2000 to 27 million in 2020 and 99 million in 2050. The group that comprised 13 percent of the elderly population in 2000 will comprise 30 percent of the population in 2050, growing faster than any other cohort.[4]

The aging population will present serious policy challenges in terms of dependency ratios and pension obligations that the state will be required to meet. The structure of the population will be what Chinese researchers refer to as a "4-2-1 family," with four grandparents, two parents, and one child. Children will have no siblings, and they will have to carry a heavy burden of support. The aging population will also require a significant increase in medical costs. In reviewing the situation in the United States,

Barbara Torrey estimates the cost of long-term care for this group to be 14.4 times higher than that for the 65–74 age group.[5] The Medicare costs are 77 percent higher than those for individuals aged 65–69.

These shifting demographics will have major consequences for dependency ratios and pension obligations. In 2004, official figures showed that the total dependency ratio was 38.63, with that for the elderly at 11.87, but the ratio of the working to nonworking population was dropping fast, at 6:1 in 1991 and anticipated to be 2:1 by 2020. However, as Hussain has perceptively pointed out, an exclusive focus on the dependency ratio of the elderly, which has been at the center of the debate over pension costs, is misleading. This ignores the large economic plus that comes from the declining dependency ratio of children (26.76 in 2004) that will bring benefits before the aging costs really begin to impact heavily. It is calculated that by 2020, children (0–14 years of age) will have dropped from 40.4 percent of the population in 1964 to 19.3 percent.[6] The United Nations Development Program (UNDP) calculates a slightly steeper drop, to 18.5 percent by 2015.[7]

The need to invest more in pensions and higher medical costs will mean that the Chinese leadership will have to hope that the economy keeps growing fast enough to generate the revenues needed to cover these costs. China's future leaders will find themselves in the familiar "guns versus butter" debates. Experience elsewhere, including South Korea and Taiwan, suggests that social welfare expenditures will increase further if political liberalization occurs.

In addition to aging, another adverse consequence of China's family-planning policy is the distortion in the male-female ratio. The most recent census (2000) shows that the ratio of males to females is 106.74:100, resulting in 41.27 million more men than women. However, at birth the ratio is 119.92:100, and by age four it is 120.17:100. Jiangxi and Guangdong have ratios of 138:01:100 and 137.76:100, respectively, with rural Guangdong at a rate of 143.7:100.[8] The ratio for those in the 10–15 age group is much lower, at 112.43:100. This clearly indicates a strong trend in a further imbalance in the ratio over the next ten to fifteen years and beyond. These ratios will mean that at least 1 million men per year will not be able to find a marriage partner,[9] and more recent figures suggest even higher numbers. One assessment calculates that there may be as many as 100 million Chinese bachelors by the year 2020.[10] Such skewed ratios will have significant consequences for family structures and also for the capacity of families to take care of the elderly, perhaps requiring the state or civil society organizations to take on greater responsibilities. Other consequences will be the increase in dowry price in the rural areas and increased illegal trade in women and in prostitution. If large numbers of males who cannot find a bride drift into cities looking for work, there will be increased demand for the services of commercial sex workers, and this will likely increase the spread of HIV/AIDS.

Over the next two decades China will become much more urbanized. The leadership seeks to move between 300 million and 500 million people from the rural areas to towns and cities by 2020, providing an urban population of around 800 million. In fact, urbanization is seen as the best way to provide a long-term solution to the problems of inequality that stem primarily from urban-rural differences. The main debate has been over how to manage this process; proponents are divided over whether the focus should be on developing major megalopolises along the coast with these cities as the destination of migrants or on small-town expansion in the countryside. Whereas policy makers have generally favored the latter, reality is likely to favor the former, and this will demand that China's urban areas become much more efficient, as they have in Japan.

The third major demographic shift is the increased urbanization that has accompanied continued economic growth and is anticipated to accelerate in the future. The move out of agriculture has been important to improve livelihoods, but the population shifts have presented challenges in terms of integrating the new populations into effective urban environments. With the return to family farming under the household responsibility system, a large pool of labor was released to work in rural small-scale industry as well as to provide the migrant labor to underpin the urban construction and services boom. The 2000 census noted 144 million (12 percent of the population) living away from their registered abode. Of these, 79 million were long-distance migrants, up from 7 million in 1982 and 22 million in 1990. In a province such as Guangdong, migrants make up 25 percent of the population, whereas in Shanghai they constitute over 10 percent of the population.[11] China's future stability depends on how effectively these migrants are integrated into new urban centers and provided with effective education, housing, and medical services. If China's rising middle class is able to buy or is provided with effective services while new urban entrants are excluded or provided with inferior services, the politics of envy and resentment are likely to increase and provide a reservoir of discontented citizens that could be mobilized by contentious political factions.

The challenge should not be underestimated. At the Seventeenth Party Congress (November 2007) it was stated that "city clusters with mega-cities at the core" are the new poles of economic growth. This suggests that the program of urbanization will move ahead despite the continued commitment to policies to "build a new socialist countryside."

The 2000 census calculated an urban population in China of 455.94 million (36.09 percent of all Chinese).[12] This was a 9.86 percent increase over 1990, the year of the previous census. However, getting an accurate count of China's urbanization is very difficult because of different counting systems that are used.[13] If we take the census figure in comparative terms, China is "under-urbanized" as a result of the previously controlled urban flow and the household registration system. Other transitional societies have higher rates of urbanization—such as Hungary (64 percent) and Russia (73 percent)—as do the remaining socialist countries—Cuba (75 percent) and North Korea (59 percent).[14] Over the next ten years the urbanization rate is expected to increase to 40 percent at current rates of growth. But with current policy favoring urbanization, it is likely to be higher, perhaps reaching the 55–60 percent range.[15] Given the level of industrialization, the urbanization rate in China should be around 60 percent. Interestingly, on the sidelines of the Seventeenth Party Congress, Guo Shuqing, chair of the board of the Construction Bank of China, made the comment that if one used the World Bank criterion of those who worked in the cities for at least three months of the year no longer being farmers, then China's urbanization rate was already 60 to 65 percent. This is a significant difference, with major consequences for effective government investment and service provision. Meeting the urbanization goals will present major challenges for the government in terms of investment in urban infrastructure and planning. It will also present significant challenges for job creation and the provision of social welfare. The programs for infrastructure development will provide employment opportunities, but whether the service industries will be expanded sufficiently to deal with this increased urbanization and will be able to accommodate the estimated 150–200 million surplus laborers in rural China remains to be seen.

This means that there must be new avenues of employment growth. The Development Research Center of the State Council calculates that the Chinese economy needs to generate around 24 million jobs to absorb the new labor force, laid-off workers, and college graduates, and it does not see the employment pressure alleviating for twenty to thirty years. The best option for employment growth is the service sector, which in China employs a smaller percentage of employees in comparison with other countries at a similar level of development. Allowing effective foreign investment into this sector could generate a boom of 40–50 million jobs. The other main option for employment expansion is enhanced development of the private sector. Geographically, private enterprises are heavily concentrated in the coastal areas, with Jiangsu, Guangdong, Zhejiang, Shanghai, and Beijing home to 54 percent, and the western provinces only 14 percent. Those provinces with a higher growth rate and standard of living are also those with a higher level of private enterprise.

Prospects for the Economy and the Relationship with the United States

To a large extent the potential for future U.S.-China relations depends on the trajectory of the Chinese economy. As other chapters in this volume have demonstrated (especially Chapter 3), the vitality of the two economies has become inextricably linked. A slowdown in the U.S. economy will have an impact on China's capacity to export, as will appreciation of the Chinese currency and the increase in prices for raw materials.

Although trade frictions and currency wrangling will remain for some time, strong growth is essential for China via the creation of new higher quality jobs. A major challenge for China will be whether it can move up the production chain, generating higher paid employment for its citizens to replace many of the low-wage manufacturing jobs that have fuelled the economic boom to date. This would see China emulating the economic development pattern of its neighbors in East Asia.

A faltering economy would be problematic for all concerned. Obviously, future economic development depends on a number of assumptions being fulfilled, and a number of problems could throw these assumptions off course. First, there must be no domestic or external shocks that would derail growth. A global economic downturn resulting in major trading nations deciding to raise trade barriers on Chinese products would have malign effects. China might then turn to other ways of improving its political lot.

Even under favorable circumstances, the growth rates of the Chinese economy of 10 percent and more in recent years will inevitably decline to around 4.5 to 5.5 percent by 2030. The Chinese currency should have doubled or tripled in value over this period of time, achieving at least 4 RMB = US\$1. As the economy matures, the growth rate should settle down to a lower, more sustainable level; this will be aided by a shift to domestic consumption as the main driver of growth. However, this would still mean that the Chinese economy will be the first or second largest in the world by 2030, having overtaken Japan by around 2015. This measure, of course, is total gross domestic product (GDP), not per capita GDP, and on the latter figure China will still remain far short of 2007 OECD levels. Its current \$2.2 trillion GDP (at nominal rates) should grow to \$4.7 trillion in 2015, \$7.0 in 2020, and over \$14 trillion by 2030. In purchasing power parity (PPP) terms, the rise would be from about \$10 trillion in 2007 to \$44 trillion a generation later. Depending upon U.S. growth rates, this could equal or surpass U.S. GDP (at 3 percent growth rates, current U.S. GDP would achieve \$26 trillion only in 2032). This would mean a nominal Chinese GDP per capita of $9,800 in 2030. In PPP terms it would be around $29,300. Thus, a major consequence will be a substantial expansion of the middle class, an issue we will return to.

The structure of the economy will also look different, with a high percentage engaged in the service sector and less in primary production. The Development Research Center calculates that already by 2020 less than 5 percent of the labor force will be engaged in the primary sector, with 45.5 percent in the secondary sector and 49.5 percent in the tertiary sector. In the future, continued growth in the economy will rely on increases in capital stock and total factor productivity. It is clear that China needs to shift the main engine of growth to the service sector. The bottom line is that, despite the reassessment of the GDP figures on the basis of the new economic census, the development strategy that has worked for the China in the past will not function as well in the future. To realize its growth potential, China must generate new demand to bring increased production. Over the past decade, the two principal drivers have been the growth of state investment and the growth of net exports, followed by consumption. If we look to the future, investment—especially in infrastructure and industry—will remain important, but there is no room for the ratio of investment to GDP to rise. Though China's exports are likely to continue expanding given the current scale, the rate of increase is bound to diminish. China's total trade is already around 70 percent of GDP, a ratio usually found in small export-driven economies (ASEAN and Taiwan) and not in continental economies.[16] Meanwhile, with production growing, imports are booming, and the overall trade surplus will be small if not eroded altogether.

This leaves consumption as the main driver of China's economic growth. Effective expansion of consumption has been held in check by the high rates of savings because of people's legitimate needs to save for retirement, medical care, and education. If these were provided by the government, consumption would greatly increase as savings declined. Government sterilization of incoming funds from the export surplus also has stunted consumption. The savings rate in China climbed to over 43 percent of income in 2004 from about 26 percent in 1985, and this is not likely to increase further. In major OECD economies, the household savings rate averages around 10 percent (with the notable exception of the United States, under 1 percent). China is on a par with Singapore, but much of Singapore's savings consists of mandatory contributions to a social security program. To meet the consumption objective, China will have to integrate its domestic market with the outside world and to develop more effective financial instruments and credit arrangements.

The shift to domestic consumption together with the changing demographics will lead to slower growth rates over time. Further constraints will be set by limits on energy resources and water supplies. Last but not least, continued high growth runs the risk of creating an environmental nightmare. What is worrying is that such major environmental problems of water and air pollution (two out of three cities fail to meet resident ambient air quality standards, and 10 percent of adult deaths in Shanghai have been attributed to air pollution) have developed so early in the transition—per capita income is only $1,100, and still over half of the population is living in rural areas. To reduce energy demand, the government set a target of using 20 percent less energy for each percentage point of output growth—a target that is unlikely to be met.

A smoothly growing China will focus on its position in the world economy and have less reason to think in territorial terms. However, the "rise of China" will raise questions for the United States, particularly as a "hegemonic transition" in the position of the two countries approaches in 2030 and afterward. Even more difficult might be a sudden check to Chinese growth—as a result of recession and/or the increase in worldwide tariffs. In a country largely dependent upon resources obtained from outside, some leaders might think in terms of regional access in Russia or Southeast Asia and plan military strategies accordingly. In the 1930s Germany and Japan charted their expansionist strategies in a context of worldwide economic restriction. Even if China's growth does not face obstacles, the United States will have to find ways of accommodating China's interests in the broader international system. Britain failed to do this vis-à-vis Germany in 1890, though it was more successful in regard to the United States (see Chapter 1). The accommodation of China's demands should not be an insurmountable problem and is certainly a strategy that is preferable to trying to frustrate them. On the whole, China has increasingly accommodated its international behavior to international norms, even if this has taken some time and external pressure to bring about.[17]

Political Developments:
The Demand for Inclusion

The creation of an urban middle class has been a key product of Chinese reform. The response of this class to policy will be a crucial determinant of China's future direction. The CCP's policy of co-optation of the population has worked very well to date, and there is no sign that the middle class demands rapid political reform. However, little research has been conducted on the middle class, and both its size and opinions are unclear. The Chinese Academy of Social Sciences in a 2003 survey calculated that the group amounted to 19 percent of the population and could grow to 35 percent of the population by 2020.[18] A report by the *McKinsey Quarterly* calculated that by 2011 the lower middle class (earning between 25,000 and 40,000 RMB annually) would amount to 290 million (accounting for 44 percent of the urban population). More impressively, by 2025 the upper middle class (annual income 40,001 to 100,000 RMB) will amount to 520 million (50 percent of the urban population). They will have a disposable income of 13.3 trillion RMB.[19] Obviously, they have a lot riding on continued economic growth and stability and could form the backbone for a positive relationship with the United States.

As long as the economic growth persists, the growth of this middle class should exert a stabilizing influence if its members can be co-opted successfully by the CCP leadership. Following President Jiang Zemin's speech on July 1, 1999, greater numbers of the middle class, including private entrepreneurs, have joined the party, and a law expanding the protection of private property has been passed. If politically cultivated, the middle class will not necessarily be a force to quicken the pace of democratic change. Most research shows that during the process of transition, the middle class favors stability and a gradual approach to change within the existing economic and political system. However, this class is likely to expect an increase in transparency, particularly at the local level, and a reduction in corruption. The middle class can become a support base for the expansion of civil and political rights if its economic interests so dictate. We have seen, however, a burgeoning social activity around environmental and quality of life issues. For example, citizens in middle-class neighborhoods in Shanghai protested the extension of the Maglev train system to link the city's two major airports. In Xiamen, Fujian Province, a largely middle-class protest successfully stopped the opening of a chemical plant. Such protests are not regime threatening in the way that those of the poor or marginalized groups could be, but they may lead to calls for greater transparency and accountability in the political system and a more regularized application of the rule of law.

This status-quo orientation of the middle class at the present time will be reinforced by the aging of Chinese society. An older society tends to mean a more stable and conservative attitude. This also argues for a gradual approach to change within the Chinese political system. More of the state's finances will have to be invested in care for the elderly, and social welfare expenditure will rise. This means there will be fewer funds available for military purposes.

These trends would argue against the views of those who feel that the "rise" of China will inevitably set the United States and China on a collision course. However, China's continuing economic growth and its increasing role in global politics will cause concern for U.S. policy makers, who will have to make space for China's legitimate interests. Energy scarcity or differences over Taiwan could still provide the spark for a more contentious relationship, but ultimately the state of the relationship will be improved by smoothly functioning economic interactions.

Set against this has been the strident outbursts of nationalism that have broken out, often fuelled by citizens whipping up interest through the Internet. This is difficult for the leadership to handle, and in a number of instances it has had to acquiesce to citizen pressure for action against foreign countries, usually waiting a decent period of time before moving to calm the situation down before foreign relations are damaged too seriously.

However, it is a dangerous game to play, as a government retreat might be interpreted as weakness by nationalistic xenophobes. With the decline in belief in the official orthodoxy of Marxism-Leninism, China's leaders have sought ways to bolster their legitimacy beyond the ephemeral fruits of economic growth. The promotion of nationalism has occurred not only through pride in China's achievements over the past fifteen years but also by the patriotic education campaigns that were promoted after the suppression of the student-led demonstrations of 1989. This has been a particular problem in China's relations with Japan.

We have seen a huge upsurge in protests over foreign countries for their criticism of China's human rights record in the run-up to the 2008 Olympics; France came in for particularly harsh criticism online for the demonstrations against the Olympic torch relay in Paris. This led to attempts in China to organize a boycott of the retailer Carrefour. Similar online criticisms were launched against what was seen as Western bias in reporting about the spring 2008 riots in Tibet; CNN even had to apologize to the Chinese government for negative comments made by one of its journalists about the nature of the Chinese leadership. It is clear that in these protests, citizens do not distinguish between criticism of the Chinese leadership and that of the Chinese nation and people as a whole. This creates a volatile situation that may force the Chinese leadership into a stronger antiforeign stance than they may see themselves as desirable. It is also a resource that China's leaders could draw on if reforms and the economy bog down. The antiforeign card could be played to strengthen their weakening position.

China's political system could witness major structural change between now and 2030. How the leadership manages the next phase of reform will prove crucial for the relationship. The current central leadership is aware of this and has responded with calls for better and more transparent government and for the party to monitor itself and the government more effectively. At the CCP plenary session in September 2004, the party formally recognized its shift from a revolutionary to a ruling party. CCP documents and speeches of leaders refer frequently to the need to promote democracy and the rule of law, with an emphasis on boosting inner-party democracy and developing a broader form of consultative democracy and perhaps extending electoral competition to levels above the village. The key question, however, is whether the party can develop the governing capacity to deal with the multiple challenges it faces (inequality, social unrest, and corruption) or whether it will reach a level that will overwhelm the politico-administrative system. If the leadership rejects what it terms "Western-style" political structures, it will be incumbent on them to develop the kind of institutions within the framework of one-party rule that cannot only continue to stimulate economic growth but also deal with the social tensions, provide sufficient transparency to reduce corruption, and make officials accountable to the citizens who pay their wages. Liberalization will have to be at least a partial substitute for full democratization. This will require further progress in developing the legal system and legal rights, including greater protection of property rights (including intellectual property rights), stricter enforcement of anticorruption rules, and greater consumer protection. If this is achieved, the CCP will be the first titular Communist movement in world history to manage a peaceful political transition that co-opts the middle class.

It is in this area of political systems and the understanding of individual rights that there is the greatest divergence in views and mistrust between the United States and China. In the foreseeable future, both nations will continue to disagree on fundamental values. However, further Chinese liberalization will lessen misunderstanding and contribute to a greater U.S.-Chinese consensus. Some political divergences may be too great to be bridged in the short run, but on some concrete issues and governing practices there are greater common interests. Local governments in both countries, for example, are wrestling with how to provide better public services for their citizens within increasing financial constraints. In this and other areas, such as social welfare provision and the role that nongovernmental organizations can play in providing goods and services, there are fruitful areas for cooperation.

However, the CCP has acknowledged the need for greater democracy, the rule of law, and good governance to retain the support of its citizenry.

Yet for the foreseeable future, China's party leadership is unlikely to be subjected to demands for full democracy in the Western sense. But if the United States and China are to avoid conflict over the longer term, it is imperative that the growing Chinese middle class receive at least informal inclusion in leadership decisions and policies. As an example, in the late nineteenth century the German middle class was split, and government by the middle class was never achieved. Aristocratic and administrative influences permeated society. The nationalists were primarily govern-ment workers, high industrialists, and the military; they did not include workers, peasants, or the petit bourgeoisie.[20] The predominantly eco-nomic fractions of society did not achieve a preponderant influence upon German leadership. Some form of incorporation of the emerging Chi-nese middle-class and economic stratum will ensure that Chinese policy is not determined by nationalists—those on the periphery and somewhat excluded from the mainstream of political-economic life.

Conclusions

It is not possible to chart the course of the future U.S.-China relation-ship, but a number of scenarios can be drawn from the analysis pre-sented in this chapter. If current policy continues, the relationship will not suffer unduly, but it will be subject to instabilities. The differences in culture and political system and the underlying nationalist sentiment will mean that the relationship is vulnerable to the impact of external events. It is uncertain whether there will be sufficient mutual trust to ride through a crisis such as the EP–3 incident or the NATO bombing of the Chinese Embassy in Belgrade without disruption. Pragmatic rea-sons will push politicians on both sides to ensure that the relationship does not spiral downward and out of control, but it will be difficult to forge a genuine equal partnership. The CCP could still flirt with a stri-dent form of nationalism in order to bolster the national consensus. Friction with the United States will continue, and a full rapprochement is improbable. Policy will continue to harbor the tensions between ap-peasing the new economic elites and trying to provide support for those who have been left behind by the reforms. Politicians on both sides are likely to blame policy shortcomings on the actions of the other party, whether this be the hollowing out of U.S. industry or China's problems in accessing sufficient raw materials.

Continued economic growth in China and the inclusion of the middle class into the political structures, combined with further liberalization in the social and political spheres, would, of course, be the most beneficial to a sound relationship. Should there be a democratic breakthrough with China following the path of others in the region, this would reduce tensions and place the relationship on a sound footing. Optimists would like to see China following in the footsteps of its East Asian neighbors, with a transition to "soft authoritarianism" followed by a democratic breakthrough as a natural corollary of economic growth. Although this is desirable from the point of view of the United States, it does not seem likely in the short term.

A third scenario would see the current leadership becoming sufficiently disturbed by the potential for unrest and what it interprets as U.S. attempts to isolate it internationally that it would adopt a more nationalistic policy combined with an inefficient authoritarianism domestically. Then the party would be dominated by new elites who would read any opening up of the political system as leading to erosion of their privileges and benefits. A strident nationalism might provide a minimal level of social glue to give the new regime a residue of support. A more likely variant would be the emergence of a predemocratic Latin American-style political system. Under this scenario the inequalities would continue to rise, with the CCP becoming the preserve of the elites, whose power would be backed up by the military. The lack of political reform would produce a permanent underclass in both urban and rural China that would be portrayed as a threat to stability and continued economic progress. This would be the worst outcome for U.S.-China relations.

The problems that confront United States and China as they reach the top of the power pyramid are not new ones. France and England, Germany and the United Kingdom, the Soviet Union and the United States confronted each other with war or cold war as the result. Only exceptionally have two Great Powers negotiated a transition without major conflict. England and the United States did so between 1890 and 1910 (see Chapter 1). They were enabled to do so at least in part because of firm connections between their societies in economic, cultural, and political terms. China and the United States will probably not be as culturally or linguistically close as were the United States and Britain, but they can substitute for this greater differentiation with extensive and programmed efforts to bring the societies closer together. Governments are ultimately tied to societies. Social links then can help to bring stronger governmental ones.

CHAPTER SEVEN

STRENGTHENING THE STRATEGIC DIALOGUE BETWEEN CHINA AND THE UNITED STATES ON CORE POLITICAL VALUES

Yu Keping

GENERALLY SPEAKING, SINO-U.S. CONFLICTS OVER SOME POLITICAL issues originate from the underlying differences between them on such basic political values as democracy and human rights. Such an argument seems to have been proved in practice. The U.S. government has been critical of the Chinese government's handling of human rights and democracy issues, asserting the massive violation of human rights in China and even ruling that China cannot be included on the list of global democratic countries. China has retaliated as a result. China reiterated that the existing social system fits China's domestic conditions best, that the Chinese people have the right to choose their own road toward political democratization, and that democracy and human rights are domestic issues that foreign countries have no right to meddle in. Moreover, China attacked the U.S. government for using "dual standards" on the issues of human rights and democracy, arguing that a massive violation of human rights exists in U.S. society if it is assessed by criteria used to judge China. After the U.S. State Department issued its annual white book of *Country Reports on Human Rights Practices,* the State Council Information Office of China issued its own annual white books, *Progress of China's Human Rights Practices* and *Records of Human Rights Practices in the U.S.*

Both China and the United States are Great Powers with significant influences on the world historical process. Conflicts between the two countries over core political values would not only damage their national interests but also impede the stability of international community and advancement of global democracy to some extent. Core political values such as democracy and human rights can decisively influence the domestic political life and deeply shape the foreign policy of a country as well. As permanent members of the United Nations Security Council, China and the United States shoulder significant responsibilities to the international community. In this modern globalization era, the Sino-U.S. strategic dialogue on core political values is especially conducive to the sustained stability of international community and the realization of a harmonious world.

It is fair to say that China and the United States share elements of agreement concerning democracy and human rights, although fundamental differences also exist between them. I will explore the shared elements firstly by examining the political system, constitutional principles, and dominant discourses within both countries.

First, both China and the United States place human rights at the top of their political agendas. The constitution of the People's Republic of China explicitly states that the people are the origin of all political powers of the PRC, and the people's congresses at various levels practice state power on behalf of the people. The Chinese government has been increasingly attaching importance to safeguarding the human rights of ordinary citizens. At the end of 2003, the Central Committee of the CCP formally proposed to incorporate "safeguarding the human rights of citizens" into the constitution. Thereafter, the National People's Congress approved adding "safeguarding human rights" to the 2004 constitutional amendment. In 2007 the National People's Congress passed the "Property Law," the first one in Chinese history, which stipulates that the legal private property of citizens should be properly safeguarded. At the very beginning of reform and opening up, the Central Committee of CCP came to realize that "one of the painful lessons [the] CCP should remember is over-centralization, and now democracy and decentralization should be given more prominence."[1] Deng Xiaoping also argued that socialist modernization would hold no hope without democracy.[2] In 2007 the report of the Seventeenth Party Congress of the CCP explicitly stated that people's democracy is the life of socialism.[3] More recently, President

Hu Jintao expressed that the CCP should hold high the banner of people's democracy. Democracy, though understood differently, is a basis of political legitimacy in both China and the United States. The democracy that the Chinese people are pursuing is defined as "people's self-mastery" or "popular sovereignty"—that is, the people are the master of the country and the origin of state power as well.

Both China and the United States believe that the rule of law is very important. The United States has a long tradition of rule of law, which together with democracy is a basic component of the American political culture. In contrast, China historically cherished the "rule of man," the "rule of virtue," or the "rule of courtesy," with much emphasis on rule *by* law rather than rule *of* law. However, the CCP and the Chinese government have been paying growing attention to the rule of law since the reform and opening up. In the 1980s CCP leaders announced that as the sole ruling party in China, the CCP must act within the framework of the constitution and laws and that no party cell or party member has the right to overstep the laws. In 1997 the Fifteenth National Congress of the CCP formally put forward the political objective of "constructing a socialist country under the rule of law." In 1998 the National People's Congress absorbed the clause "constructing a country under the rule of law" into the constitution. As referred to by the CCP and the Chinese government, *rule of law* means that law is the supreme authority within a country and that all men are equal before the law. The Sixteenth National Congress put forward the objective to "construct a socialist political civilization," the two pillars of which are democracy and rule of law. In other words, democracy and the rule of law have been widely recognized as two fundamental political principles in China's political context. For example, both Chinese leadership and intellectuals agree that democracy requires some mechanisms to make it work, such as free and open elections, checks and balances of powers, large-scale political participation of citizens, and a sound legal system.

On the other hand, the divergences between China and the United States on such core political values as democracy and the rule of law seem much more noticeable than do the commonalities between the two countries. Sometimes the standpoints of the two sides are opposite, especially in terms of the assessment of democracy and human rights. As far as the democracy issue is concerned, there are at least two typical viewpoints, both of which provoked mutual finger-pointing.

In the opinion of most American politicians and scholars, democracy must meet three minimal standards: (1) a multiparty system, with at least two parties competing for power; (2) a general election system with all eligible citizens freely voting for state leaders; and (3) checks and balances among the legislative, executive, and judicial branches. Based on these standards, U.S. observers assessed different political systems in the world, China among them. In their eyes, the CCP is the sole ruling party in China, and multiparty competition doesn't exist; neither is there a general election with "one citizen, one ballot" as its major characteristic, nor are there balances and checks among China's governmental branches. As a result, in their assessment China does not meet any of the three minimal standards of democracy. Thus they jumped to the conclusion that China is not a democratic country.

In response, the Chinese government insisted that the existing political system is the best one to safeguard the interests of the Chinese people and that practice has shown that the socialist democratic system with Chinese characteristics is a successful political system. Apart from defending the legitimacy of China's political system, some mainstream Chinese scholars also voiced two criticisms of U.S. politics. The first is based on classical Marxist theories. According to classical Marxist theories, they argued, any democracy has a class foundation by nature. Actually, in these terms democracy only means the political rights of the ruling class. Democracy and dictatorship are two sides of the same coin. Democracy for the ruling class is tantamount to dictatorship for the ruled classes. As a result, they concluded, all capitalist democracies, including the United States, are hypocritical in nature. Democracy is only a tool the ruling class uses to cheat the people. The second criticism is based on politics. Some Chinese scholars blame the American democratic system for its intrinsic defects, as many government policies do not necessarily reflect the will of the majority of the people. Severe violations of human rights exist in American society, and the U.S. government also compromises the human rights of people in other countries under the guise of protecting human rights and promoting democracy. As a result, these scholars concluded that the United States—the mouthpiece of human rights in the world—is actually the most formidable threat to the world human rights cause.

What makes China and the United States so different from each other in terms of core political values? I believe the basic reasons are the different tradition of political culture and the different level of socioeconomic development. In addition, misunderstanding and prejudice between the two sides exacerbate the difference. This latter can actually be mitigated by communication, dialogue, and cooperation.

In the view of many Chinese scholars, U.S. politicians and scholars misunderstand democracy in China. For example, many Americans simply label the party system in China as "the dictatorship of one party." In fact, the party system in China is "one-party rule, multiparty cooperation." According to this institutional arrangement, on the one hand, the Communist Party of China, like any other ruling party in the world, tries to maintain its leadership as a ruling party; on the other hand, governments at all levels from the center to localities are coalition governments between the CCP and other elements. Government at all levels includes representatives from other factions, some in leadership positions. Moreover, the CCP per se has been changing greatly. The CCP admits that it has transformed from a revolutionary party to a ruling party. It openly announced that its ruling position was not its birthright, and that the ruling position wouldn't last forever.[4] The CCP needs democracy, rule of law, and good governance to obtain the support of the people and to maintain its ruling position. Currently the CCP's political ideal is to achieve the integration of and the balance among "the leadership of the party," "the mastery of the people," and "the rule of law."[5]

Chinese scholars also believe that many Americans have ignored the progress China has made in democracy and human rights. According to these scholars, every Chinese man and woman can feel deeply that China has made great progress not only in economic development but also in political development since the reforms. China has been learning the positive elements of political civilization across the world and integrating them into the Chinese context. Even if not fully achieved, human rights, the rule of law, and democracy are now parts of the core values in Chinese politics. A number of new institutions, such as the policy-making hearing, publicity of political affairs, one-stop-shopping administrative service, presumption of innocence, and so on, have been adopted and promoted in China. These usages were usually seen as typical Western political practices.

Last but not least is the prejudice in favor of Western-style democracy. Many U.S. politicians and intellectuals take the Western (i.e., U.S.) model of democracy as the only model, measuring and judging China according to its parameters. But just as the economic and cultural life of humans is diverse, so is political life. Historically speaking, the path of China's political development is very different from that in the West, much as its economic development has been different. The model of economic development with Chinese characteristics has been successful. From this point of view, why couldn't a model of political development with Chinese characteristics be similarly successful?

Frankly speaking, in the foreseeable future, China and the United States are not likely to have convergent political values. However, it is possible to remove misunderstandings and prejudice, to increase consensus, and to mitigate divergences. In my view, both nations could shelve some political issues where consensus is unlikely to be reached. China and the United States should promote dialogue and communication in fields where there is a relatively small divergence of opinion or where there are great common interests. They should seek common ground while accepting existing differences. They should contribute to a more harmonious world by increasing the two sides' common political interests and by promoting global democracy. Following is a closer look at some of these shared interests.

Shared Interests

Globalization and Government Innovation

Government reform and innovation is a global agenda. China and the United States can jointly examine several issues by enhancing communication and cooperation: how to increase the incentives for government innovation; how to tackle the challenges posed by globalization to government management systems; how to reduce the cost of administration; how to promote the efficiency of administration; how to improve the quality of service provided by the government; how to increase transparency in the government management; how to enhance the role of e-government; and how to prevent bureaucratism and corruption among government officials.

Social Policy

China and the United States have common interests in the field of social policy. Dialogue between the two countries could help solve these concerns: how to ensure public safety; how to solve the problem of an aging population; how to improve social security; how to improve city governance; how to enhance a society's capacity in tackling emergencies; how to decrease social conflicts; how to coordinate development in urban and rural areas; how to promote social innovations; how to prevent and control crime; and how to fight against terrorist activities.

Civil Society

The two nations also have common concerns in developing a healthier civil society. For example, how can mutual trust between civil society organizations and governments be nurtured and maintained? How should civil society organizations (CSOs) be regulated? How can CSOs best be encouraged to orderly participate in the political process? How should the capacity of social organizations in self-government be enhanced? How can risk in civil society be avoided? And how can government enhance civil society's dynamics? If cooperation and trust between China and the United States are to last, the governments and the civil societies in the two countries must work together.

Public Participation

Public participation is crucial to both the Chinese and U.S. versions of democracy. Citizens of both nations can increase the capacity of self-government through dialogue, jointly examining how to tackle the challenges posed by globalization on social autonomy, how to nurture and increase citizens' capacity of participation, how to promote the role of community organizations in public participation and social autonomy, and how to coordinate citizens' political participation, economic participation, and social participation. In addition, they can determine how best to increase and strengthen the channels for public participation and social autonomy.

Ecological Governance

Domestic safety as well as global safety is at stake in ecological safety. In the field of ecological governance, the common interests between China and the United States are obvious. Both countries are facing serious problems in ecological safety caused by economic development and the improvement of living standards. Both countries must focus on communication and dialogue in this field, answering questions such as how to ensure sustainable social and economic development; how to promote education on ecological safety among citizens; how to promote the awareness of environmental protection; how to make more efficient policies for protecting ecology; how to tackle and prevent global warming; how to improve the legal system in protecting ecology; how to coordinate the possible conflicts and tensions between the two countries in international energy development and utilization; and how to develop a new type of global ecological ethics.

Conclusions

All in all, although there are significant differences in the history and culture, in the political system, in the ideology, and in the level of economic development of China and the United States, there are also many common interests. It is important to note that these common interests have been increasing in tandem with the development of domestic and foreign affairs in both countries. If the governments and the people of both nations jointly invest in maintaining and promoting healthy relations that seek common ground while accepting existing differences, the shared interests of the two countries will be enhanced. China and the United States will not necessarily be strategic adversaries. On the contrary, their strategic partnership will be consolidated, which will help promote their common interests and in turn promote global democratic governance.

PART TWO

PROBLEM AREAS

CHAPTER EIGHT

DAMPENING THE TAIWANESE FLASH POINT

Xu Shiquan and Ezra F. Vogel

THE TAIWAN ISSUE REMAINS A THORNY ONE IN SINO-AMERICAN relations. China considers it to be the most sensitive core issue, and the United States regards it as a potential "landmine."[1] Since the establishment of diplomatic relations between China and the United States in 1979, the bilateral relationship has undergone ups and downs, chiefly because of Taiwan. The signing of the August 17 communiqué in 1982 paved the way for a fairly smooth development of relations in the years that followed, whereas the visit to the United States by former Taiwanese leader Lee Teng-hui in 1995 plunged the relationship into an unprecedented crisis. China's basic Taiwan policy is consistent. Its fundamental elements include the One China principle, the policy of "peaceful reunification, one country two systems," and its refusal to renounce the use of force in the settlement of the issue. The basic U.S. policy is that the status of Taiwan is undetermined and that Taiwan's relationship with the mainland should be resolved in a peaceful manner by mutual assent. However, U.S. implementation of this basic policy has been subject to changing political considerations.

The Taiwan policies of both China and the United States have been affected by changes in the international environment and shifts in the national priorities of the two countries. In recent years, the recognition of common interests between the two countries with regard to the Taiwan issue has led to better mutual understanding in the political field, but fundamental differences still remain in the security area. This chapter traces the trajectory of these changes and pinpoints converging interests as well as differences. It then aims to address the most critical question: how can the policies of the two countries concerning Taiwan be managed to avoid an eventual conflict and to advance toward possible resolution? At stake are not only the vital national interests of the two countries but also world peace.

Evolution of China's Taiwan Policy[2]

Since the founding of the People's Republic of China in 1949, Beijing's policy toward Taiwan has undergone three major stages: liberation of Taiwan by force (1949–1955); liberation of Taiwan by peaceful means (1955–1979); and "peaceful reunification, one country two systems" (1979–present). A most important turning point was realized in December 1978, when the Third Plenum of the Eleventh Central Committee of the Chinese Communist Party decided to shift the focus of the country's endeavors to economic development. That same month, China and the United States agreed to establish diplomatic relations, with the United States acknowledging "the Chinese position that there is but one China and that Taiwan is part of China." Against this background, party leader Deng Xiaoping put forward the "peaceful reunification, one country two systems" formula, which has been the cornerstone of China's Taiwan policy ever since. The formula is known as Deng's Six Points. In plain language, they are:

1. Peaceful reunification through cooperation between the Chinese Communist Party (CCP) and the Kuomintang (KMT).
2. Postreunification, Taiwan and the mainland would pursue different political systems.
3. After reunification, Taiwan would maintain its judicial discretion, legislative power, its court of final appeal, and armed forces. The mainland would neither send civilian nor military personnel to Taiwan.
4. The mainland would not agree to "total autonomy" of Taiwan because that would mean "two Chinas."

5. Peaceful reunification does not mean annexation of Taiwan by the mainland, nor vice versa.

6. Peaceful reunification talks would be conducted on equal footing, not between the central government and local authorities. China would brook no foreign interference.[3]

As time passed, new circumstances occurred in Taiwan and the mainland as well as internationally. Among the most prominent were the advent of the "pro-independent" Democratic Progressive Party (DPP) as a rising political force in Taiwan, and the increasingly closer economic, trade, and personnel exchanges across the strait. The mainland thus readjusted its policies to cope with the new realities. In January 1995, then CCP General Secretary Jiang Zemin made important policy proposals to Taiwan, which are popularly known as Jiang's Eight-Point Proposal. Compared with Deng's Six Points, Jiang's proposal contained the following new elements:

1. The cross-strait talks would not be conducted between the CCP and the KMT alone, but between the CCP and representatives of all political parties and influential groups and organizations in Taiwan.

2. As the first step, the two sides across the strait would negotiate an official ending of hostility.

3. The mainland would separate politics from economics in handling cross-strait affairs.

4. The mainland would not take issue with Taiwan's nonofficial economic or cultural exchanges with foreign countries.

5. The mainland would regard cultural links across the strait as an important basis for reunification.[4]

When Hu Jintao became the general secretary of the CCP in 2002, he continued to implement the basic policy of "peaceful reunification, one country two systems" while readjusting and enriching it in accordance with new circumstances. His most important policy proclamation on the Taiwan issue was made on March 4, 2005, during the Third Plenum of the Tenth National Conference of the CCP. It is commonly referred to as Hu's Four Points or "4 Nevers":

1. Never sway in adhering to the One China principle.
2. Never give up efforts to seek peaceful reunification.
3. Never change the principle of placing hope on the Taiwanese people.
4. Never compromise in opposing "Taiwan independence" secessionist activities[5]

Compared with Deng's Six Points and Jiang's Eight-Point Proposal, Hu's Taiwan policy contained the following new elements:

1. He set opposition to "de jure" Taiwan independence, not reunification, as the policy goal for the foreseeable future.
2. He set peace and development as the axis of cross-strait relations.
3. For the first time, he defined "status quo" across the strait—the mainland and Taiwan belong to one China.
4. He adopted a "forward-looking" stance toward the DPP and other "pro-independent" parties in Taiwan and was willing to talk with them, regardless of past statements and actions, as long as the One China principle was met one way or another.
5. He insisted on the policy of pinning hope on Taiwanese compatriots. (This reflects Hu's thinking that the human factor is the basis for policy-making and that, to achieve reunification, the mainland should win the hearts and minds of the Taiwanese people.)
6. He upheld the position that the Taiwan issue should and could only be solved by all the Chinese on both sides of the strait; neither side should seek a unilateral solution.

The Evolution of U.S.-Taiwan Policy[6]

During World War II, Chiang Kai-shek was recognized as the leader of China, and the United States continued to recognize his government as the official government of China even after he fled from the mainland to

Taiwan in 1949. In January 1950 President Harry Truman announced that the United States would not become involved in the Chinese civil conflict, but when the Korean War broke out in June 1950 the United States moved its Seventh Fleet to prevent Taiwan and the mainland from attacking each other. At the San Francisco Peace Treaty in 1951 Japan ceded sovereignty over Taiwan, but the United States and the Allies then took the position that the status of Taiwan was not yet determined. This has remained the U.S. position ever since.

In 1972, during President Richard Nixon's visit to China, the United States and China could not reach a common agreement on the status of Taiwan. Therefore, on February 27, 1972, they released the Shanghai Communiqué, in which each side stated its views. The Chinese side said, "The Government of the People's Republic of China is the sole legal government of China; Taiwan is a province of China. . . . The liberation of Taiwan is China's internal affair in which no other country has the right to interfere; and all U.S. forces and military installations must be withdrawn from Taiwan." The U.S. side declared, "The United States acknowledges that all Chinese on either side of the Taiwan Strait maintain there is but one China and that Taiwan is a part of China. The United States Government does not challenge that position. It reaffirms its interest in a peaceful settlement of the Taiwan question by the Chinese themselves."

On November 14, 1973, China and the United States agreed that "disputes between states should be settled without resorting to the use or threat of force, on the basis of the principles of respect for the sovereignty and territorial integrity of all states, non-aggression against other states, non-interference in the internal affairs of other states, equality and mutual benefit and peaceful coexistence."[7]

On December 15, 1978, when China and the United States agreed to establish formal diplomatic relations beginning January 1, 1979, the United States agreed, according to the terms of the treaty, to give one year's notice to terminate the Mutual Defense Treaty, end formal diplomatic relations with Taiwan, and withdraw all its forces and installations from Taiwan. It agreed that all its treaties with Taiwan were null and void. The United States agreed that the PRC was the sole legal government of

China. However, the United States announced that it would continue to supply arms to Taiwan so that Taiwan could defend itself. Deng Xiaoping strongly opposed the U.S. sale of arms to Taiwan but agreed to normalization despite the U.S. intention to continue to supply arms to Taiwan. In that normalization agreement of December 15, the United States said it "recognizes the Government of the People's Republic of China as the sole legal Government of China. Within this context, the people of the United States will maintain cultural, commercial, and other unofficial relations with the people of Taiwan."

A number of legal issues remained after the U.S.-China agreement on normalization, and, to deal with these, the U.S. Congress on April 10, 1979, passed the Taiwan Relations Act. This legislation spelled out in more detail U.S. policy and gave more reassurance to Taiwan that it would deal with threats to its security than President Jimmy Carter had previously given. The act stated that U.S. policy is "to consider any effort to determine the future of Taiwan by other than peaceful means, including by boycotts or embargoes, a threat to the peace and security of the Western Pacific area and of grave concern to the United States." It said it is also U.S. policy "to maintain the capacity of the United States to resist any resort to force or other forms of coercion that would jeopardize the security, or the social or economic system, of the people on Taiwan." Furthermore, it expanded the U.S. definition of military assistance, saying "the United States will make available to Taiwan such defense articles and defense services in such quantity as may be necessary to enable Taiwan to maintain a sufficient self-defense capability."

After the United States established formal diplomatic relations with Beijing, the American Institute in Taiwan became a quasi-government organization, staffed by personnel who had been State Department officials and who returned to the State Department after completing service in Taiwan. Taiwan in turn had a quasi-governmental office (now called TECRO) in Washington that substituted for its previous embassy.

In 1981–1982, when pressed by China to reduce arms sales to Taiwan, the United States decided not to sell FX advanced fighter planes to Taiwan. On August 17, 1982, the United States signed a Joint Communiqué with the PRC stating that "it does not seek to carry out a long-term policy of arms sales to Taiwan, that its arms sales to Taiwan will not exceed, either in qualitative or in quantitative terms, the level of those supplied in recent years since the establishment of diplomatic relations between the United States and China, and that it intends to reduce gradually its sales of arms to Taiwan, leading over a period of time to a final resolution."

The Shanghai Communiqué of 1972 was written at a time when the leaders in both Taiwan and Beijing accepted the view that there is only one China. After Chiang Ching-kuo died in 1988, the United States was confronted with a new situation as Lee Teng-hui transformed the government into a more democratic one that no longer claimed jurisdiction over all of the mainland and strengthened local culture and history, which could be used to support independence from the mainland. Especially after the Tiananmen event of 1989, the growth of democracy in Taiwan seemed to the U.S. public very attractive. Lee Teng-hui's moves caused Beijing to worry about growing tendencies toward separatism. Some months after Lee visited the United States in 1995, Beijing fired missiles near Taiwan to warn about pressures toward separatism. The United States responded by sending two carrier task forces to the area around Taiwan, carefully avoiding sailing into the Taiwan Strait, which Beijing had warned would be seen as very provocative.

Some U.S. presidential candidates (notably Ronald Reagan, Bill Clinton, and George W. Bush) have been critical of Beijing during their political campaigns, and they continued to be critical of China at the beginning of their administrations. But in the end, all presidents since Richard Nixon in 1972 have supported the Shanghai Communiqué and have affirmed the One China policy.

Since the standoff in the Taiwan Strait in 1996, U.S. officials have shown great concern for avoiding conflict with mainland China over the Taiwan issue. They are aware that the military balance between Beijing and Taiwan has shifted since the mid-1990s toward Beijing, and they fear that greater confidence in Beijing about military strength might cause Chinese leaders to risk attacking Taiwan. As China has strengthened its military capabilities with the aim of deterring U.S. support for Taiwan in the event of a mainland-Taiwan conflict, the United States has aimed to maintain its military capabilities in the region, in part to deter China from attacking. At the same time, when leaders in Taiwan make statements that suggest their intention to create de jure independence, the United States has made it clear that if Taiwan leaders provoke Beijing they could not count on U.S. support. U.S. and Chinese officials recognize that they both have an interest in avoiding a conflict between the mainland and Taiwan. U.S. officials are also aware that the current situation, in which Chinese and U.S. military planners must plan for the contingency of possible conflict, limits the amount of transparency and mutual trust between the two countries and is not a desirable situation for long-term peace and security in the region.

A Comparison of Chinese-Taiwan and U.S.-Taiwan Policies

In recent years, particularly after the terrorist attacks of September 11, 2001, when U.S. national priority shifted to the fight against international terrorism, there has been growing recognition that both China and the United States have an interest in the maintenance of peace in the Taiwan Strait. This positive development can be seen in four key areas:

(1) *The Question of One China.* The position enunciated by President Truman, that Taiwan's status is undetermined, remains U.S. policy. The Taiwan Relations Act of 1979 remains one of the pillars of its China policy. The United States commits itself to its three joint communiqués with China and does not support "Taiwan independence."

China is absolutely firm on the One China principle but over the years has shown flexibility in its definition. There have been the so-called Old Three Sentences[8] and the Three Sentences. The Anti-Secession Law[9] adopts the Three Sentences: "There is only one China in the world. Both the mainland and Taiwan belong to one China. China's sovereignty and territorial integrity brook no division." This flexibility was also shown when the "1992 consensus" was reached in Hong Kong during talks between the "white glove" organizations of the Straits Exchange Foundation (Taiwan) and the Association of Relations across the Taiwan Straits (the mainland). When the Straits Exchange Foundation representative clearly stated that there was only one China, the Association of Relations across the Taiwan Straits' representative responded by saying that his association "does not agree with the Taiwan side's understanding of the meaning of 'one China'"; however, "the meaning of one China need not be discussed."[10] China has been dealing with the United States over the issue of One China in a similar manner. In fact, the two countries have lived with the reality of the One China principle and One China policy since 1972. So long as the United States does not abandon its One China policy, there should be no serious problems over this issue between the two countries in the foreseeable future.

(2) *The Maintenance of the Status Quo.* Again, China and the United States have different definitions of the status quo across the Taiwan Strait. The Chinese definition is that both the mainland and Taiwan belong to one China. The U.S. definition was given by former Assistant Secretary of State James Kelly on April 21, 2004: "For Beijing, this means no use of force or threat to use force against Taiwan. For Taipei, it means exercising prudence in managing all aspects of cross-Strait relations. For both sides, it means no statements or actions that would unilaterally alter Taiwan's status."[11] The difference suggests that the two countries are looking at different sides of the same coin: China stresses the "de jure" side of the status quo whereas the United States emphasizes the "de facto" side of it. So long as the status quo meant by both is not unilaterally changed, there should be no serious problems over the issue between the two countries.

(3) *Cross-Strait Exchanges.* This is perhaps the least problematic, since the two sides have a common understanding. The official U.S. position is: "In the absence of a political dialogue, we encourage the two sides to increase bilateral interactions of every sort. Clearly, there would be economic benefits for both sides by proceeding with direct aviation and shipping links. The increasing people-to-people contacts may also ease tensions."[12] China has been promoting the Three Direct Links[13] since 1979, believing they would be conducive to peaceful reunification. The United States has stated that it has no objections to China's "links" as long as they are achieved peacefully.

(4) *The Ultimate Solution of the Taiwan Issue.* The United States insists on a peaceful solution of the Taiwan issue, while China refuses to renounce

the use of force if peaceful efforts should be obstructed. This fundamental difference remains. But in recent years, opposition to a unilateral solution of the issue has become an important overlapping point in the Taiwan policies of both countries. China's position is that the ultimate solution of the Taiwan issue has to be decided by all its 1.3 billion people—including the 23 million Taiwanese compatriots—together.[14] The U.S. position is that "in the final analysis, the Taiwan issue is for people on both sides of the Strait to resolve."[15] If the positions of both countries remain unchanged, this reduces the risk of misunderstanding.

The reason behind the increased overlapping interests over the Taiwan issue could be attributed to the closer strategic goals of the two countries in the Taiwan Strait area. For China, its policy on Taiwan is under the overall strategy of focusing all efforts on development; for the United States, the "foremost concern is maintaining peace and stability" in the Taiwan Strait area.[16]

The area of the greatest danger of potential conflict between China and the United States concerns security. The efforts of each side to build up deterrence against the other create a vicious circle. The United States policy reflects three overall aims. One purpose of U.S. military presence in the Western Pacific is to deter China from using force to achieve reunification with Taiwan. The United States also aims to "revitalize" its security cooperation with allies in Asia and the Pacific—Japan, South Korea, and Australia, for instance—to contribute to global security. Finally, the United States aims to assist Taiwan's military ability to resist a possible mainland attack and to establish "inter-operability" between the two militaries. Since 1995 China has been accelerating efforts to modernize its national defense and build up deterrence against "Taiwan independence." It would be a waste of time to argue over which side began this vicious circle, as it would end up as a chicken-and-egg story. The critical issue is how the two countries can find a way to interrupt this circle.

Hypothetically, China and the United States might enter into direct conflict under the following circumstances: (1) China's efforts to solve the issue peacefully are frustrated by Taiwan's moves toward independence, and China, in accordance with Article 8 of the Anti-Secession Law, believing it has no other choice, uses force; the United States intervenes militarily. (2) While here is still a possibility of a peaceful solution, China resorts to force to press for reunification; and the United States intervenes militarily. (3) The United States abandons its One China policy and supports Taiwan independence militarily; and China uses force to uphold what it considers is its sovereignty and territorial integrity. Judging from our earlier discussion, neither China nor the United States would like to see these worst-case scenarios become reality.

Policy Suggestions

To avoid Sino-U.S. conflict over Taiwan and to maintain peace and stability in the area, the best policy choice should be for mainland China and Taiwan to enter into peaceful negotiations on an equal footing for a solution that is acceptable to both. To realize that, the mainland and Taiwan have to take into account each other's basic aspirations: for the mainland there has to be one China. For Taiwan, its people have to be their own masters. As far as the mainland is concerned, the "one country two systems" formula was particularly designed to meet these demands, although Taiwan would expect more rights and more international space than Hong Kong enjoys. In the near future, with the KMT candidate victorious in the 2008 election, the mainland should take the initiative to resume the cross-strait dialogue on the basis of the 1992 consensus and, as a first step, make efforts to end hostility. The mainland should try to find a new formula, apart from the 1992 consensus, that could establish the basis for the resumption of dialogue. At the same time, the mainland should not reduce its efforts to promote cross-strait trade and economic, personnel, and other exchanges.

The main concern of the United States is its possible involvement in a conflict between the mainland and Taiwan. It would be helpful if the United States were to confirm its support for agreements between Taipei and Beijing regarding the status of Taiwan that are arrived at peacefully and without coercion.

CHAPTER NINE

GLOBAL WARMING: THE ROAD TO RESTRAINT

Pan Jiahua and Kelly Sims Gallagher

THE UNITED STATES AND CHINA ARE NOW THE TOP TWO GREENHOUSE gas emitters in the world, and their actions in fighting global warming will be decisive in post-2012 global climate regime building. Under the framework of the United Nations climate convention (formally, the Framework Convention on Climate Change) and the Kyoto Protocol, however, the two countries belong to different political blocs: developing and developed nations. Both China and the United States share the common goal of protecting the climate under the UN climate convention, but their responsibilities are different under existing regimes.

As a large developing economy, China has to formulate its energy and climate policies in a comprehensive and strategic way so as to meet increasing energy demand, achieve energy security, protect public health, and reduce China's impact on the world energy market. Energy consumption in China increased from 1.35 billion tce (tons of coal equivalent) in 2000 to 2.64 billion tce (or approximately 1.85 billion tons of oil equivalent) in 2007. Industrialization and urbanization are still dramatically accelerating in China; each year during the next two decades, the increase in urban population will be more than 11 million. Per capita GDP (constant 2005 RMB) has grown from 1,595 yuan to 17,100 yuan during the past thirty years. Double-digit growth in the industrial sectors is likely to continue. Clearly energy and climate policies in China are not merely environmental and domestic issues, but economic, social, development, and international issues as well.

Similar to China, the United States must formulate its energy and climate policies comprehensively and strategically to support economic growth, spur job creation, achieve energy security, and protect public health. As the most advanced and strongest economy in the world, the United States has enjoyed high levels of per capita income for many years, growing from $14,500 to $33,000 between 1980 and 2005 (constant 2000 dollars). U.S. energy consumption and greenhouse gas emissions in terms of both aggregate and per-capita levels are high—totally different from the situation in any developing economy and many industrialized ones as well. Total energy consumption in 2006 in the United States was 2.3 billion tons of oil equivalent. The rate of growth of energy consumption is much smaller in the United States than in China, largely because the United States is in more of a replacement mode, substituting its existing energy infrastructure with new, more modern facilities. Per capita greenhouse-gas emissions in the United States are five times larger than per capita emissions in China, even though the aggregate total in both countries is now roughly the same.

Future Greenhouse Gas Emissions in China and the United States

China began a high economic growth phase at the end of the 1970s, and the momentum has been sustained ever since. Compared to the 1980 level, China's real GDP expanded tenfold by 2005: from $0.18 trillion (using a 2000 exchange rate) to $1.89 trillion, with an average annual economic growth rate of 9.86 percent. The growth in China's energy demand was far slower than the GDP growth due to energy conservation measures. Nevertheless, China's energy consumption in 2005 was 4.3 times the 1980 level, and the average annual energy consumption growth rate was 5.7 percent. Although the U.S. economy was already highly developed in 1980, in real terms the size of its economy doubled between 1980 and 2005, from $5.2 trillion to $11 trillion (in 2000 dollars), at an average annual growth rate of 3.1 percent during the period.[1] With respect to energy consumption in the United States, the number increased from 2.59 billion tce in 1980 to 3.34 billion tce in 2005, with an annual rate of growth at 1.02 percent. Evidently, the rates of growth in China have been much faster, but in terms of absolute amounts, China still accounts for a fraction of the U.S. total in the size of the economy, per capita income, and energy consumption.

According to statistics from the International Energy Agency (IEA), China's CO_2 (carbon dioxide) emissions from fossil fuel combustion[2] increased from 2.21 billion tons in 1990 to 5.06 billion tons in 2005, an increase of 128.9 percent during the 1990–2005 period.[3] U.S. CO_2 emissions grew from 4.85 billion tons in 1990 to 5.82 billion tons in 2005, an increase of 19.9 percent. In aggregate terms, total emissions from China and the United States were rather close in 2005, but in per-capita terms, the numbers are strikingly different, being at 3.88 t/c (tons of coal) and 19.61 t/c respectively.

The projections for future emissions in China provide diverse numbers. Li Zhizhong at the Institute of Energy Economics, Japan (IEEJ), estimates that Chinese CO_2 emissions will go up to 9441 Mt by 2030 in the reference scenario.[4] Hu Xiulian did a similar study with the projections extended to 2050.[5] Table 9.1 provides the results of reference scenarios from the U.S. Energy Information Administration in its publication *International Energy Outlook 2006*.

Table 9.1 shows that the European Union (EU) actually experienced a reduction in emissions between 1990 and 2005, but in the United States the rate of increase has been steady but moderate. The case of China looks quite different: rapid historical growth in emissions, with a growing share of global emissions. For future emission projections under business-as-usual scenarios, the EU is projected to have little growth, the United States to have some growth, and China is projected to increase substantially. Absent new policy measures, the International Energy Agency projects that, together, the United States and China will account for 45 percent of global carbon dioxide emissions by 2030.[6]

Understanding the Factors Behind Increasing Greenhouse Gas Emissions

Generally, the key drivers of energy consumption and greenhouse gas (GHG) emissions include population size and growth, imperatives for social and economic development, technological advancement, natural

Table 9.1. Reference CO2 Emission Scenarios to 2030*

	Unit	1990	2000	2005	2010	2020	2030
World	CO2 (Mtc)	21.02	23.49	27.14	30.36	36.75	43.68
U.S.	CO2 (Mtc)	4.85	5.70	5.82	6.39	7.12	8.12
	% World Total	23.07%	24.27%	21.44%	21.05%	19.37%	18.59%
China	CO2 (Mtc)	2.21	3.04	5.06	5.86	8.16	10.72
	% World Total	10.51%	12.94%	18.64%	19.30%	22.20%	24.54%
EU–27	CO2 (Mtc)	4.10	3.90	3.98	4.47	4.74	5.12
	% World Total	19.51%	16.60%	14.67%	14.72%	12.90%	11.72%**

*Historical emissions are based on statistics by the International Energy Agency (2007), and future emission projects follow the projections by the Energy Information Administration, U.S. Department of Energy (2006) under reference scenarios. For future emissions for the EU–27 region, OECD-Europe is used from the EIA projections.

**Sources:* Energy Information Administration, International Energy Outlook (Washington, DC: U.S. Department of Energy, 2006); and International Energy Administration, CO2 Emissions from Fossil Fuel Combustion, 1971–2005 (Paris: OECD, 2007).

resource availability, and environment protection measures. As such, the future pathways of both the United States and China's energy and emissions scenarios will be determined by assumptions regarding many important factors, including population growth, urbanization, GDP growth, economic structure, energy efficiency, environmental policy, technological innovation, and trade policy.

Population and Urbanization

One of the biggest and most important differences between the United States and China is the size of their populations. China is the most populous country in the world. With great efforts by the Chinese government to implement family planning policies since the 1980s, population growth was muted (see Table 9.2), but even so, the Chinese population is projected to grow until it reaches 1.5 billion around 2030.

Table 9.2. Population Trend and Urbanization Rate, China and the United States, 1975–2030*

		1975	*2005*	*2015*	*2030*
World	Population (millions)	4,067.01	6,514.8	7,295.1	8,203.0
	Urban Rate	37.2%	48.6%	52.8%	N.A.
U.S.	Population (millions)	220.2	299.8	329.0	365.0
	Urban Rate	73.7%	80.8%	83.7%	N.A.
	Net Change (millions)	0	79.6	108.8	144.8
China	Population (millions)	927.8	1,313.0	1,388.6	1,446.0
	Urban Rate	17.4%	40.4%	49.2%	N.A.
	Net Change (millions)	0	385.2	460.8	518.2
Japan	Population (millions)	111.5	127.9	126.6	123.0
	Urban Rate	56.8%	65.8%	68.2%	N.A.
	Net Change (millions)	0	16.4	15.1	11.5

Sources: Figures for 1975 to 2015 are calculated based on data taken from the UN Development Program, *Human Development Report, 2007/8: Response to Climate Change—Human Solidarity in a Divided World* (New York: UNDP, 2007); projections for 2030 are taken from Energy Information Administration, *International Energy Outlook* (Washington, DC: U.S. Department of Energy, 2006).

Compared with China, the size of the U.S. population is relatively small at 299 million as of 2006, and it is projected to grow to approximately 360 million by 2030.[7]

One critical factor is the urbanization process, which is accelerating in China. China's urbanization level has increased from 26 percent in 1990 to 43 percent in 2005.[8] It is expected to reach about 55–60 percent by 2020. Even if the urbanization level increases by only 1 percentage point per year in the first twenty years of this century, China will still see its urban population increase by about 13 million every year. There is also a trend of increased urbanization in the United States—in 1950, 64 percent of the population lived in urban areas, but as of 1990 the figure had reached 75 percent. In China, accelerated urbanization will be accompanied by several significant related potential pressures, including increased demand for employment,[9] higher consumption patterns, and massive need for infrastructure construction, all of which result in great challenges for China in the coming decades.

Accelerated urbanization in China means expansion of existing cities and creation of new towns and cities. Both require large-scale construction of infrastructure and buildings. Infrastructure and buildings typically use energy-intensive materials such as steel, cement, and chemicals. Because of demand from the construction sector, the likely continued growth of these energy-intensive industries will have significant impacts on China's energy demand and emissions in the future.[10] Residential energy consumption now contributes to about 11 percent of China's total, and it is the second-biggest energy consuming sector following the industrial sector. Empirical analyses indicate that currently the annual per capita energy consumption of urban Chinese residents is 3.5 times that of rural inhabitants due to changes in living style. Substituting biomass with commercial forms of energy services like electricity, for example, will expand residential energy consumption.

Economic Growth, Structure, and Global Integration

Most scenarios about the future assume that China maintains a high level of economic growth, but this is by no means assured. Realization of the national plan to quadruple 2000 GDP levels by 2020 requires that the average GDP growth rate be about 7.2 percent annually. By contrast, economic growth projections in the United States are much more modest.

In the coming decades, one might see rather dramatic changes in the economic structure of China, but currently heavy industry dominates. Since 2002, the ratio of heavy industries to light industries[11] has been greater than 60 percent (this figure reached 60.9 percent and 64.3 percent in the years 2002 and 2003, respectively). Currently, the industrial sector consumes almost 70 percent of total primary energy in China. This is in contrast to the United States, where industry accounts for one-third of total energy consumption. The Eleventh Five-Year (2006–2010) Plan in China emphasizes the need to move toward lighter industries—the "tertiary" sector. Structural changes such as growth in the tertiary sector and deployment of energy efficiency technologies in energy-intensive industries have great potential to reduce the energy intensity of the economy.

In our globalized world, China has become increasingly integrated into the world economy and is now highly dependent on international trade. Total imports and exports amounted to $2.17 trillion in 2007 (accounting for two-thirds of China's total GDP). China is now a major manufacturing base for the world. Since China is at the lower end of the international division of labor, the majority of the country's imports are high value-added products and services, whereas exports are mostly products from energy-intensive manufacturing industries. As such, the intensity of the embedded energy of its imports is generally lower than that of its exports. This causes an international mismatch of energy demand (and supply in the case of certain fuels). Under such an import and export structure and given the expectation of inevitable growth in import and export volumes, China will probably continue to increase its energy consumption for products destined to be consumed outside China. Although estimates are difficult to make based on available data, a recent study by the WWF indicates that for bilateral trade between China and the United States in 2002, the energy embedded in goods exported to the United States amounted to 84.55 million tce, as compared to 9.16 million tce of energy embedded in imports to China, with a net export of embedded energy of 75.39 million tce. As the volume of exports to the United States had more than doubled between 2002 and 2006, the amount of energy embedded in goods exported to the U.S. from China is estimated to be over 150 million tce.[12]

Natural Resource Endowments

All countries' energy strategies are subject to the constraints of their unique natural resource endowments. Despite the fact that China consumes more than twice as much coal each year, the United States actually has much larger coal reserves than China. The United States holds 27 percent of the world's coal reserves, and China holds 13 percent, but coal is by far both countries' most abundant fossil fuel resource. China accounts for only 1 percent of world oil and gas reserves. The United States accounts for 2 percent of world oil reserves and 3 percent of world gas reserves.[13] China's relative scarcity in oil and gas resources is one reason why it relies so heavily on coal, which accounts for nearly three-quarters of primary energy supply. Since coal is the most GHG-intensive of all the fossil fuels, this represents a huge challenge for China in terms of GHG mitigation. The United States relies on coal for approximately one-half of its electricity supply, but overall, coal accounts for one-third of U.S. energy consumption.[14]

Environmental Policy

Environmental policy directly affects energy consumption in both the United States and China. Pollution-control standards can require the installation of pollution-control equipment, and they can increase the cost of energy production and consumption. Direct coal burning is one of the main sources of air pollution in urban areas in China, especially in northern China during the winter heating period. Air pollution from motor vehicle use is a major contributor to urban air pollution in China's richer cities as well. China is the world's largest sulphur dioxide emitter, with 25.49 million tons emitted per year as of 2005, 27 percent higher than that in 2000.[15] For China's 600 million urban residents, 64 percent are exposed to some form of air pollution. Acid rain pollutes more than one-third of China's territory, and the long-distance flow of pollutants has led to international concern in East Asia. The United States has much more strict pollution-control standards than China for all pollutants except carbon dioxide. To combat acid rain, the U.S. government issued the Clean Air Act (later amended), which created an emissions trading regime and set strict targets for emissions from power plants and industrial facilities. Pollution from motor vehicles is also strictly regulated through the Tier I and Tier II emissions standards. Both countries have issued numerous energy-efficiency standards for motor vehicles, appliances, and industrial uses, and in fact, China's passenger car fuel-efficiency standards are much stricter than U.S. vehicle fuel-efficiency standards. Neither country has imposed CO_2 emission standards at the federal or central level.

Technological Innovation

Investment in innovation of low-carbon energy technologies has the potential to make the overall climate challenge much more manageable. First, innovation can bring down the costs of already available low-carbon technologies such as solar, efficiency, nuclear, and wind technologies. Innovation may also bring newer technologies to commercialization, such as carbon capture and storage technologies that can be coupled with fossil-fuel technologies to reduce the carbon emissions associated with burning fossil fuels. Development and deployment of energy-efficiency technologies, for example, could allow growth in the economy without an accompanying growth in greenhouse-gas emissions from energy consumption. U.S. government investments in energy research, development, and demonstration as a whole for fiscal year 2008 amounted to $3 billion. Efficiency and renewable funding accounted for 42 percent of the total.[16] Chinese government investments in research and development are smaller, although advanced coal (including more efficient coal technologies) and advanced vehicle technologies are high priorities of the Ministry of Science and Technology. Failure to invest adequately in innovation could make the task of carbon mitigation more expensive or difficult.

Compatibility of Climate Protection with Energy Security and Development Goals

Increases in energy consumption and emissions are often, though not necessarily, linked to the expansion of the economy and improvement in living standards. Thus, emission-reduction requirements for climate protection can sometimes be in conflict with the conventional paradigm of development. However, the mitigation of climate change demands improvements in energy efficiency, greater diversification of the energy supply mix, and a more sustainable development of the economy, taking into account environmental considerations. Viewed from the positive side, climate protection can certainly be compatible with energy security and development goals, both of which are highly desired by both the United States and China. Yet, there are a number of actions that might improve energy security or enhance economic growth but would make climate change much worse. Greater use of coal, for example, could easily cause increases in greenhouse-gas emissions, especially if used inefficiently or without carbon capture and storage technologies.

With its dominance within the energy mix, coal combustion is responsible for many key pollutants that have environmental, economic, and social impacts. According to statistics, 70 percent of soot emissions, 90 percent of sulphur dioxide, 67 percent of nitrogen oxides, and 70 percent of carbon dioxide in China are from burning coal. Studies show that economic losses arising from air pollution are equal to 3–7 percent of GDP. According to the World Bank in 2001, sixteen of the twenty most seriously air-polluted cities in the world are situated in China. The World Health Organization notes that only 31 percent of Chinese cities met WHO standards for air quality in 2004. Within the eleven biggest cities, soot and fine particulates in the air are estimated to cause the premature death of half a million people every year and leave 400,000 people with chronic bronchus inflammation.

One of the worst pollutants from burning fossil fuels is sulphur dioxide (SO_2), which has local (health and acid rain) as well as regional (acid rain) implications. WHO estimated that more than 600 million people are exposed to SO_2 levels above the WHO standards. SO_2 mixing with nitrogen oxides (NOx) causes acid rain. In 2004 WHO estimated that acid rain seriously affects 30 percent of China.[17] A recent study found that a reduction in carbon emissions of 5 percent every year would save local health expenditures by 0.2 percent of GDP annually.[18]

Energy security can be defined as having energy available at all times in desired forms and sufficient quantities, and at reasonable prices. The issue of energy security is expected to become increasingly critical because of growing oil imports on the part of both China and the United States. China's oil imports have been growing more rapidly than U.S. oil imports, but in aggregate, China's net oil imports were 3.4 million barrels per day in 2006, compared with 12.3 million barrels per day for the United States.

China is already a global manufacturing base. The process of urbanization is closely linked with that of industrialization. On the one hand, the role of being a major global producer provides an opportunity for China to achieve high-speed economic growth and increased social welfare. On the other hand, China is consuming more and more energy resources as it industrializes. Although China has large coal reserves, it depends strongly on foreign supplies for oil and gas. China became a net oil importer in 1993 and a net crude oil importer in 1996; China's total imports exceeded 100 million tons in 2004 and 163 million tons in 2007.[19] Crude oil import dependence surpassed 40 percent in 2004, was close to 50 percent in 2007, and is expected to reach 60 percent in 2020. To the Chinese government, oil security is a top priority. Although coal imports are very small, it is noteworthy that China became a net coal importer in 2007 for the first time. Energy diversification in order to optimize the energy mix is one of the central objectives of Chinese energy strategy. The main considerations for the promotion of energy diversification are energy security, environmental protection, and sustainable development.

For both the United States and China, oil supply lies at the heart of energy security. Oil insecurity could result from a series of risks, such as increasing world oil prices, resource shortages, marine transport disruptions, and political instability in oil-producing regions. Environmental protection is another important reason to promote energy diversification. Overdependence on coal without compensating environmental policy will result in serious environmental impacts. Experts estimate that 90 percent of the sulphur and 70 percent of the smoke and dust in the atmosphere come from coal combustion. Although the dominance of coal in China seems unchangeable in the foreseeable future due to constraints on natural resources and the lack of cost-effective substitutes, energy diversification would undoubtedly help to improve air pollution and environmental quality.

Renewable energy development could also play an important role in the provision of energy services in remote areas, where centralized power networks cannot be economically extended. China is geographically large with uneven development levels among different regions. As of 2001, 30 million residents of more than 20,000 villages were without access to electricity. Some of them were without the guarantee of basic energy supply. Combustion of traditional biomass energy is the primary method of consuming energy in most remote rural areas. The Chinese government has made great efforts to promote electrification in rural areas and integrate the provision of modern energy services into poverty alleviation and sustainable development. Renewable energy development has turned out to be an efficient way to solve this set of problems, as demonstrated by several projects that deliver power to rural areas.

China enacted its Renewable Energy Law early in 2005; it entered into effect on January 1, 2006. A new "Medium and Long-term National Planning of Renewable Development" plan has been ratified by the National Congress and will be issued soon. According to the new plans, the installation capacity of renewable energy generation is targeted to reach 30 percent of total generation capacity by 2020, of which hydro, wind, solar, and biomass generation should account for 300 gigawatts (GW), 30 GW, 1.8 GW, and 30 GW respectively. Renewable energy supply will be 400–500 Mtce, accounting for about one-seventh of primary energy consumption assuming the total primary energy consumption will be around 3.5 billion tons of coal equivalent. This target is more ambitious than that of the "Outline of New and Renewable Energy Development (1996–2010)" published in 1996.

On November 6, 2005, the first assessment report on the status and outlook of wind-power generation development in China was published. The projections of this report were very ambitious. It is declared that China could realize 40 GW of installed capacity by 2020. Under this proposal, wind power would generate 80 billion kilowatt hours annually to meet the demand of 80 million people, thereby avoiding 48 million tons of CO_2 emissions. If these goals could be achieved, wind power would assume a greater share of total electricity generation than nuclear power. China's nuclear power development is drawing the attention of the international community. According to official planning, by 2020, installed capacity should reach a target of 40 GW, supplying 4 percent of total installation capacity for power generation in China. To reach the target, about thirty reactors would need to be constructed, each having a 1 million kilowatt capacity.

Besides renewable energy and nuclear power, natural gas may offer another option for energy diversification in China. The production and consumption of natural gas reached 40.8 and 39.0 billion m³ respectively in 2004 but accounted for only 2.6 percent of the overall energy mix in 2004. In recent years, the consumption of natural gas has increased rapidly. It is estimated that the demand will go up to 200 billion m³ by 2020, with estimates for further growth in the medium and long term. This growth would largely need to be met by imports, which raises some energy security concerns.

Energy diversification has great potential for GHG avoidance in both countries because it could cause substitution of lower-carbon fuels for carbon-intensive coal. The energy efficiency of oil and gas utilization is estimated to be 30 percent and 23 percent higher than coal use respectively. According to the guidelines of the Intergovernmental Panel on Climate Change for emissions inventories, the emissions coefficients of coal, oil, and natural gas are 0.7476, 0.5825, and 0.4435 respectively.[20] As some have proposed, however, if there is increased coal utilization for coal-to-liquids, for example, the carbon intensity of the economy could dramatically increase.

The compatibility of climate protection with energy security and development goals in the U.S. context is different in some respects from the situation in China. The United States already has a diversified fuel mix, with oil and gas accounting for 45 percent of total energy supply, nuclear for 11 percent, and hydro and other renewables for 8 percent. Still, greater diversification away from coal would help to reduce the carbon intensity of the economy. Currently the U.S. government and industry are each investing considerable research, development, and demonstration dollars into carbon capture and storage technologies that would enable the extended use of coal for some time into the future. As in China, energy security proponents often advocate for expanded use of coal, which could make the climate change problem worse.

Greater progress on energy efficiency and expanded use of low-carbon energy sources are likely to be key strategies for mitigating climate change in the United States. The 2007 Energy Independence and Security Act mandated stricter fuel-efficiency standards for passenger cars (35 miles per gallon by 2020) and created a renewable fuel standard of 36 billion gallons of renewable transportation fuels by 2022. A renewable electricity portfolio standard was considered but ultimately failed to be included in the legislation. The federal government is now actively considering climate change legislation, with two major bills in the U.S. Senate. Senate bill S. 2191, the Lieberman-Warner Climate Security Act (L-W CSA),[21] known as the Lieberman-Warner bill, voted out of the Environment and Public Works Committee, is considered the more stringent in terms of its targeted emissions reductions, and has the support of the environmental community. Another bill, known as the Bingaman-Specter bill, has arisen from the Energy and Natural Resources Committee, and though it is weaker than the Lieberman-Warner bill, it has the support of the U.S. labor movement. A key challenge for successful passage of climate legislation in the United States will be the support of the labor unions, which are concerned about international competitiveness and impacts on the U.S. manufacturing sector.

Approaches for Joint Action on Climate Change

The analysis in the previous sections indicates that China and the United States share many common challenges and possible solutions with respect to climate protection. In addition, they clearly share common but differentiated responsibilities with respect to climate protection. The United States contributed a large fraction of the historical carbon dioxide emissions in the atmosphere, but both countries will be major emitters in this century absent new policy measures. Although negotiations continue regarding the post-Kyoto framework, there is no reason why China and the United States could not begin work together now.

There are currently major differences between the United States and China in the context of international negotiations. At the political level, the Bush administration has called for China as a major emitter to go hand in hand with the United States to take mitigation action. As early as 2000, when President Bush refused to ratify the Kyoto Protocol, the exemption of China and other major developing countries from emission caps was given as one of the three key reasons.[22] The increase in emissions by large developing countries has indeed been fast, and the efforts to reduce emissions by some developed countries are currently being offset by such increases in the developing world. Also, U.S. experts often argue that the cost of GHG emission mitigation is low in China and other developing countries as compared to mitigation costs in the developed world. However, China and other developing countries have not accepted the U.S. approach. In addition to stating their concerns about the lack of financial and technological resources to reduce emissions, the Chinese government has stated that the United States as an advanced industrialized country should take the lead and demonstrate to the poor countries that mitigation is feasible and would not have negative impacts on economic development and the improvement of living standards.

A second political disagreement between China and the United States lies in how a global climate regime is to be built. The Chinese government's preference is for all international climate change agreements to fall under the UN Framework Convention on Climate Change, but the Bush administration has advocated joint actions outside the climate convention process. Since the UNFCCC entered into force in 1994, global negotiations on climate change have been mainly under the auspices of the UN climate convention. After rejecting the Kyoto Protocol, the United States has been attempting to build regimes outside the climate convention process. So far, the United States has advocated a number of processes, including the Asia-Pacific Partnership on Clean Development and Climate (AP6), the Major Economies Initiative, Asia Pacific Economic Cooperation climate initiatives, and the Group of 8 Plus 5 (G8+5) Summit. Whereas China would like to keep climate negotiations in the climate convention channels, the United States has been actively involved in the climate regime-building process outside the convention.

At a more technical level, China and the United States disagree on a number of key elements as well. Together with the EU and other developing nations, China would like the developed nations, the United States included, to commit to mandatory, quantified emission reduction targets. But the Bush administration has repeatedly rejected the notion of quantifiable mandatory emission reduction targets—as demonstrated by the Bali Action Plan, in which the target number was removed at the insistence of the United States, and President Bush's April 2008 announcement that he would commit the United States to stop growth in U.S. emissions by 2025 with the use of policy incentives. President Barack Obama has stated, however, that he is committed to mandatory emissions reductons in the United States. A second major difference was the role of the market. The U.S. government emphasized the potential of the market for effective and efficient emission reductions whereas the Chinese government believed that the government is able to play a constructive role in mobilizing resources for promotion of technology transfer and to create the incentives for emission reductions in the developing world. A third technical disagreement was the role of technology. The U.S. government believed that the climate change solution lies with technological innovation and progress. Although the Chinese government agreed that the technological potential could be substantial, the lack of technological capacity, the relatively high costs of low-carbon technologies, and current trends of technological "lock-in" in the developing world may prevent effective development and deployment of advanced low-carbon technologies.

Despite the differences, both China and the United States are taking actions domestically and internationally to fight against climate change. The major bills in the U.S. Congress were already discussed. In June 2007 the Chinese government published its national climate change program, and during its Seventeenth Congress, the Chinese Communist Party committed to contribute to global climate protection. In October 2008, the Chinese government issued a new white paper on climate change policy.

China and the United States already cooperate to some extent on technological innovation through their protocols on cooperation in fossil, energy efficiency, and renewable energy technologies. There is much scope for enhanced technological cooperation in low-carbon technologies on both a bilateral and multilateral basis. With their large coal reserves, advanced coal and carbon capture and sequestration (CCS) technologies are two areas where there could be greatly expanded research and development cooperation. The same is true for increased cooperation on energy efficiency and renewable energy technologies. Increased joint efforts to promote accelerated deployment of low-carbon technologies are warranted as well.

In summary, there are many ways that China and the United States can join efforts to protect the global climate, including enhancing mutual understanding of domestic actions and climate change regime building both outside and inside the UN climate convention process. It is unlikely, however, that China will adopt exactly the same policies that the United States, as a developed country party to the UN climate convention, may take.

Conclusions

China and the United States are key players in the fight against climate change. As a developed country, the United States is expected to increase its emissions in the coming decades at a moderate rate if no policies are implemented to reduce emissions. As a developing country that is currently rapidly industrializing, China has experienced a concurrently rapid growth in energy consumption and GHG emissions. Both are projected to continue for years to come. Due to differences in national circumstances between the two countries, differentiation of responsibilities is inevitable in the near-to-medium term.

The scientific reality is that dramatic reductions in global greenhouse gas emissions are needed within two decades. The current political reality is that both countries believe that the other should do more. It is unlikely that China and the United States will implement the same exact policies, but there are many possibilities for enhancing cooperation between the two countries for climate change mitigation. Cooperation on global climate regime building both inside and outside the UN climate convention process is one example. Technological and institutional cooperation may prove to be concrete and fruitful as well. China is making progress to protect the global climate, but cooperation and support from a country like the United States would certainly help China to go farther to reduce emissions.

In climate cooperation, both countries will have to integrate the threat of climate change into other strategic policy challenges, including energy, trade, and development policy. Globalization is leading to an international restructuring of industries, and China is currently the world's workshop. Trade disputes can and will be easily linked to energy and climate change issues.

There are many lessons that China might learn from the U.S. experience, but there is one thing that the Chinese will have to avoid: the American lifestyle as it is presently lived. In the United States, per capita emissions are about twenty tons of CO_2, five times the amount generated by an average Chinese person. As most energy-intensive industrial sectors have been relocated outside the United States, U.S. emissions are mainly from the transport and buildings sectors. This is in dramatic contrast to China, where emissions mainly come from the manufacturing sector. As China develops, there is a possibility that the Chinese will wish to duplicate the lifestyle of Americans today, with big, inefficient houses and private ownership of inefficient cars. Whereas Americans have to work on greening their consumption patterns, Chinese must invent a new pathway to develop a truly sustainable lifestyle.

CHAPTER TEN

AVOIDING CRISIS BETWEEN THE TWO GREAT POWERS

Yang Jiemian

SINCE THE END OF THE COLD WAR, GREAT CHANGES HAVE TAKEN place in international relations, thus posing both opportunities and challenges to the international society. Being two of the most important actors in global affairs, China and the United States are trying hard to use the opportunities and meet the challenges in their relationship as well as in the their relationships with other countries and associations. As the twenty-first century unfolds, the world is undergoing tremendous changes in the configuration of powers, which has resulted in new styles of strategic thinking and crisis management. The Sino-U.S. relationship has continually expanded, going from bilateral to multilateral, regional, and now global concerns. Crisis management between the two nations constitutes an important step toward the systematic buildup of global crisis management, especially vis-à-vis nontraditional security threats. Moreover, in the era of globalization and information, strategic trust between the two countries becomes more important than passive reaction in Sino-U.S. crisis management.

Peaceful Transition of the Contemporary International System

Historical Opportunities

Prior to the end of the Cold War, changes to the international system were realized by great wars—for example, the Treaty of Westphalia that ended the Thirty Years' War, the Congress of Vienna after the Napoleonic Wars, the post-World War I Versailles-Washington system, and the Yalta system following the conclusion of World War II. The Cold War's end and the subsequent rise of globalization presented a historical opportunity. The international society peacefully transitioned to a new international system for the first time in 350 years. The main contributing factors can be summarized as follows:

First, the international society has realized the catastrophic consequence of nuclear conflict and the reality of interdependence in the globalization era. Therefore, states now seek peaceful means instead of war to satisfy their interests and redistribute power. The major powers of the world have agreed to control conflicts and to avoid world war and massive regional wars.

Second, the previous international system survived the end of the Cold War by peaceful and gradual transformation. At the end of the Cold War, most actors widely agreed that the United Nations, World Bank, International Monetary Fund, and the General Agreement on Tariffs and Trade/World Trade Organization should continue to function. Beginning during the Iraq War (2003) and continuing through Iraq's rebuilding, the majority of the international society defended the UN's authority by rejecting U.S. efforts to unilaterally change the existing international system.

Third, the majority of the international society supports transforming the system in a peaceful and gradual manner. Through protracted and strenuous negotiations, international actors have succeeded in setting up new mechanisms concerning world trade, nonproliferation, climate change, and so on. Regional and subregional cooperation has made substantial progress, such as the enlargement and consolidation of the European Union, the fairly normal and effective operation of the African Union (AU), the birth of the charter of the Association of South East Asian Nations (ASEAN), the development of the Shanghai Cooperation Organization (SCO), and Mercado Comun del Sur (Mercosur), to name a few.

Fourth, the emerging powers do not seek an overhaul of the international system but prefer to improve and update it. Contrary to predictions of inevitable conflict between rising and established powers, the emerging powers prefer to change the current international rules, norms, laws, and codes of conduct through negotiation and dialogue. As an example, the G8 conducts regular dialogues with major emerging powers within the core states of China, India, Brazil, Mexico, and South Africa. Dialogues are often begun over relatively easier and more urgent subjects and sectors of low politics such as trade and climate change.

Last but not least, peaceful transition is extremely popular to the people of the world. The world's residents are pursuing peace, seeking development, and broadly enjoying the "dividends" brought about by the system's peaceful transition. It is their preference that dictates, to a large extent, the decision-making of their governments. Against this background, most governments consider economic and social development to be their top priorities. Nowadays, putting the wealth and health of the people first has become a catch word for most statesmen and politicians in designing, planning, and implementing their policies.

Sino-U.S. Perspectives on War and Peace

Since the rapprochement of the early 1970s, China and the United States have had similarities as well as differences on the question of war and peace. The main similarities lie in the avoidance of major wars between Great Powers. In their three basic communiqués—in 1972, 1979, and 1982—China and the United States stressed the importance of maintaining peace and stability in the world. The Seventeenth Congress of the Chinese Communist Party in 2007 reaffirmed this fundamental strategy by expressing its determination of adhering to the road of peaceful development and mutual benefits with other countries. In the two National Security Strategy reports, the Bush administration stressed the fact that the present time sees the first opportunity of major power cooperation instead of war competition. Even so, China and the United States do not see eye-to-eye on such issues as the role of the UN Security Council, missile defense, and root causes of terrorism. On balance, however, the two countries have many more commonalities than differences on the question of war and peace.

In the Asia-Pacific region, China and the United States cooperate or coordinate their policies toward the Korean nuclear issue, Iranian nuclear issue, Pakistan, Myanmar, and others. However, these policies differ on the regional security architecture. China poses no challenges to the U.S. military presence in the region as a historical legacy and present reality but prefers multilateral frameworks based on a new security concept of mutual trust, mutual benefit, equality, and cooperation. China attaches particular importance to the subregional mechanisms by promoting the ASEAN Regional Forum (ARF) and the SCO. The United States insists on its leadership in regional security matters and tries to preserve its bilateral alliances. It also advocates value-based alliance and is weaving a network of allies, partners, and coalitions of the willing and is seeking to shore up its "hub-spoke" security system in the region.

As regards their positions in the fields of the military and security, China and the United States are of one attitude: that is, they are trying to avoid direct military conflict by strengthening their own military power in order to dissuade the other side from venturing into war. This negative conflict evasion is a result of mutual suspicion. The two countries still treat each other as potential adversaries. China shows grave concerns over U.S.-Taiwan military relations and U.S. strategic deployment around China. The United States has adopted a hedging policy toward China with a special eye on China's growing military power. The main Pentagon strategic documents paint China as a country approaching a strategic crossroads and suspect China's intentions more than its capabilities, which serves the so-called hedging policy toward China.

Crisis Management and Mechanism-Building

Bilateral Crisis Management

Following President Richard Nixon's trip to China in 1971, China and the United States gradually entered into a period of cooperation against Soviet expansionism, which actually kept their mutual problems from becoming crises. However, the end of the Cold War had put the two countries into a situation of strategic suspicion. China and the United States confronted one crisis or near-crisis after another, such as the *Yinhe* incident in 1993, the Taiwan Strait confrontation in 1995 and 1996, the bombing of the Chinese Embassy in Belgrade in 1999, and the aerial collision in 2001.

While standing firmly on its principles and safeguarding its national interests, China exercised self-restraint and looked for solutions instead of escalation of the crises. The United States also showed concern for damage control and avoidance of a military showdown. Frequent crises had made the two countries look for effective crisis management.

Multilateral Crisis Management

In addition to the aforementioned bilateral crises, China and the United States now confront multilateral crises of a different nature. The two nations have had more overlapping interests and conducted greater cooperation in dealing with, among others, the Gulf War crisis in 1991 and 1992; the Indo-Pakistan nuclear crisis in 1998; the September 11, 2001, terrorist attacks; North Korean nuclear issues since 2002; Iranian nuclear issues since 2003; and the Darfur crisis in recent years.

Some of their driving forces merit further discussion. First of all, globalization stands out as the most important factor in the change of mind-sets and practical handling of crisis management. If the existence of nuclear weapons served as an effective deterrence to the outbreak of war between the two superpowers during the Cold War period, then globalization has interwoven the benefits and damages to all the major actors into an interdependent entity. Most actors believe that peaceful means are the best way to achieve their interests. Only occasionally, someone like President George W. Bush would advocate and practice preemptive strategy and regime change by force, which have already been proved a failure.

Besides, multilateral crisis management has provided China and the United States with more platforms for consultation and cooperation not only between themselves but also with other actors. These interactions among the major actors have transcended ad hoc reaction and entered into systematic construction. The major powers are tapping the full potential of existing institutions, such as the UN Security Council (UNSC). Furthermore, they are creating new ones adapted to the new conditions of our times. China hosted the Six-Party Talks on the North Korean nuclear issue and joined the "5+1" (five permanent members of the UNSC plus Germany) on the Iranian nuclear issue.

It can be said that the Sino-U.S. cooperation in multilateral crisis management has served a breakthrough in the chains of bilateral crisis management. For instance, their effective cooperation in the Gulf War, September 11 attacks, and Korean nuclear issue played an important role in stopping the vicious cycle of bilateral crises at different times. Indeed, now their interactions in multilateral and bilateral crisis management have entered a new stage of mutually reinforcing each other. As they carefully handle multilateral crises where vital interests are at stake, China and the United States have increasingly been cooperative in dealing with the so-called Taiwan independence. In turn, parallel efforts in containing the Taiwan "independence forces" lay some basis for their cooperation in tackling hot spots, thus contributing to the maintenance of world peace and stability.

Changes and Readjustments

Contextual Changes

The post-Cold War era has witnessed great changes of crisis management at various levels in the context of the Sino-U.S. relations. At the global level, changes are taking place with respect to power basis, actors, and agendas. The configuration of powers is gradually but definitely shifting from that of one superpower and some major powers into that of multipolarity. Major powers now include traditional powers, emerging powers, and resource-rich powers. The U.S. capability to lead global affairs is waning. The emergence of developing powers is one of the most important developments of our times. Some other countries have become important actors because of their strategic resources, such as oil, gas, and certain metals. Presently both state actors and nonstate actors are important participants in global affairs. The global agendas are also changing; both traditional and nontraditional security issues now threaten the peace and stability of the world.

Crisis management at the regional level sees its main changes in the increasing role of regional cooperation in the economic, diplomatic, and security fields. Some regional mechanisms of crisis management are emerging. The Six-Party Talks on the Korean nuclear issue have played a role of crisis prevention. The SCO has made counterterrorism one of its major tasks. The EU and AU both pay great attention to crisis management. However, compared to Sino-U.S. cooperation at the global level, the Sino-U.S. cooperation at the regional level is relatively weaker and needs more coordination. China lacks capability in regions other than Asia. The United States is generally not interested in regionalism and collective security.

In terms of bilateral crisis management, China and the United States are confronted with the challenge of translating their intentions into reality. In terms of mechanisms, neither country is fully prepared to deal with possible crisis and near-crisis resulting from the challenges of, among others, financial security, energy security, and public health problems. In terms of legal preparation and norm setting, the two countries are not yet capable of achieving common basis. For instance, they are sometimes each obsessed with how to define terrorist groups in their common struggles against terrorism.

Conceptual Changes

By confronting and handling these crises and near-crises, China and the United States have gradually undergone several conceptual changes. First, they have realized that they cannot afford the catastrophe of failed crisis management in their overall relationship. Second, they have understood the importance of effective communications of ideas and thoughts over crisis management. Third, they need effective institutions for crisis management, and as a first step they have worked to overcome the mismatch of their respective mechanisms. Fourth, because they cannot agree on the causes of their bilateral crises, both sides have lacked sufficient trust of the other. Finally, the two countries have added a new dimension to their attitudes toward international crisis management. As China has become more proactive, the United States has deemed China to be an important partner in international crisis management. Both nations now view crisis management as their responsibility both in terms of their bilateral relations and as members of the international society.

Furthermore, the two countries have come to realize that they do not only need to manage crisis on an ad hoc basis but also make their crisis management part of system building in international society. The would-be international system consists of generally accepted norms and rules, effectively operating institutions and mechanisms, and popularly shared values. Accordingly, their efforts in crisis management should be taken as a part of the system building in the long run.

China and the United States are facing such historical tasks as removing the root causes of strategic distrust and building a solid basis of strategic cooperation. Although they have begun to show concern toward each other's core interests, the two countries still suspect one another's strategic motives and so adopt hedging measures. On the one hand, Chinese sensitivities have expanded from the U.S. policy toward Taiwan to the strategic prevention of China's peaceful rise. There are plenty of examples that can be interpreted as such; the so-called color revolution and American military presence at the door of China's western border, the much-discussed "Concert of Democracies" and "value-based diplomacy, and the "four-nation mechanism" of the United States, Japan, Australia, and India are but three. On the other hand, the United States sees a rising China as a challenge to its global primacy and tries to maintain its superiority in military capability vis-à-vis China. In the United States, some political forces look at China's every move through an ideological prism: some strategists take China as a threat in political, economic, military, and cultural aspects, and some media sectors instigate an anti-China feeling whenever possible. It goes without saying that deep-rooted suspicions are the breeding grounds of crisis. Therefore, the removal of strategic distrust would ease, if not remove, the root causes of bilateral crisis and facilitate the handling of multilateral crisis.

Concrete Changes

The two countries have also made concrete changes in the way they handle crisis management. Actually, they have avoided bilateral crisis since the September 11 attacks. Moreover, they even saw the importance of turning potential crisis into opportunities of cooperation. For instance, both China and the United States deemed Chen Shui-bian's efforts to join the UN under the name of Taiwan as "provocative" and adopted parallel measures to prevent the situation in the Taiwan Strait from getting out of control. The EU and Japan also expressed their opposition to this provocation by the Taiwan authorities, thus making a joint effort of the international society, which led to the general election in Taiwan in March 2008.

Institution building by China and the United States is also developing in the direction of cooperation rather than confrontation. Some unique mechanisms are taking shape. China and the United States have, by and large, established institutions of timely and effective crisis management. The two countries are attaching greater importance to building mechanisms of strategic dialogue, both at the summit and functional levels. The two presidents have conducted regular and effective communications via summits, meetings on the sidelines at international conferences, phone calls, and correspondence. At senior levels, the strategic/senior dialogues have become regular platforms for strategic discussions and drivers for implementing strategic thinking. To a certain extent, these efforts have helped to prevent the reoccurrence of bilateral crises. Additionally, dozens of mechanisms—ranging from military maritime consultation to bilateral talks on climate changes—contribute to enhance mutual trust and reduce suspicion. All these contribute constructively and positively to crisis prevention and management.

Obviously, there exist differences and discrepancies between China and the United States, such as domestic constraints, conflicting national interests, different priorities of respective agendas, coordination problems, different decision-making processes, structural mismatches, and difficulties in coordination with other major actors in multilateral crises. But with more prominent demands on multilateral crisis management, China and the United States have professed to common rather than conflicting interests in handling various hot spots—existent or potential. Their efforts can be characterized into trilateral, multilateral, subregional, regional, crossregional, and global ones. China and the United States work together on the North Korean nuclear issue at the UN Security Council and during the Six-Party Talks, with the Iranian nuclear issue at the UNSC and P5+1, with the Darfur issue at the UNSC and with the AU, and with the terrorism issue at various levels. Their efforts have contributed to the easing of tensions and better management of crisis. Looking down the road, the two countries will develop even more integrated and coordinated efforts.

Here lie more challenges in both regional and functional terms. China and the United States do not share any subregional security cooperative framework. In East Asia, China and the United States do not agree on the necessity of constructing a multilateral security framework, which could see a constructive coexistence of China-proposed subregional mechanisms and the U.S.-led bilateral alliances. In the Central Asian subregion, China and the United States are associated with two different organizations: the SCO and NATO. Here the thinking of zero-sum is still somewhat prevalent. Furthermore, China and the United States need to work with other major actors in institution building in the broader scopes, such as regional, cross-regional, and even global ones. The traditional powers, emerging powers, important groups of small and medium countries such as the ASEAN and AU, and resource-rich countries all need to work together to deal with existent and potential crises, especially those related to the nontraditional security threats of our times. China and the United States also need to cooperate institutionally in dealing with the potential crises in energy safety, financial safety, environment protection, and climate change.

Strategic Vision and Earnest Implementation

Upholding Their Strategic Vision

Looking into the future, the Chinese and U.S. governments need to convince their respective citizenship of the advantages of cooperation as well as show the world the benefits of working toward a new international system that is fairer and more fitting to the changed and changing conditions. The next five to ten years are crucial to the two countries to build up strategic trust that will result in constructive cooperation between an emerging power and an established one. China and the United States should further enhance their economic interflows, political consultation, diplomatic partnership, and cultural exchanges. In terms of crisis management, the two countries have both near- and mid-term tasks. In the near term, China and the United States need crisis prevention regarding such sensitive issues as Taiwan and Tibet. In the mid-term, the two countries should work for the systematic buildup of crisis management strategically, institutionally, and practically so as to pave the way for even higher levels of cooperation leading toward consensus on values.

The two countries should put their crisis management in the context of the global situation. Major actors in the world are currently attaching greater importance to improving the existent international system and exploring the possibilities of a new one. Most countries are calling for a multipolar world based on sovereign states, multilateralism, and rules. Many nonstate actors are promoting global governance, especially in nontraditional security matters. The international society's related efforts are centering on the reform of the United Nations, the expansion of the G8 platform, the maintenance of the nonproliferation system, and follow-up to the Kyoto Protocol.

However, completing the transition to a more global and comprehensive system is difficult due to several constraints. To start with the least difficult ones, the traditional and emerging powers, the major global and regional organizations, and other key state and nonstate actors are working in some selected regional and functional subsystems. Regionalism is an important supplement and prelude to the global system. China and the United States are exploring their relationship by working together with Asia-Pacific Economic Cooperation (APEC) in the Asia-Pacific Region. China and Japan are interacting within the framework of "ASEAN+3." China, Japan, India, and major European countries are all members of ASEUM, an Asian-European consortium. In addition, there are many more nonstate actors contributing to regional cooperation. Functional subsystems are established in line with the ever-proliferating and specialized domains of global affairs. The international society is confronting the urgent need to regularize the new challenges of the times in the absence of overall norms, rules, codes of conduct, and laws. Sector by sector, trade by trade, and issue by issue, the international society is building up various functional subsystems, such as the WTO and the (post-) Kyoto Protocol system.

In the context of globalization and the information age, the traditional and emerging powers and other actors are readjusting their relationships through new concepts, ideas, theories, and practices. China has put forward a number of new concepts concerning security, peaceful development, and a harmonious world. In designing future major power relations to ensure peace and stability of the world and to set up a favorable environment for prevention and management of crises, China is building various partnerships with Russia, the EU, India, and Brazil. The United States in the second term of President George W. Bush turned toward selective multilateralism. The United States is strengthening its alliances with European countries and Japan and is readjusting its coalitions of the willing and able. Some European powers are emphasizing the importance of global governance. Most members of the international society have accepted interdependence and win-win goals as the guiding principles of international relations. This partly explains why the international society as a whole has avoided large-scale war and has instead managed crises in an effective way. However, some actors are still influenced by the conventional ideas of *realpolitik*, geopolitics, and Cold War mentalities. Their ideas and actions contribute to the occurrence of some crises.

Crisis Management and Opportunity Utilization

China and the United States have already learned important lessons through previous crises. Facing the emergence of new actors, new agendas, and new challenges, they and other major actors need to agree on major strategic thinking and coordinate their efforts to manage or prevent future crises. Major powers may have great differences yet not resort to war for their solution: China, Russia, France, and Germany severely criticized the United States during the 2003–2004 Iraqi crisis and war, but they ruled out a total break with the United States from the very beginning. Some countries are confronting existent or potential crises in prudent fashion: India and Pakistan have so far defused several crises since the beginning of this century and will need to do more. China and Japan agreed to peacefully solve their territorial disputes in the East China Sea. China and the ASEAN have agreed to a code of conduct in peacefully settling their disputes in the South China Sea.

China and the United States are confronted with new tasks of coordinating their guiding principles and strategic thinking. As regards guiding principles, the two countries have special responsibilities to maintain peace, stability, and prosperity in the world. Their governments agree to be both stakeholders and constructive cooperators. But their positions on multilateralism, sovereignty, and noninterference in internal affairs are still far apart. As regards strategic thinking, China and the United States have recognized the necessity to work together in dealing with many important issues but still hesitate to trust each other. Therefore, they cannot cooperate with other major actors in a strategic and systematic way. These differences have created difficulties in the Sino-U.S. management of crisis.

Effective Management of Crisis

In terms of crisis management, the challenge for the two countries is not *whether* but *how*. Both China and the United States have recognized the importance of crisis management and established a number of mechanisms accordingly, ranging from hotlines to maritime consultations. Even so, the two sides do not have sufficient coordinating mechanisms in dealing with the crises of nontraditional security threats. For instance, they did not cooperate well during the 2005 tsunami crisis in the Indian and Pacific oceans. In addition, owing to differences in political culture, security apparatus, military structure, and practical handling, the established mechanisms do not always function effectively, such as what happened in the wake of the U.S. bombing of the Chinese Embassy in Belgrade in 1999 and the Sino-U.S. aerial collision in 2001.

What has come to prominence in Sino-U.S. crisis management in the new century is increased coordination in the crises concerning third parties. In this respect China and the United States are looking for institutional solutions by working at the UN on Iranian and Myanmar issues, setting up the Six-Party Talks, and naming special envoys on the Darfur issue. But the countries are only at the initial stage of coordination, and they need to work together more on the basis of international laws and regulations.

Attaching Greater Importance to Opportunity Management

Sometimes there are elements of opportunity in the process of crisis management. The timely translation of these opportunities into realities should be included in the calculation of Sino-U.S. crisis management. The following three ways merit our attention.

First, China and the United States can work together more effectively to realize potential opportunity out of crises. China and the United States seized upon their respective potential opportunities when the first Persian Gulf crisis broke out in 1991 and when the second Korean nuclear stalemate occurred in 2002, thus benefiting their core interests. Currently the two countries could have similar opportunities in the crises of climate change and endemic diseases by achieving more social and economic benefits. Faced with the challenge of Taiwan independence in recent years, China and the United States cooperated in opposing Taiwan's attempts to bid for UN membership and succeeded in bringing a new opportunity for cross-strait peace and development.

Second, the two countries together with other actors can turn their cooperation in war evasion into institution building as part of improving and updating the international system. They can pool their wisdom and resources in designing and realizing cooperative frameworks in dealing with both traditional and nontraditional security threats. There have already been some successful instances of narrowing or even removing differences, such as peacekeeping, nonproliferation, and "8+5" dialogue. Particularly, the two countries could take up the crisis or near-crisis in low politics as opportunities to forward their mutual benefit. Those possibly include a Northeast Asian security cooperation framework and Asian monetary cooperation.

Third, the two countries can make both opportunity management and crisis management a regular content for their strategic dialogues and set up official or unofficial task forces to design the policies and assess the results. Given the fact that more numbers of actors are involved in the multilateral crisis management, these official and unofficial consultations should enlarge the scope and intensify the content, especially in respects related to transnational issues. The Sino-U.S. crisis management could and should be extended into conflict prevention and resolution. Generally speaking, major powers do more negotiations, and small and medium-sized countries do more mediation in terms of conflict resolution. This shows another aspect that China and the United States could work together on in the new century.

Conclusions

The Asia-Pacific region has seen the emergence of a number of important international actors, including China, India, and ASEAN, along with the United States and Japan. As two major powers in the region and the world, China and the United States have a special responsibility to maintain peace, development, and cooperation. Only through this strategic and overall perspective can the two countries chart the general direction of their relations and effectively manage crises. As regards crisis management, China and the United States have traversed the first phase of probing to develop crisis management on ad hoc and specific cases. Now they have entered into a more mature phase of institutional improvement and concept building. In spite of their progress in crisis management, more crises are expected in the future course of Sino-U.S. relations. Therefore, both sides need to take them into consideration. Obviously the stable and prudent coordination of these two major powers in crisis and opportunity management facilitates the regional and global peace and prosperity.

COMMENTS ON YANG JIEMIAN'S "FROM CRISIS MANAGEMENT TO STRATEGIC COOPERATION"

Graham Allison

I COMMEND MY COLLEAGUE YANG JIEMIAN FOR HIS THOUGHTFUL review of crisis management in Chinese-U.S. relations from a Chinese perspective. There is much in Yang's chapter with which I agree, as well as a number of points that look quite different through an American lens. Points of disagreement, at least from this American perspective, include: his account of the end of the Cold War (which Americans call "victory") and the transition to a new international system (which to me appears incomplete and uncertain); the interpretation of the waning of American power and rise of multipolarity (which appears to me uneven); and the Bush administration's first-term unilateralism aside, his assertion that the "United States is generally not interested in regionalism and collective security," which I believe is inaccurate. On this last point, I note that in 2005 the United States applied for observer status in the Chinese-led Shanghai Cooperation Organization—but was rejected.

Much more important than these differences, however, are Yang's major points, where I substantially agree with him. In this comment, therefore, I will focus on these major propositions in the hope of complementing his excellent work and extending his analysis. My comments are organized under five headings.

Recognition of Shared National Interests

Recognition of shared national interests provides a solid foundation for effective crisis management. As Yang writes, China and the United States have "realized that they could not afford the catastrophe of failed crisis management in their overall relationship." This recognition of shared vital interests has led over time to prudence, mutual restraint, strategic dialogue, agreement on rules of the road (including, for example, incidents at sea), enhanced communications such as the hotline, practice in crisis management, and even early thinking about crisis prevention.

As we reflect on the central question of this book and explore whether and how the United States and China can avoid the fate of Germany and England in that late nineteenth- and early twentieth-century hegemonic challenge, what is the major ground for hope? I join Yang in his judgment that it is this recognition of vital shared interest in avoiding a war in which the United States and China would both be victims. In 1914 a relatively inconsequential action (the assassination the Austrian archduke by Serbian terrorists) set off a spark. But the combustible fuel that allowed the spark to ignite World War I was found in prevailing views and illusions of leaders and policy influentials in key judgments. As historians have noted, if the key protagonists in 1914 had been able to see the future in a crystal ball, each would have understood that the war would end with their nations, their regimes, and their own lives in shambles. By 1918 the Austro-Hungarian emperor was dismissed and his empire dissolved; the Russian czar was overthrown by a Bolshevik Revolution that changed Russia's regime; the German kaiser was disgraced, and Germany was defeated and occupied; France was humiliated and prostrate; and Britain had exhausted the financial reserves that it had accumulated over centuries, fatally weakening its empire. In 1914, none of these leaders had that foresight. Each thus allowed their own government's reaction to initiatives by others to end in a war none would have rationally chosen.

Reflecting on the beginning of the war, British prime minister David Lloyd George said, "When a collision seemed inevitable, engine drivers and signal men lost their heads and pulled the wrong levers. The stokers alone did their work. . . . War ought to have been, and could have been, averted."[1] I join Professor Yang in the belief, and hope, that the leaders of China and the United States are wiser today.

Peace and Development Versus Rapid Economic Modernization

Yang notes that the "main theme of this era is peace and development." As the founding leader of modern Singapore, Lee Kuan Yew, has frequently explained, China's overriding operational objective for the next twenty years is *rapid economic modernization* through the magic of market-based capitalism and export-led growth within the framework of the global economy established by the dominant powers.

Within this economic framework embodied today in the WTO, China has enjoyed double-digit growth for more than three decades and aspires to sustain this historically unprecedented performance. According to the "rule of 72," one can answer the question of how long it takes for an economy to double by dividing the rate of growth into seventy-two. Thus, at a growth rate of 10 percent per year, the Chinese economy has been doubling every seven years. This means that over the past thirty years, the Chinese economy has grown sixteenfold. As the World Bank has noted, this growth has lifted hundreds of millions of people from desperate poverty to more sustainable lives—the most dramatic example of mass poverty reduction in the history of human beings' life on Earth. If China is able to sustain this level of growth, some individuals living in China today will, in their own lifetime, experience a 100-fold increase in their standard of living. The benefits for such an increase could include individuals moving from one meal a day to three, moving from no health care to hospitals, and moving from moderate incomes to unimagined wealth.

Although the benefits of China joining the global economic framework are evident, so, too, are the risks and vulnerabilities. According to China's de facto social contract, sustained high rates of economic growth are an essential precondition for China's domestic stability and for the population's deference to the current Communist Party-dominated government. Sustaining this high rate of economic growth is only possible in a benign, open, global trading system.

To put the point bluntly, the Chinese government is, in effect, betting the future of China's domestic stability and requires control on a benign, open global marketplace that is vulnerable to interruption either by events (a major global recession) or deliberate actions (American protectionism that limits Chinese exports to American markets).

To hedge against these risks, China has become the essential supplier of American consumer goods through globalized, just-in-time supply chains that begin in Chinese factories and end in local Wal-Marts across the United States. China also holds more than $1 trillion of American debt. Thus, more as a consequence than deliberate choice of either government, there has emerged a version of what in the strategic nuclear arena was in the Cold War called Mutual Assured Destruction. In strategic nuclear strategy, this refers to conditions in which one nation cannot attack another without triggering a retaliatory response that assuredly destroys the attacker. In such circumstances, each nation's survival requires avoiding a nuclear war of which both would be the first victims. Winston Churchill observed the "sublime irony" that made safety "the sturdy child of terror, and survival the twin brother of annihilation." It would be instructive to pursue this analogy, particularly questions about the stability, or potential instability, of MADE: Mutual Assured Destruction of Economies.

Demand for Energy

China's sustained rapid economic growth has fueled demand for rapid increases in supplies of energy, especially oil and gas—imports that doubled in six years and are projected to triple again by 2030. On the one hand, China's search for oil has led it to actively invest in Sudan, Iran, and other points of potential conflict with the United States. On the other hand, China has chosen, or least accepted, an energy strategy that will leave it dependent on sea lanes that deliver two-thirds of the world's daily consumption of oil—sea lanes that are today, and will be for decades to come, dominated by the U.S. Navy.

Thus again, to put the point bluntly: the success of China's chosen strategy requires as a prerequisite a *benign security relationship* with the

United States that will be essential for (1) receiving energy supplies that are essential for (2) the high economic growth that is needed for (3) domestic stability and regime survival.

Beneath the surface of debates about "engaging," "hedging," or "engaging but hedging," leaders of both China and the United States seem to have largely missed a more fundamental point. China's chosen strategy has bet its highest priority operational objective on benign conditions in both the economic and security realm—conditions of which the United States is the principal protector and arbiter.

The Taiwan Issue

In addressing the single most challenging issue in U.S.-Sino relations, namely Taiwan, both governments deserve high marks. Each has recognized this as the only flashpoint that could lead to war among Great Powers in the current international system. Today, the risk that reckless action by a Taiwanese government could trigger a war is much lower than it was a decade ago, in substantial part because of mature, joint management of crises and substantial cooperation in anticipating and preventing crises.

China's sophistication in helping shape the politics of Taiwan to avoid crises includes its evolution in its declaratory policy from "rapid integration" to "containing" Taiwan's independence movement, its relaxation of timetables, and its encouragement of more enlightened politics in Taiwan. Should these trends continue, it is possible to foresee the elimination of this danger in the relationship between the United States and China. As my colleague Ezra Vogel has advocated, in the aftermath of recent elections in Taiwan, "The United States should declare categorically support for any agreement that Taiwan and Beijing reach peacefully and actively encourage both sides to reach agreements."[2]

Yang wisely calls for moving beyond crisis management to strategic cooperation. He highlights positive recent developments in this area, pointing in particular to the Six-Party Talks on North Korea. Although I join him in applauding recent developments that have closed Yongbyon, preventing North Korea's production of additional plutonium, I believe that the fact that at this point North Korea has ten bombs worth of plutonium and has conducted a nuclear weapons test constitutes a *major failure* in U.S. and Chinese national security policy.

As Henry Kissinger has noted, a cardinal challenge for statesmen is to recognize "a change in the international environment so likely to undermine national security that it must be resisted no matter what form the threat takes or how ostensibly legitimate it appears."[3] North Korea's emergence as a nuclear weapons state would constitute just such a change. Consequences for both the nonproliferation regime and the threat of nuclear terrorism would seriously undermine the national security of both the United States and China.

As the UN High-Level Panel on Threat, Challenges, and Change warned: "We are approaching a point at which the erosion of the nonproliferation regime could become *irreversible* and result in a cascade of proliferation." North Korea's defiance, not just of its nonproliferation treaty (NPT) commitment but of the United States, China, and the world, is one area of serious erosion. Recall the recent history. North Korea withdrew from the NPT—with impunity. It illegally removed the 8,000 fuel rods from Yongbyon in January 2003—with impunity. It reprocessed those fuel rods to extract plutonium for six additional weapons—with impunity. And though U.S. intelligence warned in the fall of 2006 that North Korea was preparing to test a nuclear bomb, the Bush administration demanded that it halt this "unacceptable threat to peace and stability in Asia and the world," and China threatened "serious consequences," Kim Jong Il proceeded with his nuclear weapons test that October. If a state as small, poor, and weak as North Korea can successfully stiff the United States, China, and the international community, what does that say about the state of the international order?

The more urgent threat is that of nuclear terrorism: terrorists successfully exploding a nuclear weapon and devastating one of the great cities of the world. Could Kim Jong Il sell Osama bin Laden a nuclear weapon or the fissile material from which terrorists could make a nuclear bomb? Absolutely. During talks in Beijing in April 2003, North Korea's deputy director general for U.S. affairs, Li Gun, told Assistant Secretary of State

James Kelly that Pyongyang not only possessed nuclear weapons but might also export them, saying, "It's up to you whether we . . . transfer them." An economically desperate Mafioso state, North Korea has demonstrated its willingness to sell anything to anyone who will pay. After repeatedly crossing Bush administration red lines without retribution, Kim could plausibly imagine that he could get away with selling a nuclear bomb to Al-Qaeda. With its arsenal of ten weapons, the sale of one or two would have little impact on North Korea's deterrent posture.

As Lenin asked, "What is to be done?" North Korea's nuclear arsenal has to be eliminated. This is an ambitious goal, but it is not unprecedented. Four states had nuclear weapons and then relinquished them. South Africa built six nuclear weapons by the 1980s and, prior to the transfer of power to the postapartheid government, dismantled them. Three of the successor states to the Soviet Union—Ukraine, Kazakhstan, and Belarus—together had more than 4,000 strategic nuclear weapons on their territories when the Soviet Union dissolved. In 1994 they agreed to return the weapons to be dismantled in Russia, and they have done so.

If China and the United States are serious about collaborating to eliminate North Korea's arsenal and the threat of nuclear terrorism, they should lead in creating a new Global Alliance Against Nuclear Terrorism. The alliance's mission should be to minimize the risk of nuclear terrorism anywhere by taking every action physically, technically, and diplomatically possible to prevent nuclear weapons or materials from falling into the hands of terrorists and from being used to destroy one of the great cities of the world. In *Nuclear Terrorism*, I describe in depth the common undertakings that are required for this alliance. Together, they would seek to shape a new global nuclear order governed by a doctrine of Three Nos: No loose nukes, No new nascent nukes, and No new nuclear weapons states.

The threat posed by North Korea should serve as an impetus for joint action. To deter Kim Jong Il from the extreme act of selling a nuclear weapon to terrorists, the United States and China, ideally in concert with other members of the new Global Alliance Against Nuclear Terrorism, should act now to convince him that North Korea will be held fully accountable for every nuclear weapon of North Korean origin. Here they could take a page from John F. Kennedy's playbook in the Cuban Missile Crisis.[4] The announced policy of nuclear accountability for North Korea would warn Kim and his successors directly and unambiguously that the explosion of any nuclear weapon of North Korean origin on the territory of these states or their allies will be met with a full retaliatory response that assures this could not happen again.

Furthermore, North Korea must be persuaded to actually fulfill in a verifiable manner its February 2007 commitment of "abandoning all nuclear weapons and existing nuclear programs and returning, at an early date, to the Treaty on the Non-Proliferation of Nuclear Weapons and to IAEA [the International Atomic Energy Agency]." The only country that can make this happen is China. To do so, it will have to employ a complete arsenal of both sticks and carrots.

In its dealings with North Korea, the Bush administration's primary objective has been regime change. This, however, is China's worst nightmare. Collapse could send millions of refugees into China and lead to the absorption of North Korea by South Korea, thus eliminating the buffer between a military ally of the United States and China. In Beijing's narrative, preventing that outcome was the reason China entered the Korean War and pushed U.S. forces back to the current divide between North and South Korea. China's seriousness in pursuing North Korea's denuclearization will thus be dependent upon a credible U.S. commitment to subordinate regime change to denuclearization.

Kim Jong Il's overriding objective remains regime survival, including the survival of the leader and his family. The key stick, therefore, must be China's readiness to interrupt the oil lifeline that keeps his desperate economy afloat and his iron grip intact.

Few are aware that the first American ever to win a Nobel Prize was President Theodore Roosevelt. Early in the twentieth century, as the leader of an emerging American superpower, Roosevelt brokered a peace treaty after weeks of contentious negotiations between Japan and Russia to conclude the Russo-Japanese War of 1904–1905. For this extraordinary undertaking he won the 1906 Nobel Peace Prize.

As an emerging superpower and, potentially, a future target, China has an opportunity to lead in preventing nuclear terrorism and proliferation. As has been repeatedly demonstrated in recent years, China is the only party that could plausibly orchestrate the complete, verifiable elimination of North Korea's nuclear arsenal. If Beijing can lead the current Six-Party process to produce a Korean Peninsula free of nuclear weapons, President Hu Jintao, like Roosevelt, would richly deserve a Nobel Peace Prize.

CHAPTER ELEVEN

ARMS CONTROL AND THE SPREAD OF WEAPONS OF MASS DESTRUCTION

Gu Guoliang and Steven E. Miller

SINCE THE END OF THE COLD WAR, THERE HAS BEEN A SUBSTANTIAL, albeit incomplete, convergence in the U.S. and Chinese approaches to issues of arms control and nonproliferation. In that earlier era, China was largely an outsider to the relevant negotiations and regimes. Particularly in the realm of nuclear nonproliferation, China did not sign the NPT or join most of the relevant institutions. It was an outspoken critic of the NPT system, which it regarded as a discriminatory arrangement designed to advance the interests of the other major powers. The United States was concerned about China's alleged cooperation with countries such as Pakistan and North Korea. Given China's disaffection from and opposition to the norms and regulations associated with the NPT regime, it was inevitable that nonproliferation issues would be a serious point of friction in Sino-U.S. relations.

However, this picture has changed rather dramatically. Starting in the early 1990s, China adjusted its policy and began to join treaties and institutions it had previously spurned.[1] It made a commitment to support the nonproliferation regime and undertook efforts to bring its behavior and its domestic legislation into conformity with the requirements of the system. Accordingly, the governments in Washington and Beijing now share a broad objective—preventing the spread of nuclear weapons (and other weapons of mass destruction)—and operate within the confines of the same international legal and institutional framework. Where once friction was inevitable, now cooperation is possible.

There exists today not only an opportunity for the United States and China to cooperate but also an imperative to cooperate on arms control and nonproliferation issues. In recent years the international situation has undergone profound and complex changes. New challenges have come to the fore, bringing greater uncertainty and unpredictability to the international security environment. From both traditional and non-traditional security perspectives, the threat posed by the proliferation of weapons of mass destruction (WMD) and their means of delivery to world peace and stability is increasingly salient and raises great dangers to U.S. and Chinese interests. Therefore, it is an urgent task for both the United States and China to find ways to work together to effectively check such proliferation. In some instances, as with the North Korean nuclear crisis, cooperation between China and the United States may be both essential and necessary if the situation is ever to be resolved in a satisfactory manner. More generally, it will be difficult for the international community to respond effectively to proliferation challenges or to fashion a strengthened arms control framework if the United States and China are not acting in harmony. The extent of collaboration between Beijing and Washington is one of the critical factors that will determine the fate of the world's arms control and nonproliferation efforts.

Cooperation is possible and important, but it is not inevitable or easy. Though the United States and China now share broad nonproliferation objectives, their perceptions and interests are not identical. They will often have very different relationships with countries such as North Korea and Iran—two states that Washington views with unremitting hostility while China has maintained close relations with both. Even when pursuing a common objective, Beijing and Washington may differ on the preferred approach to achieving that objective; China has been skeptical of sanctions and the use of force as remedies to nonproliferation crises, for example, though these have been at the center of recent U.S. policy toward proliferators. Moreover, on a number of other issues, from no-first-use to missile defense to the military use of space, the United States and China still do not see eye-to-eye. Thus, though the prospects for cooperation are much greater than in the Cold War past, the potential for friction and disagreement remains. The great challenge ahead—and the most constructive and fruitful approach to Sino-U.S. relations—will be to exploit and maximize the promise of cooperation in realms of common interest while learning to address, circumscribe, and minimize or eliminate areas of disharmony. Chinese and American policies on WMD proliferation, though still not fully congruent, are aligned today to a degree that would have been unimaginable twenty years ago. Careful tending of the relationship and further attention to the hard work of collaboration may promote further convergence in the years ahead.

China Joins Up

Until the early 1990s, China did not participate in international nonproliferation regimes. (In 1984 it did join the International Atomic Energy Agency and ratify the Biological Weapons Convention, but these were the only exceptions to the general pattern.) Since the early 1990s, however, China has undertaken a dramatic change of course that brought it into the arms control mainstream on WMD proliferation issues, made it a significant player in these regimes, and resulted in a considerable overlap in the policies and perspectives of Beijing and Washington.[2] Several categories of behavior illustrate this change.[3]

First, China began to join treaties it had previously criticized and to participate actively and constructively in multilateral arms control negotiations. Most notable here, China joined the NPT in 1992, thus acceding to a treaty that it had long criticized as a device to perpetuate the predominance of the superpowers. In 1995 it supported the indefinite extension of the NPT. In addition, in 1996 it signed the Comprehensive Test Ban Treaty (CTBT). Beijing also signed (in 1993) and subsequently in 1997 ratified the Chemical Weapons Convention (CWC). Where once China was out, now it is in.

Second, China has increasingly sought cooperation with and membership in the institutions associated with international nonproliferation regimes. In 1997 it became a member of the Zangger Committee (a longstanding informal group of NPT members who coordinate on the export of sensitive nuclear technology). Most important, it joined the Nuclear Suppliers Group (in May 2004). It has applied for membership in the

Missile Technology Control Regime (MTCR) and has established cooperative consultation with other institutions such as the Wassenaar Arrangement (which coordinates export controls on conventional weapons and dual-use nuclear technology) and the Australia Group (which seeks to prevent the spread of chemical and biological weapons). Here again, it is evident that China is making the transition from outsider to insider.

Third, China has gradually but steadily put in place domestic export control legislation that brings its internal legal infrastructure into conformity with its growing international nonproliferation obligations.[4] In 1997, for example, China issued Regulations on Nuclear Export Control that incorporated the Nuclear Suppliers Group control list, though China itself was not yet a member of the group. In the subsequent decade, Beijing has on a number of occasions sought to revise and strengthen its domestic export control system. In 1998 it established regulations governing the export of dual-use items. In 2001 it augmented its nuclear export control list. More recently, in 2006 and 2007, Beijing approved new regulations covering export of nuclear materials (that is, the fissile material that could contribute directly to the manufacture of nuclear weapons) and sensitive nuclear technologies, while also increasing the penalties for violating these regulations. Similar stories can be told about Beijing's evolving regulatory framework for controlling exports relating to chemical and biological weapons and missiles. Thus, China is not only joining international nonproliferation regimes but has been taking appropriate steps to adjust its internal laws and policies so as to be compatible with international obligations. This is another, and particularly meaningful, way in which China has become a supporter rather than a critic of international nonproliferation efforts.

Few if any states have a perfect record when it comes to compliance with and enforcement of WMD export controls—not least because it is difficult for governments to monitor the behavior of individual firms, which often have incentives to break or bend rules in order to gain lucrative contracts. As is true of other states, China's record is not perfect in this regard. In addition, there are often gray areas that allow different interpretations of what is or is not a permitted export. There remain areas in which Washington and Beijing disagree. It would not be correct to say, in the U.S.-China context, that all points of contention over proliferation issues have been eliminated.

But the far more important point is that the United States and China are both members of key nonproliferation regimes, their perceptions coincide to a considerable degree, and (unlike in the Cold War) their broad objectives and commitments are no longer in fundamental collision. Instead, Beijing and Washington share a belief that WMD proliferation is undesirable and contrary to both national and global interests, and they share a stake in the health and effectiveness of existing nonproliferation regimes. In what has become a well-known phrase, Washington has urged China to become a "responsible stakeholder" in the global order. In the realm of nonproliferation, to a large extent China has done so. As one expert has concluded:

> Since the early 1990s, and especially over the last five years, China's arms control and nonproliferation policy has become increasingly compliant with the international and multilateral conventions and regimes as Beijing recognizes the risks posed by the proliferation of weapons of mass destruction. . . . Beijing has made great strides in becoming a stakeholder in the international community's efforts to stem, prevent, and combat WMD proliferation.[5]

Given this new reality, collaboration, cooperation, and perhaps eventually even partnership are clearly possible. Moreover, there is no doubt that the nonproliferation outcomes Beijing and Washington both prefer are far more likely if they are working together than if they are working at cross-purposes. But the prospects for future collaboration depend on the balance of factors favoring and inhibiting cooperation.

Factors Promoting Cooperation

The United States and China have emerged from an adversarial past, but their relationship remains uneasy, unsettled, and ambiguous. Fears (and expectations) of future rivalry are evident on both sides. What reason is there to think that the two wary powers will be able to cooperate in managing critical aspects of the global security order? Several broad considerations, rooted in common interest, suggest that Washington and Beijing should be able to coordinate and collaborate on WMD proliferation issues.[6]

China and the United States share a common perception of the new international security environment.   After the end of the Cold War, with the change of the international security situation, the threat perception of the United States changed. Following the terrorist attacks of September 11, 2001, the United States made clear in its 2002 National Security Strategy that "America is now threatened less by conquering states than we are by failing ones. We are menaced less by fleets and armies than by catastrophic technologies in the hands of the embittered few." It reckons that the gravest danger it faces "lies at the crossroads of radicalism and technology."[7]

China also recognizes that the international security situation has undergone major changes since the end of the Cold War. With nontraditional security threats on the rise and intertwined with traditional ones, security problems of various kinds have become more transnational and interrelated. The proliferation of weapons of mass destruction and their means of delivery is detrimental not only to world peace and stability but also to China's security. China does not wish to see the emergence of the new countries possessing WMD in the world, not to mention in its neighborhood. As development is the first priority for China for many years to come, and as China becomes more closely linked with the rest of the international community, the achievement of its development objectives will rest more on a long-term peaceful and stable international environment.

Both China and the United States recognize that the security of one nation today is even more closely related with that of the region and of the world as a whole. Only through international cooperation can we effectively address the common security problems facing all countries. China and the United States need each other's support and cooperation in countering global terrorism and proliferation of WMD.

China and the United States have common ground and common interests in countering WMD threats. After years of common efforts by the international community, a relatively complete international nonproliferation regime has been put in place. Both China and the United States benefit from and are firmly committed to the international nonproliferation regime. Prevention of the proliferation of weapons of mass destruction and their means of delivery is conducive to regional and global peace and development and serves the common interest of both China and the United States.

Therefore, both nations support strengthening the integrity and authority of the existing international arms control and nonproliferation regimes. China and the United States are each state parties to the Nuclear Non-Proliferation Treaty, the Biological Weapons Convention (BWC), the Chemical Weapons Convention, and the Comprehensive Test Ban Treaty. Both countries are members of the International Atomic Energy Agency (IAEA) and have voluntarily placed their civilian nuclear facilities under IAEA safeguards. They are also members of the Zangger Committee, the Nuclear Supply Group (NSG), and other international nonproliferation regimes. Both countries have committed themselves in earnest to implementation of the obligations of the treaties. Furthermore, both countries recognize that international instruments on arms control and nonproliferation provide a legal basis for international nonproliferation efforts and place them on a just and reasonable premise.

Under the current situation, China and the United States attach great importance to export control. As noted earlier, China for its part has over the past years promulgated a series of laws and regulations and established a complete set of export control mechanisms, covering nuclear, biological, chemical, and missile fields.

Both China and the United States attach great importance to the role of the United Nations in its nonproliferation efforts. As the core of world collective security mechanisms, the UN plays an irreplaceable role in international cooperation to ensure global security. The fight against terrorism and proliferation of WMD requires full play of the leading role of the UN and its Security Council.

China and the United States have had good cooperation and fruitful interactions in the field of arms control and nonproliferation. The possibility of U.S.-China cooperation on nonproliferation issues is confirmed by the reality that such cooperation has actually occurred. Recent years have witnessed a number of instances in which the two powers worked together in pursuit of a common end (although not always successfully and not always without disagreement).

The most prominent illustration is China's prominent role in managing the crisis over North Korea's nuclear program. Though it was acutely concerned about North Korea's emerging nuclear capabilities and was outraged by the eventual detonation of a North Korean nuclear weapon, the Bush administration essentially "outsourced" the management of the crisis to Beijing.[8] The Bush administration has been unwilling to engage in bilateral talks with a regime it regards to be a "rogue," and the United States possesses few instruments for effectively influencing Pyongyang. Under the circumstances, the Bush administration deferred to Beijing, which possesses advantageous connections with Pyongyang and more potent levers of influence. As Yoichi Funabashi stated, "The United States decided to leave to China most of the responsibility for promoting peace on the Korean Peninsula, particularly the settling of the North Korean nuclear issue."[9] China has been convener and host of the Six-Party Talks to address the North Korean crisis. In that capacity, China has recurrently played a constructive role, pushing the recalcitrant North Koreans to participate despite Pyongyang's frequent hostility to the process, pressing a reluctant Bush administration to be more flexible in its dealings with a North Korean regime loathed in Washington, and occasionally intervening forcefully to break negotiating deadlocks. It has been a fitful process, full of disappointments, but much is owed to Beijing for the grudging progress that has been achieved. More recently, the Six-Party Talks in Beijing have achieved important progress. This symbolizes the successful cooperation between China and the United States in handling the issue of proliferation, although much hard work is needed to reach a final peaceful solution to this issue. China has played an important part in bringing about the Six-Party Talks and made great efforts in persuading North Korea to give up its nuclear program.

Other examples include:

1. China and the United States have had good cooperation at the NPT review conference. Through joint efforts, the indefinite extension of NPT was achieved.

2. China and the United States had good cooperation in handling India and Pakistan's nuclear tests. After India and Pakistan successively conducted nuclear tests in May 1999, China and the United States held close consultations both through hot lines and at the P5 foreign ministers' meeting in Geneva. The leaders of the two countries issued a joint statement asking India and Pakistan to stop nuclear testing and join the CTPT.

3. China and the United States have also had extensive interactions in dealing with Iran's enriched uranium program. In intense negotiations, China and the United States (along with other permanent members of the UN Security Council) have been able to reach common ground on sanctions resolutions against Iran. The results of these negotiations have not been to the perfect satisfaction of either Washington or Beijing, but they show that dialogue and compromise are possible. From China's perspective, the progress of the Six-Party Talks has shown that the same approach should also apply to the solution of Iran's uranium enrichment program. Continuing dialogue is a better approach than imposing sanctions, not to say resorting to military force.

4. Mechanisms of dialogue and consultation between the two countries have been established at different levels. Dialogues at both the top and working levels have been established between China and the United States. The Arms Control and Disarmament Department of the Chinese Foreign Ministry and the Nonproliferation Division of the U.S. State Department have held strategic dialogues on political and security issues including arms control and nonproliferation. There have also been dialogues between the Chinese Commerce Department and the U.S. Commerce Department on various issues of arms control and nonproliferation.

Potential Frictions and Impediments to Cooperation

Divergent Strategic Interests

Washington and Beijing will inevitably view each nonproliferation crisis through the lens of their own interests and strategic calculations. Though they desire the same nonproliferation outcome, they will frequently have very different perceptions of the urgency of the crisis, different fears, different assessments of how their national interests can best be advanced, and different instincts about what are the acceptable solutions and intolerable scenarios. For example, whereas Washington very badly wants to see, and hopes to cause, the failure of the North Korean regime, Beijing fears that a collapse of the North Korean state would bring enormous problems to its border.

This problem arises in acute form in the case of Iran. The United States has had no diplomatic relations with Iran since 1979, has had sanctions in place for some two decades, has pursued a policy of regime change against a government it regards as evil, and has openly raised the possibility of the use of force against Iran. Washington invariably pushes for a harsh policy toward Tehran and is deeply skeptical of the value of diplomacy given its view of the character of the Iranian regime. China sees things very differently. Though there is no reason to doubt that Beijing prefers a nonnuclear Iran, it has had good, and even steadily improving, relations with Tehran. More fundamentally, given China's large and rapidly growing need for energy imports, Beijing has a strategic interest in Iran's enormous reserves of oil and natural gas. Thus, over the past several years, while the Bush administration has been urgently pressing its P5 colleagues to negotiate more draconian sanctions to impose on Iran, China and Russia have stood for more dialogue and less harsh sanctions against Iran. China has reached several large energy deals with Iran—in amounts that cumulatively exceed $100 billion.[10] Whereas George W. Bush's Washington has wanted to isolate and coerce Tehran, Beijing has preferred to engage and reach deals with Iran. The

Bush administration regards Iran's present nuclear policy to be, as the president has many times said, intolerable and unacceptable; China, in contrast, has responded to the Iranian nuclear challenge in a more temperate fashion and does not offer the same frantic opposition found in Washington.

Although they share the goal of countering proliferation of weapons of mass destruction, the United States and China do not share the same assessment of the character and urgency of the problem. Nor do they share the same assessment of what approach to the Iranian nuclear challenge is preferable and likely to be effective. Nevertheless, Washington and Beijing have tried to work together on this crisis, particular in the context of the P5 sanctions negotiations and, as noted earlier, it has been possible to find some ground for agreement. But given their divergent perspectives on critical aspects of the issue, it should be no surprise that the process of finding agreement has been frustrating and painful and that the results have not been hugely satisfying to either side.[11] When all the relevant perceptions and interests are not in alignment, collaboration on nonproliferation challenges will not be easy.

Different Approaches to Managing Nonproliferation Crises

China and the United States have the common goal of countering proliferation of WMD. However, China stands for the proper solution of the nonproliferation issues by diplomatic and peaceful means, and it supports limited sanctions to persuade countries to comply with their obligations. China's government does not think sanctions can solve the issue of proliferation.

China's approach stands in marked contrast to the much more aggressive approach preferred and pursued by the Bush administration. The United States has focused very heavily on sanctions and believes that if sanctions can be made painful and punitive enough, proliferators can be compelled to change their ways. The reluctance of China (and other powers) to support strong sanctions has been a source of great frustration for the Bush administration. Conversely, the administration's instinct to isolate and punish what it sees as nonproliferation sinners causes dismay in Beijing and other capitals. This contrast explains why sanctions negotiations among the P5 and between China and the United States are typically difficult.

Accompanying Washington's recent preference for harsh sanctions is a policy of preemptive strikes and regime change. The Bush administration has argued that it is necessary and appropriate to use force to eliminate WMD threats emanating from proliferating states. This was one of the primary rationales for the invasion of Iraq (though it was discovered after the attack that Iraq possessed no WMDs). Further, the Bush administration has argued that truly effective nonproliferation policy must eliminate not only the offending WMD program but the offending regime. Washington has openly articulated a policy of regime change with respect to both North Korea and Iran—a policy objective that inclined the Bush administration to find ways of undermining or overthrowing these regimes rather than sincerely negotiating with them. It has, however, reached a nonnuclear deal with Libyan leader Moammar Khadafi's HBYA. Whereas Washington prefers sanctions, force, and regime change, Beijing prefers diplomacy and deals. Perhaps a new administration in Washington will change the emphases of U.S. policy, but so long as the current priorities remain in place there will be significant differences in the U.S. and Chinese approaches to coping with nonproliferation challenges.

Disagreement on Arms Control Issues

China stands for no-first-use policy whereas the United States insists on the first use of nuclear weapons as the last resort to counter nuclear, biological, and chemical threats. China is concerned about the U.S. ballistic missile defense (BMD) program, which may negate the credibility of China's small nuclear arsenal and destabilize the situation in Asia. In addition, China and the United States have different perceptions on the issue of prevention of an arms race in outer space. Furthermore, U.S. arms sales to Taiwan have had a negative impact on the cooperation of China and the United States in the field of arms control and nonproliferation. Efforts thus need to be made to narrow the differences between the two countries in the field of arms control and nonproliferation.

Conclusions

What is desirable for the future? Clearly the goal should be to shape even more cooperative future relations between China and the United States in the field of arms control and nonproliferation. If achievable, this would be good for U.S.-China relations, good for the national interests of the two powers, and good for global security. Today, much more than in the past, such cooperation appears to be possible.

As permanent members of the UN Security Council and nuclear-weapon states, China and the United States share common obligations and interests in the nonproliferation area. Against the backdrop of increasing nontraditional security threats, China and the United States have much more room to cooperate in the field of arms control and nonproliferation. Following is an important and constructive agenda for U.S.-China collaboration.

First, China and the United States should work together to strengthen the NPT regime. The nonproliferation treaty is the cornerstone of the global nuclear nonproliferation regime. As the two major nuclear-weapon state parties to the treaty, China and the United States should fulfill their undertakings stipulated in Article VI "to pursue negotiations in good faith on effective measures relating to cessation of the nuclear arms race at an early date and to nuclear disarmament, and on a Treaty on general and complete disarmament under strict and effective international control."

To comply with their undertakings, both nations should reduce the role of nuclear weapons in their national security considerations. The two countries should support the conclusion of an international legal instrument on the complete prohibition and thorough destruction of nuclear weapons. Before the goal is achieved, they should refrain from researching new weapons designs and developing and possessing new low-yield weapons that will lead to a reduction in the threshold of nuclear weapons use.

The two countries should undertake not to use or threaten to use nuclear weapons against nonnuclear-weapon states or nuclear-weapon-free zones and support the conclusion of a legally binding NSA convention. They should reach common agreements on no-first-use of nuclear weapons against each other and any other countries, and they should strive for an early ratification of the CTBT and an early start to the negotiations for the Fissile Material Cutoff Treaty (FMCT), with a view of concluding the treaty.

Second, China and the United States should work together to make the NPT more effective and credible. The NPT has loopholes including the ambiguous definition of "peaceful use." A balance should be struck between nonproliferation and peaceful uses. China and the United States should work together to find the way to guarantee the legitimate rights of the nonnuclear states for peaceful use of nuclear energy, and to effectively prevent nonnuclear states from pursuing proliferation activities under the pretext of peaceful uses. Measures should be taken to enhance the IAEA's safeguarding and verification processes.

A good reward and punishing mechanism should be established. More incentives should be given to those who abide by the treaty, and heavier punishing measures should be taken to restrain those who violate it, including those who withdraw from the treaty.

Finally, both countries should strive for enhancing the universality and the authority of the NPT. Measures should be taken to encourage and reward those countries that are outside NPT to accede to the treaty and isolate and punish those countries that refuse to join or that withdraw from the treaty.

Third, China and the United States should have more active and effective cooperation in preventing proliferation of WMD. The two countries should continue their cooperation in dealing with North Korea's nuclear program and the Iran enriched uranium issue.

Fourth, building strategic trust between China and the United States will further promote cooperation in countering the proliferation of WMD.

Regular strategic dialogues can help China and the United States gain a better understanding of the other party's threat and security perceptions, and clarify their strategic intentions and thus avoid misjudgment. China and the United States should, through strategic dialogue, achieve strategic reassurance and reach the strategic common understanding of not regarding the other party as its adversary. Both sides should acknowledge the existence of their common strategic interests. Each side should acknowledge the basic strategic interests of the other side.

In sum, the United States and China should establish a stable nuclear strategic relationship. With the growth of China's economic power, some individuals in the United States have expressed concern over the modernization of China's national defense. Meanwhile, the U.S. Department of Defense's "Resolution in Military Affairs" and development of the strategic force of the United States have also received close attention in China. Nuclear development and the future role of nuclear force in both countries have a direct bearing on the future of China-U.S. relations. Establishing a stable nuclear strategic relationship is the requirement of and guarantee for maintenance of long-term stable and sound China-U.S. relations; it also serves the strategic interests of both countries. China and the United States should assure each other that the nuclear force each side possesses is neither directed against nor constitutes a threat to the other side.

China and the United States should reach the understanding that a nuclear war cannot be fought or won. The two countries should discuss what type of nuclear relationship they want to have, exploring such issues as the framework of their nuclear forces and ways to avoid and manage conflicts, accidents, and crises.

China and the United States can carry out positive and effective cooperation in the fields of maintenance of nuclear safety and prevention of nuclear accidents and loss of nuclear materials.

The United States and China should have substantial talks on the U.S. ballistic missile defense program, especially its planned deployment of BMD in Asia. This will help remove the sense of insecurity on the part of China. The United States should change its positions on China's application to the MTCR.

Confidence-building measures such as dialogues at all levels including high-level talks, hotline contacts, and crisis management between the two countries should be taken so as to avoid misjudgment or accidents, which may lead to military conflict neither side wants.

China and the United States may exercise asymmetrical military transparency with a view to reducing distrust. The United States should make its nuclear strategy, targeting, and development plans transparent and should inform China of its missile defense developments in a timely manner. China should take measures to increase its military transparency. As a country with only limited nuclear force, China's transparency of the scale, structure, and development plans of its nuclear force can only be a gradual process.

In conclusion, China and the United States have major common grounds and common interests in the field of arms control and nonproliferation despite some differences. The scope of cooperation in this field is expanding, and this cooperation will continue to play an important role in promoting general Sino-U.S. relations.

CHAPTER TWELVE

COOPERATION IN GOVERNANCE: THE REGIONAL DIMENSION IN A U.S.-CHINA SHARED VISION FOR THE FUTURE

Zhang Yunling and Alan S. Alexandroff

In 2005 Zheng Bijian, chair of the China Reform Forum, an influential advisor to the Communist Party, and a leading figure at the Central Party School, wrote an article that appeared in the pages of the prestigious U.S. Council on Foreign Relations journal, *Foreign Affairs*. In it he raised the image of "China's peaceful rise" (*heping jueqi*) to Great Power status (*da guo*).[1] As he noted, this rise had become a subject of heated debate in academic, policy, and international circles. It remains so.

In 2008 Princeton University professor G. John Ikenberry in the same journal pondered again the consequences of the rise of China for the international community. In his opening paragraphs Ikenberry raised the key questions of China's rise and the consequences for the current leading international relations power—the United States: "Will China overthrow the existing order or become part of it? And what, if anything, can the United States do to maintain its position as China rises?"[2] China's rise today remains a key imponderable for contemporary international relations.

This chapter examines the potential common interests between the United States and China as well as the significant challenges and obstacles that the two Great Powers face. The chapter focuses on regional governance and how regional governance in the Asia-Pacific could be a dimension in building and reinforcing a collaborative U.S.-China relationship.

In examining regional governance, we remain alert to the architecture of international relations. As a legacy of the Cold War, there is deep U.S.

179

regional involvement across the globe but especially in Europe and in Asia. Thus, in examining China's increasing involvement in regional governance in Asia we are drawn to a central structural question for China—its relationship with the United States. Once focused on the U.S. relationship, and given the current U.S. leading role globally as well as regionally, the scope of our examination includes China's role at the regional governance level and also at the global level, influenced by the U.S. assessment of China's global leadership.

The Rise of China

China entered the twenty-first century as a rising power. Historically, rising powers have been regarded as challengers to the existing order and the dominant powers in the international system. In China's case, its success to date is based primarily on its integration into the global economy through its reform and opening-up policy. As one scholar recently wrote, "China has become an insider in the international system."[3] Further, China has committed to follow a peaceful development road and strived to build a harmonious world of lasting peace and common prosperity.[4] Thus, China has thus far escaped a more searching examination as a challenger and a possible threat to the United States.

China attaches great importance to its relationship with the United States. Although China does not agree with all the practices of the United States, especially its unilateral interference, as China sees it, the two powers have many interests in common across many issue areas, as we will show. As a result, the current structural relationship continues to favor and indeed tilts the relationship toward collaboration.

China's strategy is based on three principles: first, China recognizes the United States as a superpower, indeed the current sole superpower; second, China will cooperate with the United States in as many areas as possible; and third, it would seem China will continue to increase its strength, including military strength, and raise its status both regionally and globally. From China's perspective, as long as the United States recognizes and takes into account China's interests, China is unlikely to challenge the overall U.S. leadership role. In the final analysis, the most significant question for China is, how can it balance its support for democracy, domestically and externally, with a defense of sovereignty whether in Taiwan, Central Asia, or the Asia-Pacific generally?

The Asia-Pacific represents the large regional area of intersection between these two Great Powers. As Wang Jisi, dean of International Studies at Peking University, wrote not long ago, "There is one region where the United States is most likely to come into close contact with China, leading to either major conflicts of interest or real cooperation (or both): in Asia and the Pacific. Driving relations between the two countries therefore requires a comprehensive analysis of the forces in the region."[5] Cornell's Peter Katzenstein has argued persuasively that contemporary global politics is built on a global "structure of regions, embedded deeply in an American imperium."[6] There is no question of the importance of regions, especially the Asia-Pacific, and the continuing influence of the United States regionally and globally. For China and the United States regional governance presents a challenge, a point of friction, perhaps, but also an opportunity and a possible collaborative setting for their relations.

David Lampton, a longtime scholar of China, puts China's growing regional influence and the reaction of U.S. policy in the following terms: "These changes require alterations in U.S. policy and behavior at the same time that China is developing a stake in a stable yet dynamic status quo in East Asia and beyond. East Asia is not becoming Sinocentric, but it is becoming a place which Chinese interests and influence cannot be disregarded.[7]

China recognizes, also, that there remains a limit to China's scope for global political influence. The regional context, in fact, provides China more immediate political influence. As Zhang Yunling and Tang Shiping wrote, "China reasons that the best way to achieve regional political influence is through cultivating an image as a responsible (regional) Great Power that is constructively involved in addressing and alleviating various regional issues."[8]

The definition of "responsible power" is problematic and still strongly debated in influential circles in both China and the United States. The debate has been taken up principally on China's role and influence in the global governance setting. But it is evident as well that regional and global governance cannot be easily divorced.[9] For both powers, actions in either can impact on the other and on overall prospects for U.S.-China collaboration.

The emergence of an energetic Chinese regional strategy has not come without criticism. In particular, in those regional organizations where the United States has not been included, most notably the Shanghai Cooperation Organization, China has been accused of developing its own power sphere or returning to a "Middle Kingdom Order." But such accusations appear to ignore China's stated aversion to power alliances. As Chu Shulong, a Chinese security specialist from Tsinghua University, has argued, "China believes the new world order in the post-Cold War era will be a system of partnership, a system that is now in the process of replacing the alliances system."[10]

The Global Governance Equation

Recently Harvard's Richard Rosecrance, in *Can the World Be Governed? Possibilities for Effective Multilateralism,* has identified the contemporary characteristics that facilitate Great Power cooperation: "As we have already seen two things bring countries together: common goals that can be achieved only in tandem, and common opponents—states or movements—that can be opposed effectively only by co-operative action."[11]

U.S. trust and collaboration toward China will be built on global and regional governance. Positively, effective regional collaboration can reinforce trust and collaboration generally between the two powers; negatively, conflict or opposition between the United States and China in the global governance setting, in particular, has the potential to undermine trust and collaboration in both the global and the regional governance settings.

Following the U.S. invasion of Iraq, China's premier underscored China's need and intention to find a collaborative path building on the former Chinese president's insistence to focus on what he saw as a "period of strategic opportunity" (*zhanlue jiyi qi*). Speaking to a Harvard audience in 2003, Premier Wen Jiabao argued, "If we don't grasp it, it will slip away. We are determined to secure a peaceful international environment and a stable domestic environment in which to concentrate on our own development, and with it to help promote world peace and development."[12] The Chinese leadership has seen the need for China to become a responsible Great Power (*fuzeren de daguo*). American officials, however, including Robert Zoellick, then U.S. deputy secretary of state, called on China to become a "responsible stakeholder."[13] Implicitly the United States was calling on China to show a higher level of commitment and leadership for global governance organizations and matters. From a Chinese perspective, this shows that China is recognized as an important member of the international community on the one hand, yet on the other hand, doubt remains in the United States over China's willingness to take on international responsibilities.[14] How then can these Great Powers design and build a broad enough collaboration in the face of such challenges to ensure common effort and built trust?

Focusing on "common goals" of global growth and prosperity represent an ideal set of areas where both nations can establish and promote leadership to their benefit and improve conditions for other states and enhance U.S.-China collaboration. In trade and investment, globally we should look to China-U.S. cooperation in the WTO. And regionally we should look to APEC. Finally, we should look at the bilateral U.S.-China economic relationship itself. Both countries could improve their economic relationship by considering a U.S.-China free trade agreement. What would it take? Should we also look at how China could—with its significant sovereign wealth funds (SWFs) and huge foreign exchange reserves—improve the health of the global economy and improve the economic relationship between these two economic powers? As Harvard's Larry Summers notes, however, there are concerns that governmental influence could arise from these SWF investments. Such risks could, according to him, be mitigated by SWFs investing through intermediary asset managers.[15]

Environment and climate change represent additional arenas for global governance collaboration. There are indications, recently, that both countries are prepared to examine the reduction in energy use and may be willing in the not-too-distant future to tackle climate change problems.

Global security has shifted significantly since the Cold War years. The focus in that era was principally on restraining Great Power conflict. Today most international conflict is within states. Preventive diplomacy, humanitarian intervention, and postconflict transformation challenge the Great Powers to maintain stability. With growing calls, however, for the protection of international human rights, a major area of contention between China and other Great Powers appears to exist over the question of when it is appropriate for human security concerns to override norms of national sovereignty. As Chu Shulong puts it, "China is one of the few countries in the world which strongly defends traditional principles of national sovereignty and opposes most types of foreign intervention in the internal affairs of nation states."[16]

Though the potential for collaborative action is real, the tensions arising from very traditional notions of sovereignty, defended vigorously by the Chinese leadership, challenge the capacity of China to act in concert with other powers in maintaining or restoring international stability in conflict regions. Chinese leaders have vigorously defended national sovereignty; they have urged the mutual respect for sovereignty of every state; and they have insisted on noninterference in the affairs of other states. Chinese leaders have suggested that national sovereignty is in fact the guarantor for individual human rights. Former president Jiang Zemin argued in 2000 at the UN Millennium Summit, "History and reality tell us that sovereignty is the only premise and guarantee of human rights within each nation." However, China has become still more active in participating in international peacekeeping activities under UN auspices and a contributor to UN peacekeeping forces. Future cooperation may be possible.

Focusing on "common opponents" brings yet another list of potential collaborative issues. First and foremost is the common effort to eliminate Islamic extremism. Such terrorism threatens international stability worldwide. It resonates strongly in both China and in the United States. Fighting terrorism would appear to encourage collaboration at both the regional and the global level.

In addition, there is the effort to avoid nuclear proliferation and eliminate the use of weapons of mass destruction. China and the United States have joined together in the Six-Party Talks in Korea to eliminate the prospect of a nuclear-armed Korea. Indeed, the Six-Party Talks may well be a precursor to greater East Asian security collaboration.[17] To have that occur, however, will require an interest on the part of both Great Powers to create a more permanent security organization in Northeast Asia.

One of the great challenges for the two is the threat perception of the other in their respective strategic policy communities. We have seen in the United States the "China threat" expressed openly in the Washington Beltway and beyond. The "China threat" view challenges the optimistic "peaceful rising" perspective. It argues that China's rise poses a threat to U.S. preeminence that needs to be defended with appropriate strategic defense and hedging. We anticipate that the equivalent "U.S. threat" community in Beijing argues equally forcefully with the Chinese leadership that the United States poses a present and future threat to China. If these communities are not handled adroitly, their hedging views could impair the relationship between these two Great Powers.

Regional Governance

The Asia-Pacific is a vast region within which both the United States and China possess vital interests. A striking phenomenon is the growing impact of regional organizations and institutions that are shaping the political and economic order along with the relations among the states. Some of these regional governance organizations are Asia-Pacific based and involve both the United States and China. Others are only in Asia or limited to North America. In many of these only one of the two Great Powers is a member (see Table 12.1).

Whither APEC?

In 1989 a big step was taken when the Asia-Pacific Economic Cooperation was established. APEC—the largest of the regional organizations— was designed to promote liberalization and facilitation of trade and investment and economic cooperation in the Asia-Pacific region. APEC

Table 12.1. Key Regional Institutions in the Asia-Pacific Region

Name	Nature	Involvement
APEC (Asia-Pacific Economic Cooperation)	forum	U.S., China
ARF (ASEAN Regional Forum)	forum	U.S., China
CSCAP (Council on Security Cooperation in the Asia-Pacific)	forum	U.S., China
Six-Party Talks	functional	U.S., China
ASEAN (Association of South East Asian Nations)	organization	
ASEAN +3 (ASEAN, China, Japan, ROK)	forum	China
EAS (East Asia Summit; ASEAN+3, India, Australia, New Zealand)	forum	China
SCO (Shanghai Cooperation Organization)	organization	China
NAFTA (North American Free Trade Agreement)	agreement	U.S.
Asia-Pacific Agreement (China, India, Laos PDR, ROK, Sri Lanka, Bangladesh)	agreement	China
China-ASEAN Free Trade Agreement	agreement	China

set up the Bogor goal for achieving "free and open trade and investment in the Asia Pacific" by 2010 or 2020. At the same time, APEC is considered to be a useful organization in reducing the gaps in economic development in the region. Fred Bergsten, the head of the Washington-based Peterson Institute, has suggested that APEC can realize "shared prosperity in the region" and thus "elevate the objective of equitable development to a status fully equivalent to that of free trade and investment. Implementation of this parallel goal would help counter the resistance to pursuit of the initial Bogor objective."[18]

APEC has been challenged, however. In the past few years the emerging bilateral and subregional free trade agreements (FTAs) have become separate arenas for economic integration. Due to the differences in principles, structures, and timetables, these many agreements create obstacles to the development of a broader regional market. The new call for a

FTAAP (FTA of the Asia-Pacific), which will bring the United States and China into a broad integrated regional agreement, seems not to be feasible in the near future.

East Asia Regionalism

In East Asia, ASEAN is a pioneer in developing the regional grouping. ASEAN was established in 1967 and now consists of ten member states—Indonesia, Malaysia, the Philippines, Singapore, and Thailand (the original five), Brunei Darussalam, Vietnam, Lao PDR, Myanmar, and Cambodia. ASEAN's objectives include the acceleration of economic growth, social progress, and cultural development. In addition, ASEAN promotes regional peace and stability through respect for the rule of law and encourages adherence to the principles of the UN Charter. In 2003 at the ASEAN Leaders Meeting the member countries agreed to establish an ASEAN Community comprising three pillars: an ASEAN Security Community, an ASEAN Economic Community, and an ASEAN Socio-Cultural Community. In 2007 the ten ASEAN members signed the ASEAN Charter, which set an agenda for realizing the ASEAN Community by 2015. ASEAN has emerged as a regional organization designed to integrate South East Asia, but also East Asia, by its active initiatives through multilayered frameworks of ASEAN+1, ASEAN+3 (APT) (China, Japan, and the Republic of Korea [ROK]), and ASEAN+6 (China, Japan, ROK, India, Australia, and New Zealand). As scholars observed, "ASEAN members initiated the regional grouping and each year the summit meeting takes place on ASEAN soil. ASEAN essentially sets the APT agenda."[19]

Based on this variety of frameworks, East Asia has moved quickly in formulating regional trade agreements (RTAs). In 2001, China made its first free trade approach to this regional grouping.[20] In 2002 the two sides signed a Close Economic Partnership Agreement (including an FTA). In 2005 China and ASEAN signed an agreement for trade in goods, and in 2007 the two signed an agreement for service liberalization. As a response to China's initiatives, other countries in Asia—Japan, the ROK, and India—quickly engaged ASEAN negotiating FTAs.[21] At the same time, a pan-East Asian FTA was also called for. In 2004, APT economic ministers agreed to launch a feasibility study on an East Asian FTA (EAFTA), while Japan proposed the establishment of a close economic partnership agreement based on the East Asia Summit (ASEAN+6). A Joint Expert Group, led by Zhang Yunling, completed an EAFTA study report. The report recommended that the EAFTA should be developed from APT and then extended to other countries. It seems that, as suggested by Kawai Masahiko, "China regards ASEAN+3 as a natural grouping for East Asia's trade and investment cooperation," while "Japan regards the . . . ASEAN+6 as an appropriate grouping for East Asia's trade and investment." [22] The challenge lies in how China and Japan could coordinate their different strategies.

East Asian cooperation goes beyond FTAs. In the financial area, ASEAN+3 has developed a regional financial and monetary mechanism commencing in 2003 with the Chiang Mai Initiative and now extending from bilateral SWAP arrangements to an integrated financial web (linking all bilateral commitments together). In 2007, China proposed creating a regional exchange reserve pool in order to prevent a future Asian financial crisis. All regional members supported this proposal. Furthermore, the East Asian Vision Group[23] in its report recommended that the final goal of regional cooperation was an East Asian Community.

Does an integrated East Asia without the involvement of the United States pose a challenge to U.S. interests in Asia? Some have questioned China's underlying intentions in promoting East Asia integration and cooperation. These critics have suggested that China's regional initiatives are designed "to push the United States out of Asia and assert regional dominance."[24] Yet as observed by David Shambaugh, "No Asia states . . . wish to see the American presence and role in Asia diminished. . . . Asia is certainly big enough for both powers to exercise their influence and power. . . . On balance, the United States and China find themselves on the same side of many of the key issues affecting the future of [the] Asian region."[25]

China's regionalism to date has shown an open, pragmatic, and flexible character. The United States can engage East Asia or Asia through many bilateral and regional approaches. Indeed, the United States has concluded several FTAs with individual Asian countries—for example, with Thailand, Singapore, Malaysia, and the Republic of Korea. A significant future step, as noted earlier, would be the negotiation and the successful conclusion of a U.S.-China FTA. There are many complementary regional organizations, especially APEC. As Yeo Yong Boon George, Singapore's foreign minister, stated, "In fact, ASEAN, China, Japan and Korea are all happy to pursue these three tracks simultaneously—APEC, EAS and ASEAN+3—at the same time. The difference is one of emphasis which we can live with."[26]

In the Asia-Pacific, military alliances led by the United States used to be key to the regional security architecture: the U.S. military presence provided an important regional security guarantee. With the ending of the Cold War, however, a number of new security institutions have arisen. These organizations are based on new security concepts and do not appear intended to replace the existing security organizations. Do these security organizations represent obstacles to future U.S.-China cooperation?

A New Security Concept (Xin anquam guan)

China faces a number of threats to regional stability. Beyond Great Power politics, China is concerned with the threats posed by the "three forces" (*sangu shili*)—separatism, terrorism, and (Islamic) extremism. China lacks the power and abilities to address all of these problems unilaterally. Although Beijing has built many strong bilateral relationships based on security interests, such ties have been deemed insufficient to address these developing new threats. Therefore, China's approach to multilateral security has softened, and China has become involved in organizations that discuss security matters on a more regional scale, including the SCO, the ARF, and the less traditional Council on Security Cooperation in the Asia-Pacific (CSCAP).

In March 1997, Foreign Minister Qian Qichen at the ARF's Confidence-Building Conference in Beijing articulated the "New Security Concept." Broadly the policy sought mutual reassurance based upon comparative security, dialogue, and mutual economic benefit. This concept was refined in 2002. Jiang Zemin described the formal elements of the New Security Concept to German policy leaders as consisting of abandoning Cold War-era views; establishing confidence building as the foundation of security; using economic and trade cooperation to enhance security, and vice versa; and establishing a regional collective system to fight international terrorism and crimes. At a conference held in late 1997 the core of the New Strategic Concept (a view endorsed in 2004 by Hu Jintao) was identified as the Four Nos (*si bu*): no hegemonism, no power politics, no alliances, and no arms races.[27]

Some analysts argued that the New Security Concept is simply designed to undermine the U.S. Asian regional role and weaken the U.S.-Japan strategic alliance. Though he admits that the concept has that possible impact, Chu Shulong suggests that it is much broader and reflects a strong regional component "because China's new security concept does stand against the 'old thinking' represented by military blocs. Yet the search for a new security concept, doctrine, and strategy also represents a Chinese view of the region and the world, which is different from that of the past and reflects China's search for a national security strategy and a regional security arrangement for the Asia-Pacific region for the future."[28]

It is evident that there is a significant regional aspect to the New Security Concept. Regionally a variety of measures have been employed, including joint military exercises with neighbors, using confidence-building measures (CBMs), and moderating various stances on contentious maritime and/or territorial disputes with India and South China Sea claimants, plus Vietnam, Russia, Tajikistan, and Kazakhstan. China has contributed leadership in the Six-Party Talks over North Korea's nuclear program, emphasizing that Beijing does not seek to drive the United States from East Asia militarily.

On the security front these ideas were also elaborated upon within China's National Defense White Paper, which stressed that "multilateral security dialogue and cooperation in the Asia-Pacific region should be oriented towards and characterized by mutual respect instead of the strong bullying the weak, cooperation instead of confrontation, and seeking consensus instead of imposing one's will on others."[29] China is likely to continue to make use of strategic institutions to both further develop and promote its new thinking and as a means to counter the development of alliances and hierarchical security institutions around China's periphery.

Thus, potential tensions remain between the United States and China as China emerges as a regional player and in some instances a regional leader in various organizations and institutions. The tensions arise particularly where the regional organization is led by China and the United States may be excluded, as in the case of the SCO or in ASEAN+1, APT, and the East Asia Summit. To the extent that the United States perceives China's growing regional influence and leadership as purely a zero-sum game—that China's growing influence comes at the cost of U.S. influence—then tensions may well be magnified. According to Zhang Yunling and Tang Shiping, the avoidance of a U.S. zero-sum calculation will require the United States to abandon the following views: "(1) that because the United States is the 'indispensable nation,' it has to lead all global and regional initiatives all the time; (2) that China seeks to push the United States out of the region and reestablish the 'Middle Kingdom order' in East Asia; and (3) that a divided East Asia is in the interest of the United States."[30]

Ameliorating the distrust of the United States in the face of a growing Chinese regional interest is but one consequence of China's increasing regional presence. In addition, there remains a residual distrust of China among Southeast Asia's leadership. Though such distrust may possibly blunt Chinese initiatives, more positively it leads these states to encourage the continued U.S. presence in the region. In the end the key to U.S.-China collaboration is a U.S. conclusion that growing Chinese influence does not come at the cost of American presence or influence.

Role of ARF

In the security area, the ASEAN Regional Forum is the principal forum for security dialogue in the Asia-Pacific. ASEAN established the ARF in 1994. The ARF is designed to develop in three broad stages: it is to promote CBMs, then promote development of preventive diplomacy, and finally to articulate approaches to conflict resolution. The membership today consists of Australia, Brunei Darussalam, Cambodia, Canada, China, the EU, India, Indonesia, Japan, North Korea, the ROK, Lao PDR, Malaysia, Mongolia, New Zealand, Pakistan, Papua New Guinea, the Philippines, Russia, Singapore, Thailand, the United States, and Vietnam. The ARF discusses major regional security issues, including nonproliferation and counterterrorism, and also nontraditional security issues such as transnational crime and South China Sea security.

China understands the security dimensions of ASEAN, in particular the ARF and CSCAP, to be that of "maintaining and strengthening regional peace and stability through economic development and the promotion of economic, political, and security dialogue and coordination among Asia-Pacific countries."[31] An article published in *Jiefangjun Bao* (PLA Daily) has called the ASEAN way a "security through dialogue" model. However, the United States wants to see more action-oriented endeavors. As Robert Zoellick, then deputy secretary of state, noted, "The Asian Regional Forum ought to be concerned with confidence-building measures. But, it has also emphasized the role of preventive diplomacy. This is something that we encouraged, and indeed we are also encouraged that countries in the region look for ways that they can take direct action."[32]

Considering the great diversity of the region, China seems to support a gradual and soft approach. As "the challenges facing the Asia Pacific region are becoming more complex and interrelated," the challenge is how "the ARF should move forward at a pace comfortable to all."[33]

The SCO

The Shanghai Cooperation Organization in Asia is one of the only regional security institutions lacking U.S. participation. It was formed in June 2001 when Uzbekistan joined with the original Shanghai Five—China, Kazakhstan, Kyrgyzstan, Russia, and Tajikistan. The development of the Shanghai Five-turned-SCO as a regional security community therefore represented a mechanism for China to address security issues with five like-minded governments. The SCO was established to handle the new security problems facing China, Russia, and the new Central Asian countries after the disintegration of the Soviet Union. The new security threat mostly comes from nontraditional security, like separatism, extremism, and other cross-border illegal activities that go beyond just bilateral handling. The major points of the Shanghai Agreement are: (1) military forces deployed in the border region will not attack each other; military exercises will not be targeted at each other; (2) the sale, scope, and number of military exercises will be restricted; there will be information exchanges and notification of important military activities carried out within 100 km of the border, with individual concerns receiving proper explanations; invitations will be extended to each other to observe military exercises of certain scales; and (3) efforts will be made to prevent dangerous military activities; and friendly exchanges between military forces and frontier guards in the border region will be strengthened. SCO member countries are considered to be "united under the banner of the 'Shanghai Spirit' which embodies mutual trust and benefit, equality, consultation, respect for cultural diversity and a desire for common development."[34] The SCO has a secretariat in Beijing and an antiterrorism center in Tashkent. The organization has extended beyond the original members by inviting observers (Mongolia, India, Pakistan, and Iran).

China played a key role in initiating the SCO. Beijing has shown a great deal of enthusiasm for formalizing the regime, not in the direction of creating a Eurasian NATO but rather with an eye to creating a regional community that goes beyond security issues and also addresses issues of trade, joint development, and culture. SCO members are working on more than 100 joint projects covering the areas of trade, investment, customs, finance, taxation, transportation, energy, agriculture, technology, telecommunications, environment, health, and education. At the annual meeting in 2003 the organization broadened its scope to include economic cooperation. Premier Wen Jiabao suggested at the meeting that the members consider a free trade arrangement. In addition he proposed a series of proposals to reduce nontariff barriers in a number of areas. In 2006 during an SCO summit, leaders agreed that the goals of the SCO in economic cooperation are to realize the free flow of goods, service, capital, and technology among its members by 2020. The United States has not been allowed to participate in the SCO, even as an observer.

However, due to both the ongoing threat of extremism and terrorism in the region, coupled with a possible longer-term U.S. interest in the area as part of its international operations against terror, security matters remain at the heart of the SCO's activities. In light of the fact that the SCO is currently styling itself as an institutional means to policy coordination on strategic and political matters in Central Asia rather than as a traditional alliance, the organization may prove a useful partner in international efforts to promote greater peace in what is developing into a highly unstable region. The United States has important interests and its own presence in the region. Could the SCO find a way to engage the United States—for example, through an SCO forum, or by inviting more countries, including the United States, in as observers?

Conclusions

The subtext of the narrative of Chinese-U.S. regional and global governance involvement is this: challenge and opportunity. The successful collaborative equation starts with the acknowledgement and accommodation of a rising China. In this current setting the United States, in particular, needs to avoid adopting a "China threat" perspective. To maintain the openness needed to build collaboration, each Great Power must remain skeptical of the voices advocating a "rising threat" presumption. The hedging strategies embedded in "rising threat" perspectives will inevitably erode collaboration between the United States and China.

If strategic threat perceptions don't hinder the capability to act collaboratively, then, as we have pointed out, there are many opportunities in global and regional governance to act cooperatively on significant issues—economic, environmental, and security—and in a variety of global and regional organizations and institutions. Indeed, some of the newer challenges especially in the environmental area afford the United States and China the real opportunity to advance collaboration and broader collective governance.

But to achieve this result, the leaderships in both countries need to pay attention to, and find accommodations in, their tactics and strategies for the other. Whether the issue is domestic or has broader regional or global consequences, each must consider the implications of their actions on the other Great Power. Both must exhibit great care especially over evident sensitive issues—none more delicate and sensitive than Taiwan.

Turning briefly to the strategic calculus, particularly on the global governance side, the Chinese must continue to reflect on the strict national sovereignty perspective adopted by the government. Though China has begun to modify its stance toward UN peacekeeping, for example, China's strict sovereignty and its noninterference in the internal relations of member states need to undergo continuing scrutiny. A "softer" stance on sovereignty will go a long way to integrating China into the global governance security organizations and underpin U.S.-China collaboration in the multilateral setting.

On the regional governance side, China has emerged as a committed actor in both economic and security organizations in the region. It is evident that China not only promotes growing regional collaboration but through its New Security Concept and Four Nos highlights a distinct approach to regional governance. A *China Daily* article describes the contrasting tactical approaches in regional security governance: "The frequent summit talks among these leaders with the pioneer trust-building agreements have set a good example for countries in other parts of the world to develop multiple good-neighborly and cooperative relations and safeguard peace and stability. It is a model different from the Cold War thinking, since the five-nation agreements are not aimed at forming an alliance nor are they directed against a third party."[35]

The Chinese leadership expresses the belief that this new security model will become increasingly acceptable in an international system. It does, however, require the United States to adopt a less skeptical view of this "dialogue and consensus" approach to regional governance relations. The tensions between the tactics favored by the two Great Powers have been evident in the Six-Party Talks on the North Korean nuclear issue. The current administration has veered from aggressive sanction and no-discussion approaches to far more open collaborative tactics. China, meanwhile, has promoted a more consistent "dialogue and consensus" approach, holding out economic benefits and proposing CBMs in the effort to resolve the North Korean nuclear question. If the Six-Party Talks represent a harbinger for a new East Asian security institution, then it would seem that collaboration might better be built on more congruent views of regional diplomacy. Without similar tactical approaches, regional organizations are likely to be shackled by U.S.-Chinese tensions and misunderstandings. Finally, Chinese efforts to find accommodation and inclusion of the United States in these regional governance organizations can only improve the prospects for U.S.-China collaboration.

Successful U.S.-China collaboration in regional governance is indeed possible. However, it is not inevitable; it is merely favored. To insure collaboration between the two Great Powers, respective leaders will have to engage in deliberate accommodative actions. With these, opportunities can trump challenges.

CHAPTER THIRTEEN

U.S.-CHINESE INTERACTIONS OVER TIME

Jia Qingguo and Richard Rosecrance

The Development of Relationships

U.S.-Chinese interactions have varied over time. Essentially they have changed from limited relationships in a few issue-areas to much more comprehensive interactions across the range of economic, political, and military spheres. At the same time, the interactions have deepened to the point where the economic futures of the two countries have become closely interlinked. Western demand sustains a whole range of Chinese industries. Chinese investments support deficit financing of major categories of American spending. China holds more than $1 trillion of U.S. debt. The United States contributes greatly to the surplus in Chinese foreign trade. As the dollar falls and the reminbi rises, these relations will become more balanced, but they will still be very significant. American failure to buy Chinese goods would put a crimp in Chinese economic growth, as the proto-recession today is likely to suggest. Chinese sovereign wealth funds are also moving into the U.S. financial market to rebalance the amount of foreign direct investment on each side.

Chinese-American ties, however, have ranged well beyond economics. China has joined the WTO and the IMF. It will in time become a member of G9 and the OECD. China has been critical to the success of the Six-Party Talks on North Korean nuclear weapons. It will have a large role to play in the outcome of Iranian nuclear policy. In 2007, China was invited to join the multinational 1,000-ship navy to safeguard the trade routes of the world. Following the traumatic Hainan air collision incident, the two militaries gradually resumed their relationship. In January 2004 General Richard Myers, chairman of the U.S. Joint Chiefs of Staff, came to Beijing. In October of that year, Cao Gangchuan, Chinese defense minister, paid a visit to Washington. In March 2007 General Peter Pace, chairman of the Joint Chiefs of Staff, visited China. General Timothy Keating, commander in chief of the U.S. Pacific Fleet, came two months later. More generally, Chinese and American leaders have toured each other's countries on an increasingly routine basis, and they frequently speak on the telephone. Despite the American visa restrictions imposed after September 11, 2001, large numbers of Chinese students continue to study in U.S. universities, and American tourists increasingly visit China. The number of flights between Chinese and American cities has multiplied in recent years. Ministerial delegations in various fields routinely proceed back and forth between the two countries.

There has been increasing cooperation on such topics as the environment, immigration, cross-border crime, intellectual property rights, and the war against terrorism. Recently, when Taiwan separatists pressed for independence, the United States and China cooperated on the Taiwan issue, seeking to avoid an unnecessary confrontation.

Toward Balance in International Relationships

Initially, the U.S.-China relationship was one between initiator and respondent; the United States proposed, and China responded. Now China often initiates the interaction. For instance, China's efforts to bring a peaceful resolution of the North Korean nuclear crisis led to an apparent change in U.S. policy and greater success in the Six-Party Talks. China's efforts to develop closer relations with Southeast Asian states have caused the United States to do the same. In short, after more than three decades of deepening contacts, the two countries are finding themselves involved in a more comprehensive engagement with extensive cooperation and balanced international interaction with one another. Both are beneficiaries of current international arrangements including membership in the UN, WTO, World Bank, and IMF. Both wish to uphold international law and to promote free trade. They seek greater contacts and solutions to world environmental problems. The liberalization of China economically and greater openness politically has narrowed value differences and provided a basis for further cooperation.

Will Increasing and Deepening Engagement Lead to Peace?

Whatever one says about the pervasiveness and depth of the U.S.-China relationship, however, it has not yet attained the status of irreversibility. Karl Deutsch of Harvard University contended that countries extremely close together in values, engaging in a multitude and reciprocal exchange of messages, very powerful trade/GDP relations (with one another), high levels of immigration, and similar cultural attitudes would eventually achieve the status of a "security community" in which war was for practical purposes ruled out between them. Deutsch believed that the United States and Canada, Norway and Sweden, and the Benelux countries had gained "dependable expectations of peaceful change" within each geographical grouping. Since then, Germany and France have certainly done so. China and the United States, however, have not yet forged such an indissoluble link.

Few Great Powers (with the possible exception of the United States and Great Britain after 1890) have established a pattern of long-term cooperation with one another. Great Britain successfully accommodated America's rise (see Chapter 1). Can the United States accept China's "peaceful rise"? Great Britain and the United States were both liberal-democratic states. China has liberalized economically but not fully democratized. Each country has a very large economy in a world that is even more globalized than Europe's was before 1914. In current circumstances, China will tend to give priority to economic development and political stability instead of freedom and civil and political rights. Because some Americans believe in the "democratic peace theory," they will press China to complete its democratic transition, as has happened in Eastern Europe. Any such pressure, however, will only slow down a U.S.-Chinese rapprochement and possibly forestall it. Since "the process of democratization" may be fraught with instability and international conflict, the United States should not want to see China undergo the late-nineteenth-century transition of a democratizing but irrational Germany or an imperial and expansionist Japan (see Chapter 5). In the short term it is enough that China develop economically liberalizing elements to foster its deeper association with the international economy.

A Realist Peace?

In short, China and the United States cannot be fully brought together by social associations or value ties. Their economic relationship will be strong but not unbreakable. The "power" elements in the equation, however, will tend to keep both nations in line. As a result of Iraq and Afghanistan the United States has come to realize how difficult major military interventions are in other parts of the world. Washington does not possess either the military or the economic strength to sustain a large imperial role in world politics that is not supported by other Great Powers. Its present operations in Iraq are paradoxically dependent upon the heavy purchase of U.S. securities by Beijing, Europe, and the Arab world. Equally, China is hemmed in by the powers on its flanks. India, Japan, and Russia, formally friendly to China, are independent nations that would not likely countenance Chinese territorial expansion should it occur. In these circumstances, neither Beijing nor Washington has to adopt the primary vocation of deterring and restraining the other. The system provides for this restraint in each case. In any event, a stable and balanced nuclear deterrent relationship between the United States and China will in time emerge to strengthen these constraints as well (see Chapter 4).

This does not mean that the two countries should not work to make their relationship closer. The nineteenth-century Concert of Europe brought in all the Great Powers and resolved the disputes between them for a period of thirty years. An international Concert of Great Powers could perform a similar function in the years ahead. China would be a crucial and essential member of this concert, and the group would constitute a forum in which China's rise in status could be accommodated and legitimized. This could be an important complement to the P5 of the UN Security Council, which operates far too much in the glare of world publicity and does not fully represent the existing Great Powers (leaving out India, Japan, and Germany).

So also can U.S.-Chinese bilateral ties be increased and deepened. Immigration links the trained labor forces of the two countries; education abroad has strengthened Chinese elites, and it could help American ones over time. At this point, however, the only prime minister of a major industrial country who studied in China and speaks fluent Mandarin is Kevin Rudd of Australia. The training of rising elites in the academic institutes of the other nation could help cement the process of long-term accommodation.

In the environmental field the two countries face similar and intransigent problems. Overuse of fossil fuels, pollution, the shortage of potable water, and decaying industrial infrastructure affect both nations. If the two do not reach agreement, they face the "tragedy of the commons" in which key resources are rapidly used up and little conservation takes place. Coal-fired power plants are not a solution to this difficulty unless carbon capture is included, and that technology is in its infancy. The two countries need to work together to achieve a solution. A substitute or extension of the Kyoto Protocol must be negotiated that includes developing as well as developed countries.

Game-Theoretic Interactions

Many game theorists and international political experts believe that the Great Powers confront "Prisoners' Dilemma" incentives in which the advantages to cooperation are partly vitiated by stronger incentives to deviate (or defect) from agreed arrangements. For example, two Great Powers would mutually benefit from reducing their arms expenditure, balancing it at lower levels, and avoiding an arms race. However, the power that maintains its forces would benefit still more if its opponent reduced armaments. Equally, two countries would mutually gain from a reduction of tariffs on trade between them. If only one country reduces its tariffs, the

Table 13.1. Prisoners' Dilemma Outcomes

Prisoner's Dilemma Outcomes (Payoffs)		
Country B	**Country A**	
	Cooperate C	**Defect D**
Cooperate C	3, 3	1, 4
Defect D	4, 1	2, 2

other can improve its terms of trade still more by retaining them. Each time one country cooperates, the other has incentives to take advantage of that cooperation, defecting from agreements.

In Table 13.1, countries can cooperate and obtain the mutually beneficial Pareto optimal outcome of (3, 3). But if Country A cooperates and Country B defects (D, C), B has the favorable outcome of (4, 1). In the Prisoners' Dilemma, outcomes are ranked in the following sequence: DC>CC>DD>CD. The game theoretic outcome (on a single play) is for each country to play D, resulting in the Pareto unfavorable outcome of (2, 2). As one can see, no country player can improve his position by shifting to cooperation. If he plays C, his opponent will remain at D.

Unless there is a way to enforce agreements, a Prisoners' Dilemma world will be one in which universal "defection" tends to take place. The Prisoners' Dilemma also applies to groups of nations. If certain advantages can be procured through international cooperation, some countries will undoubtedly participate and agree to work together. But others can then become "free-riders" on the outcomes offered by initial cooperators. A public goods problem thus arises in international politics: roads, schools, police protection, clean air, and clean water are public goods that have to be paid for. After they have been created, however, late-coming free-riders can obtain the benefit without having to pay the cost.

Within domestic society, a government can tax its citizens to provide such benefits. But there is no enforceable taxation in international relations. If international terrorism or the spread of weapons of mass destruction is stopped, most countries benefit. But it does not follow that nations will act together to prevent the spread of either terrorism or weapons. Some will be free-riders on the largesse (contributions) of others. Thus, reliable and enduring international cooperation may falter.

Two countries that devote increasing amounts of attention to each other and interact frequently can avoid such outcomes, particularly if they have continuities in leadership. If after having established a cooperative agreement, Country A defects on the first play, it may be expected to receive a defection from Country B on the second play. In game-theoretic simulations among players over time, it has been established that cooperation ultimately emerges among two particular players. Patterns of defection are overcome, and cooperation results. If two leaders get to know one another and anticipate each other's responses, cooperation occurs as long as an indefinite future extends ahead of them. The United States and China are durable players for the long term. There is no event—short of an intergalactic catastrophe—that could put an end to them. Each time a new leader comes to power, there is uncertainty until a pattern of agreed responses can be worked out. Given the military and economic interdependencies between them, U.S. and Chinese leaders benefit from greater interaction, which in turn is likely to lead to greater interdependence as ties deepen and intensify. No country can eliminate the other, militarily or economically; each will always be there, mastering most of its continent. It is in their interest to cooperate.

Conclusions

In the past, rising Great Powers often warred with established states. Prussia did so in the 1740s. Japan and Germany attacked status quo powers both before and after 1914. The United States rose economically and politically, but it was reluctant to assume the "Great Power" mantle and for a long period stayed isolated from broader world politics. After

1917, Russia underwent rapid economic growth and tried to cement its position as the dominant European, if not world, power. Russia also sought to gain greater territory in Eastern Europe. The Cold War, in part, was the result.

The rise of China may or may not be "peaceful." That outcome depends not only on China but on the rest of the world's response. The United States has been rather pro-China since the heady days of negotiations between Richard Nixon, Henry Kissinger, and Mao Zedong in 1971–1972, but that does not guarantee peace in the future. One key variable that makes the "rise" of China more acceptable is that Beijing (with the sole exception of Taiwan) has no territorial ambitions. All of the other Great Powers defined their futures in terms of gains in territory. China, in contrast, is a vertical power, not a horizontal one. It seeks improvement in terms of rising economic growth, not lateral expansion. It is fortunate that there is no case of war among Great Powers that arose solely from economic growth. Nations do not fight over the percentage of world GDP they possess. In the past, however, military expansion was the typical concomitant of economic development, and this conjuncture did lead to international conflict. Unless China should change its territorial ambitions, peace is likely. The United States could help ensure this result by actively supporting a peaceful solution to one remaining territorial issue, Taiwan, along lines sketched in Chapter 8.

This book has endeavored to put U.S.-Chinese relations in the context of future developments. China is growing rapidly, and its GDP will equal that of the United States in the next generation. Its military expenditure is also increasing at a high rate and will in time attain deterrent capability vis-à-vis the United States in both conventional and nuclear terms. China will become more integrated into its East Asian neighborhood, both politically and economically. It will also exert a more powerful role in great-power politics and is likely to participate in a range of such accords. China will be welcomed to a new G3 or G4 (including Japan and Europe). It will be a crucial and welcome player in any new agreement on global warming and the attempt to prevent further climate modification. To cope with coal power plants, China is now working hard on carbon capture and sequestration, though the outcome of that effort is as yet uncertain, as it is in the United States.

China is now joining international organizations and arrangements that it abjured in 1950. Its integration with the outside world has broadened and deepened. As China becomes an important stakeholder in existing international regimes, its relationship with the outside world and the United States departs from zero-sum outcomes. Beijing acts in part to solve the persistent public goods problem in international politics. China can then seek prosperity and status through international trade and investment. China's steady and responsible course also makes it possible for others to accommodate China's economic and political rise. The United States needs to encourage Beijing to act as a responsible stakeholder, for in a globalized world America and China can both seek mutual benefit as well as international peace and prosperity.

CONCLUSIONS: THE UNITED STATES AND CHINA TOGETHER?

Richard Rosecrance and Wang Jisi

THE U.S.-CHINA RELATIONSHIP IS ONE OF THE MOST IMPORTANT in world history. As we know from the past, the two greatest powers frequently fight for supremacy, and neither the United States nor China wishes to do that today or in the future. Top leaders in both countries have assured the world in their respective statements that they want to establish a stable and constructive relationship and to refrain from conflict.

It is, however, not a simple matter to avoid conflict by reassuring each other in words. The two countries have different political systems, ethnic composition, and cultures. They are in different stages of modernity and economic development, and they exist 6,000 miles away from each other. One is at the top of the international hierarchy, and the other is rising to it. Historically, this complex of a status quo power versus a rising power was a veritable recipe for greater conflict and antagonism. Some political analysts and advisors, in both the United States and China as well as in other parts of the world, point to the historical cases in which competition for supremacy led to war, hot or "cold," and predict that the United States and China will follow a similar path to tragedy. Furthermore, they often refer to specific causes of conflict between the two states, including different policies toward Taiwan, human rights, trade, finance, arms control, and regional security. Their argument is also based on the reality that both the American and Chinese military are making themselves ready for a major armed conflict against each other.

The difference in this case, perhaps, is that policy makers of the two nations are aware of their situation. They understand the factors that led Germany to rival Great Britain in the nineteenth century. They understand the basis of the conflict between the Soviet Union and the United States during the Cold War. They recognize that unexamined pursuit of individual interest could readily degenerate into military conflict. The key to better long-term relations is indubitably contact and communication between the two countries at all levels, from the governments to the elites and to societies. Understanding of the situation and maintaining communication between nations are the first requirement, but though they are necessary they are not sufficient to produce good long-term relations. As many scholars have shown, economic interdependence between Britain and Germany was quite high in 1913. Yet despite Norman Angell's mouthings about war as the "great illusion," it nonetheless occurred on August 5, 1914.

The second requirement, therefore, is adjustment of interests that leads to compromise. Britain and Germany never succeeded in solving their disagreement about the size of the German navy. The Soviet Union and the United States could not agree on the fate of Eastern Europe—whether it would be independent or completely under Soviet influence and control. During the Cold War, the Soviet Union and China competed in supporting North Vietnam, whereas the United States attempted to protect the regime in South Vietnam. The three nations viewed their respective interests and influences in Indochina as mutually exclusive and tried to win the conflict there "through to the end." In retrospect, the end result of the Vietnam War was disastrous to all three Great Powers.

In today's world, there are many concrete issues on which the United States and China might disagree: the legitimacy of possible use of force to compel Taiwan to recognize that it is part of China; the capabilities and transparency of the Chinese military; the ways of solving problems with North Korea, Iran, Myanmar, and Sudan; the degree of responsibility for global climate change; the need to adjust trade and investment imbalances; Chinese and U.S. roles in East Asia; how Chinese "soft power" might mitigate the effects of China's rise; how human rights issues should be dealt with internationally. In the past and perhaps in the future the U.S. government will press China to become democratic—according to the American definition of the term. China will continue to improve what it defines as democratic institutions and rule of law but resist American calls for political reform. However defined, the process of democratization can also entail greater nationalism and friction with outsiders and thus needs to be approached carefully. China also wants the United States to manage its own economic and financial affairs carefully and to restrain its expansive international behavior.

In this book the contributors have offered means by which this adjustment of interests can occur. In Chapter 1, Ernest May and Zhou Hong considered past examples of hegemonic transition that have both failed and succeeded. They recommend methods used by the European Union to keep China and the United States together. Joseph Nye and Wang Jisi observed in Chapter 2 that China's soft power has buffered the edges of its greater hard power and perhaps made it more acceptable; meanwhile, the soft power of the United States remains considerable.

With regard to economics and trade, Lawrence Lau, Mingchun Sun, Victor Fung, David Richards, and Richard Rosecrance suggest in Chapter 3 that the current imbalance (in savings and consumption) will require greater U.S. fiscal discipline and greater Chinese consumption. The currencies will adjust accordingly.

Ashton B. Carter and Chen Zhiya address the possibility of military conflict in Chapter 4. As China develops means to negate America's dominance in the Taiwan Strait, the United States may have to "hedge" to resuscitate that balance. Only a settlement of the Taiwan issue would entirely remove the need for such hedging. Xu Shiquan and Ezra Vogel consider this possibility in Chapter 8. It may not be sufficient to rely entirely on the two protagonists (Taiwan and Beijing) to settle the matter themselves. It is in the U.S. interest as well that a solution be reached, and the United States might encourage the new regime in Taipei to move in this direction.

In Chapter 5, Etel Solingen wonders whether rapid democratization is a desirable strategy either for China or the outside world. In the context of further "liberalization," a broadened CCP government might avoid the nationalistic policies that democratizing movements have encountered elsewhere. Tony Saich (Chapter 6) and Yu Keping (Chapter 7) look at the relationship among societies as a brake upon conflict. An increasingly aging, middle-class China may have greater common interests with a middle-class United States. Both nations have unresolved problems of equality, pollution, infrastructure, and energy that place them on a common footing.

Pan Jiahua and Kelly Sims Gallagher examine in Chapter 9 the need for China and the United States to solve the public goods problem involved in too much utilization of energy in the absence of protections against global climate change. Though each country seeks to use more energy, a degree of restraint is necessary on both sides. Both countries also need to focus on new means of carbon capture and sequestration.

Wars sometimes arise out of small incidents. The murder of Franz Ferdinand in Sarajevo on June 28, 1914, did not at first seem to raise questions that would involve all the major powers. No doubt Nikita Khrushchev initially believed that he could "symmetrically" put missiles in Cuba as the United States had put missiles in Turkey. But his attempt to do so led to the major crisis of the Cold War. In Chapter 10, Yang Jiemian and Graham Allison recognize that a greater consolidation of relations between China and the United States is necessary to prevent seemingly small issues leading to big crises.

China is very dependent on the United States in that its entire economy is based upon economic access to the outside world—access in essence controlled by the United States. Equally, on regional issues the United States is very dependent upon China, the only country that can guarantee that North Korea does not proceed with its military nuclear program. At the same time, China and the United States are nearing a posture of economic deterrence vis-à-vis each other. Graham Allison, Jiemian Yang, Ashton B. Carter, and Chen Zhiya consider this relationship in their chapters.

As investment, production, and labor interpenetrates each side, there might eventually develop a relationship of MADE—mutual assured destruction of the economy; this would provide an additional deterrent to MAD (mutually assured destruction) in the nuclear field. Bearing these dependencies in mind, the two countries can more readily prevent minor issues from becoming major ones in their own relations. As Gu Guoliang and Steven Miller demonstrate in Chapter 11, only recently have the two powers faced up to their common need to prevent the further spread of nuclear weapons and limiting their own military preparations against each other. China opposes U.S. missile defense because it might eventually undercut the Chinese deterrent. It does not endorse the U.S. monopoly of power in space. The United States, in turn, cannot entirely stand by and watch China develop capacities that make Taiwan's defense (under non-provocative circumstances) impossible. Each has to hedge against the other but prevent an unlimited arms race. This knife-edge balance of policy will not be easy to achieve.

As Alan Alexandroff and Zhang Yunling demonstrate in Chapter 12, China has in recent years sought specifically regional economic and political associations that at least in part exclude the United States. The SCO, ARF, and ASEAN+3 exclude the United States. Though the United States applied for observer status to the SCO in 2005, it has not been allowed into the Shanghai Cooperation Organization's meetings. Some analysts believe that China wants to develop the SCO as a Far Eastern and Central Asian alternative to NATO. Under these circumstances it is even more important for forums like APEC, the Six-Party Talks, and the G8+5 to bring the two critical nations together.

Finally, in Chapter 13 Jia Qingguo and Richard Rosecrance examine the interaction of China and the United States over time. China has come to participate much more intensively in international organizations and has come into continuing interaction with the United States. Game-theory simulations show that parties can move to greater cooperation over time if there is no specified end to their game and if the same leadership remains in power. China and the United States are stable elements in the international field. Short of intergalactic catastrophe, neither can be eliminated from the face of the world. Only major changes in leadership would be likely to predicate greater conflict between them.

Can the United States and China develop a shared vision of the future? If achieved, can they act on that vision? The contributors to this volume certainly hope so. At this point, the two countries benefit greatly from the basically stable global order and, to this degree, have similar attitudes and plans for the future of world politics. Neither country desires drastic changes in the existing global institutions, and both are faced with challenges such as financial turbulence, pandemic diseases, terrorism and other transnational crimes, trade frictions, regional tensions and civil conflicts in certain countries, energy and food shortages, ecological calamities, and environmental degradation. China and the United States also have similar domestic governance agendas in trying to bridge the gulf between rich and poor, maintain the momentum of social and ethnic integration, and improve social safety networks among their aging populations.

For all this, we strongly believe that a shared vision of the future is not only desirable but also necessary. Undoubtedly, the two nations do not agree on everything. But none of the domestic and international challenges facing them could be solved by mutual suspicions, verbal attacks, or military "hedging" against each other. Although many of their distinctive interests, national characters, and preferences will remain, possibly forever, China and the United States must cooperate and coordinate their policies. Whether they can achieve this outcome depends on an even greater intensity of their relations across the board—economic, political, societal, and in terms of defense. As analysts and scholars, we are convinced by human history that international relations are not as yet foredestined, and that our joint efforts, as shown in this volume, will help to promote a peaceful relationship between the two Great Powers.

NOTES

Introduction

1. See Walter Lafeber, *The Clash: U.S.-Japanese Relations Throughout History* (New York: Norton, 1997); and George Friedman and Meredith LeBard, *The Coming War with Japan* (London: St. Martin's Press, 1992). Samuel Huntington imagines a war between the United States and Japan in *Clash of Civilizations and the Remaking of World Order* (New York: Touchstone, 1996), pp. 314–316.

2. Jack L. Snyder, "Soviet Politics and Strategic Learning," in *Myths of Empire: Domestic Politics and International Ambition* (Ithaca, NY: Cornell University Press, 1991), p. 247.

3. See Fareed Zakaria, *The Future of Freedom: Illiberal Democracy at Home and Abroad* (New York: Norton, 2007), p. 85; and Susan Shirk, *China: Fragile Superpower: How China's Internal Politics Could Derail Its Peaceful Rise* (New York: Oxford University Press, 2007).

Chapter 1

1. The best surveys are James C. Thomson Jr., Peter W. Stanley, and John Curtis Perry, *Sentimental Imperialists: The American Experience in East Asia* (New York: Harper and Row, 1981); Michael H. Hunt, *The Making of a Special Relationship: The United States and China to 1914* (New York: Columbia University Press, 1983); and Warren I. Cohen, *America's Response to China,* 4th ed. (New York: Columbia University Press, 2000).

2. Edward S. Corwin, *The President, Office, and Powers: History and Analysis of Practice and Opinion,* 2nd ed. (New York: New York University Press, 1941).

3. Dave Wang, "Benjamin Franklin and China," *Essays and Articles for the Benjamin Franklin Tercentenary,* http://www.benfranklin300.org/essays.htm.

4. John K. Fairbank, ed., *The Missionary Enterprise in America and China* (Cambridge, MA: Harvard University Press, 1974); Thomas J. McCormick, *China Market: America's Quest for Informal Empire, 1893–1901* (Chicago: Quadrangle Books,

1967); James Reed, *The Missionary Mind and American East Asia Policy, 1911–1915* (Cambridge, MA: Harvard University Press, 1983).

5. E. J. Kahn Jr., *The China Hands: America's Foreign Service Officers and What Befell Them* (New York: Viking Press, 1975); Paul Gordon Lauren, ed., *The China Hands Legacy: Ethics and Diplomacy* (Boulder, CO: Westview Press, 1987).

6. Henry A. Kissinger, *White House Years* (Boston: Little Brown, 1979), pp. 745–747.

7. Rusk used this phrase in a 1951 speech, when heading the East Asian bureau of the State Department under Secretary Acheson. Warren I. Cohen, *Dean Rusk* (Totowa, NJ: Cooper Square Publishers, 1980), pp. 62–63.

8. Stanley D. Bachrack, *The Committee of One Million: China Lobby Politics, 1953–1971* (New York: Columbia University Press, 1976).

9. See Delber L. McKee, *Chinese Exclusion Versus the Open Door Policy, 1900–1906* (Detroit: Wayne State University Press, 1977); Reed, *Missionary Mind*; and Andrew Gyory, *Closing the Gate: Race, Politics, and the Chinese Exclusion Act* (Chapel Hill: University of North Carolina Press, 1998).

10. As Akira Iriye argues convincingly in *Across the Pacific: An Inner History of America-East Asian Relations* (New York: Harcourt Brace and World, 1967), Taft's "dollar diplomacy" was aimed less at helping American business interests than in engaging them in China in the hope that economic betterment would encourage the Chinese to welcome Christian missionaries and to evolve toward democracy.

11. See E. R. May, "The China Hands in Perspective: Ethics, Diplomacy, and Statecraft," in Lauren, *The China Hands Legacy*, pp. 97–123.

12. See Leonard A. Kusnitz, *Public Opinion and Foreign Policy: America's China Policy, 1949–1979* (Westport, CT: Greenwood Press, 1984); and Guangqiu Xu, *Congress and the U.S.-China Relationship, 1949–1979* (Akron, OH: University of Akron Press, 2007).

13. The travails of "normalization" are traced in Harry Harding, *A Fragile Relationship: The United States and China Since 1972* (Washington, DC: Brookings Institution, 1992); William C. Kirby, Robert S. Ross, and Gong Li, eds., *Normalization of U.S.-China Relations* (Cambridge, MA: Harvard University Press, 2005); and James Mann, *About Face: A History of America's Curious Relationship with China, from Nixon to Clinton* (New York: Random House, 1998).

14. See Dorothy Borg, *The United States and the Far Eastern Crisis of 1933–1938* (Cambridge, MA: Harvard University Press, 1964).

15. See "China, 1945–1948: Making Hard Choices," in Ernest R. May and Philip D. Zelikow, *Dealing with Dictators: Dilemmas of U.S. Diplomacy and Intelligence Analysis* (Cambridge, MA: MIT Press, 2007), pp.15–48.

16. Executive Session testimony by Secretary of State Marshall before the Senate Foreign Relations Committee and the House Foreign Affairs Committee, U.S. Department of State, *United States Relations with China: With Special Reference to the*

Period, 1944–1949 [usually known as *The China White Paper*] (Washington, DC: Government Printing Office, 1949), pp. 380–384.

17. The best recent account is Margaret Macmillan, *Nixon and Mao: The Week that Changed the World* (New York: Random House, 2007).

18. Mann, *About Face*, p. 22.

19. David M. Lampton, *Same Bed, Different Dreams: Managing U.S.-China Relations, 1989–2000* (Berkeley: University of California Press, 2001), pp. 135–139.

20. The best or most up-to-date accounts of these episodes are—for the turn of the century: Bradford Perkins, *The Great Rapprochement: England and the United States, 1895–1914* (New York: Atheneum, 1968); Iestyn Adams, *Brothers Across the Ocean: British Foreign Policy and the Origins of the Anglo-American "Special Relationship," 1900–1905* (London: Taurus Academic Studies, 2005); Duncan Andrew Campbell, *Unlikely Allies: Britain, America, and the Victorian Origins of the Special Relationship* (London: Hambledon Continuum, 2007); and Paul M. Kennedy, *The Rise of the Anglo-German Antagonism, 1860–1914* (London: Allen and Unwin, 1980). For the 1920s: Thomas H. Buckley, *The United States and the Washington Conference, 1921–1922* (Knoxville: University of Tennessee Press, 1970); Erik Goldstein and John Maurer, eds., *The Washington Conference, 1921–22: Naval Rivalry, East Asian Stability, and the Road to Pearl Harbor* (Newbury Park, UK: Frank Cass, 1994); B. J. C. McKercher, *Anglo-American Relations in the 1920s: The Struggle for Supremacy* (Edmondton: University of Alberta Press, 1990); Stephen A. Schuker, *The End of French Predominance in Europe: The Financial Crisis of 1924 and the Adoption of the Dawes Plan* (Chapel Hill: University of North Carolina Press, 1976); and Zara Steiner, *The Lights that Failed: European International History, 1919–1933* (Oxford: Oxford University Press, 2005).

21. From the incomplete and unpublished Lady Gwendolen Cecil, *Life of Robert, Marquis of Salisbury*, manuscript in the Cecil Papers at Hatfield House (Hatfield, England), vol. 5, chapter 5, p. 11.

22. Mark Sullivan, *The Great Adventure at Washington: The Story of the Conference* (Garden City, NY: Doubleday Page, 1922), p. 27.

23. Richard Madsden, *China and the American Dream: A Moral Inquiry* (Berkeley: University of California Press, 1995); Robert G. Sutter, *U.S. Policy Toward China: An Introduction to the Role of Interest Groups* (Lanham, MD: Rowman and Littlefield, 1998); Thomas Laszlo Dorogi, *Tainted Perceptions: Liberal Democracy and American Popular Images of China* (Lanham, MD: University Press of America, 2001).

24. Karl Polanyi, *The Great Transformation: The Political and Economic Origins of Our Time* (Boston: Beacon Press, 1957), p. 217.

Chapter 2

1. Joseph Nye introduced this concept in *Bound to Lead: The Changing Nature of American Power* (New York: Basic Books, 1990). It builds on what Peter Bachrach

and Morton Baratz called the "second face of power." See "Decisions and Nondecisions: An Analytical Framework," *American Political Science Review* (September 1963), pp. 632–642. The concept is developed more fully in Joseph S. Nye, *Soft Power: The Means to Success in World Politics* (New York: PublicAffairs, 2004).

2. This aspect is developed in Joseph S. Nye, *The Powers to Lead* (Oxford: Oxford University Press, 2008).

3. Hubert Vedrine with Dominique Moisi, *France in an Age of Globalization* (Washington, DC: Brookings Institution Press, 2001), p. 3.

4. See Steven Lukes, *Power: A Radical View,* 2nd ed. (London: Palgrave, 2005).

5. Josef Joffe, "Who's Afraid of Mr. Big?" *The National Interest,* Summer 2001, p. 43.

6. BBC poll, 2005. See also "Global View of U.S. Worsens," *New York Times,* January 23, 2007, pp. 3–5.

7. http://www.edu.cn/Newswin_1547/20060323/t20060323_159709.shtml. Searched on February 8, 2008.

8. http://travel.hlzi.com/html/071229/47016.html. Searched on February 8, 2008. This figure excludes travelers from Taiwan, Hong Kong, and Macau.

9. The official Web site of the Office of the Chinese Language Council International, http://www.hanban.org/cn_hanban/kzxy.php, searched on February 5, 2008.

10. Yanzhong Huang, Bates Gill, and Sheng Ding, "The Sources and Limits of Chinese Soft Power," *Survival: The IISS Quarterly* 48, 2 (Summer 2006): 17–36; and Joseph Nye, "Recovering American Leadership," *Survival: The IISS Quarterly* 50, 1 (February–March 2008): 55–68.

11. Joshua Cooper Ramo, *The Beijing Consensus* (London: Foreign Policy Centre, 2004). Ramo presents a sophisticated analysis of China's path of development in its reform era, but the Beijing Consensus is often referred to later as the combination of a tightly centralized government and a market-oriented economy.

12. By December 2007 China had participated in eighteen UN peacekeeping missions and accumulatively contributed 9,052 troops. As of September 2008, just under 2,000 Chinese troops were stationed in eleven areas for peacekeeping operations; this number will increase when Chinese peacekeepers are deployed in Darfur, Sudan. See *Shijie Zhishi* (World Affairs) 1 (2008): 5.

13. Joshua Kurlantzick, *Charm Offensive: How China's Soft Power Is Transforming the World* (New Haven, CT: Yale University Press, 2007).

14. Two Chinese analysts concede that China's soft power as a whole is roughly one-third of America's. See Yan Xuetong and Xu Jin, "Zhongmei Ruanshili Bijiao" (comparing Chinese and American soft power), *Xiandai Guoji Guanxi* (Contemporary International Relations) 1 (2008): 24–29.

15. The journal *Soft Power* claims to be "China's national innovation platform banner" and has a Web site at www.softpow.com.

16. http://news.xinhuanet.com/english/2007-10/24/content_6938749.htm. Searched on February 7, 2008.

17. Yan Xuetong, "Ruanshili de hexin shi zhengzhi shili" (the core of soft power is political power), in Wang Wen, ed., *Daguo Xinlu* (The Mind-set of Great Powers) (Beijing: Jinghua Publishing House, 2007), pp. 114–118.

18. Kurlantzick, *Charm Offensive.*

19. For example, Hu Jintao in his report to the Seventeenth Communist Party Congress referred over sixty times to "democracy" and stated that China "needs to improve institutions of democracy, diversify its forms and expand its channels, and carry out democratic election, decision-making and administration and oversight in accordance with the law to guarantee the people's rights to be informed, to participate, to be heard and to oversee." See http://news.xinhuanet.com/english/2007-10/24/content _6938749.htm. Searched on February 7, 2008. Wen Jiabao, in a March 2007 press conference, declared that "democracy, legal system, freedom, human rights, equality and fraternity are not something peculiar to capitalism. Rather, they are the common achievements of human civilization made in the long course of history and the common values pursued by entire mankind." See http://news.sina.com.cn/c/2007-03-16/ 125012536614.shtml. Searched on February 8, 2008.

20. A conversation between Wang Jisi and Dr. Banning Garrett, then-director of the Asia Program of the Atlantic Council of the United States, in Beijing, in December 2001.

Chapter 3

1. See the account in Kenneth Pomeranz, *The Great Divergence: China and the Making of the Modern World Economy* (Princeton, NJ: Princeton University Press, 2000).

2. See speeches by Lawrence Summers and Kishore Mahbubani, *The New Asian Hemisphere* (New York: PublicAffairs, 2008), p. 2.

3. Foreign trade amounted to about 40 percent of GDP in both cases.

4. See Ronald W. Jones, *Globalization and the Theory of Input Trade* (Cambridge, MA: MIT Press, 2000); and Stephen Brooks, *Producing Security* (Princeton, NJ: Princeton University Press, 2002), chap. 6.

5. The Li & Fung trading house illustrates this network. "Li and Fung work with 10,000 suppliers in 48 countries to source materials and makers for clients. So a fabric from India that gets dyed in China will go to Thailand to be embroidered (with sequins made in Korea and rhinestones from Brazil), and then return to China to be cut into garments. The firm adheres to a '30/30' principle: it guarantees that it will purchase at least 30 percent of the business from each supplier, but will not exceed 70 percent. This ensures that no one in the network is captive, and also that knowledge and learning permeates throughout the system. It is also a system for developing

trust. And it requires that suppliers have to go outside the network in order to survive—and thus be in a position to bring in new ideas from the outside. The results are impressive. In terms of asset productivity, Li & Fung earns a 30 percent–50 percent return on equity. Regarding personnel productivity, it earned $1 million per employee per year. And it scales elegantly: the firm took in $11 billion in 2004." See Kenn Cukier, *Rueschlikon Conference Report,* September 2007.

6. See Morris Goldstein and Nicholas R. Lardy, *Debating China's Exchange Rate Policy,* Peterson Institute (2008); and Andrew Crockett, Fan Gang, C. Fred Bergsten, and Lawrence H. Summers, "Commentary," p. 350. In the commentary, Summers writes: "The current account deficit is not the primary source of economic insecurity or slow growth in wages of American workers."

7. Nicholas Lardy writes: "A more flexible exchange rate policy would allow the [Chinese] central bank greater flexibility in setting domestic interest rates and thus increase the potential to mitigate macroeconomic cycles by raising lending rates to moderate investment booms. That [would] lead, on average, to a lower rate of investment. A reduction in the rate of investment is a critical component of the policies to transition to a more consumption-driven growth path. In the absence of a reduction in investment, increased consumption demand would lead to inflation." See Nicholas Lardy, "China: Toward a Consumption-Driven Growth Path," Institute for International Economics, Policy Briefing 06-6, October 2006, p. 9.

8. Lawrence Summers, "History Holds Lessons for China and Its Partners," *Financial Times*, February 25, 2007.

9. See Morris Goldstein and Nicholas R. Lardy, *Debating China's Exchange Rate Policy,* Peterson Institute (2008); and Andrew Crockett, Fan Gang, C. Fred Bergsten, and Lawrence H. Summers, "Commentary," p. 352. In the commentary, Summers writes: "It would be in China's interest to pursue [a] more aggressive exchange rate adjustment than it has to date."

10. "With Bold Steps, Fed Chief Quiets Some Critisism," *New York Times,* May 28, 2008. Helmut Schmidt echoed the same sentiment: "Financial instruments will have to be regulated as if they were drugs. For immediate relief, the Federal Reserve is creating liquidity of a magnitude that we have never seen before in world history." See "A Conversation with Helmut Schmidt," *The American Interest*, July-August 2008, p. 39.

11. See the calculations in R. Rosecrance, A. Alexandroff, W. Koehler, J. Kroll, J. Stocker, and S. Laqueur, "Whither Interdependence?" *International Organization,* Summer 1977.

Chapter 4

1. Salman Ahmed, Paul Keating, and Ugo Slinas, "Shaping the Future of UN Peace Operations: Is There a Doctrine in the House?" *Cambridge Review of International Affairs* 20, 1 (March 2007).

2. Li Zehou, *The History of Chinese Thoughts* (HeFei: Anhui Art Publishing House, 1999), p. 832.

3. Article 142, General Code of the Civil Law of the People's Republic of China, January 1, 1987.

4. Ashton B. Carter and William Perry, *China's Rise in American Military Strategy, China's March on the 21st Century: A Report of the Aspen Strategy Group* (Aspen, CO: Aspen Institute, 2007).

5. See Pan Guang, *Achievements Made by the Shanghai Cooperation Organization in the Construction of Regional Security: A thesis for China-Australia Dialogue* (Beijing: China Foundation for International and Strategic Studies, 2007).

6. Ron Huisken, "The Road to War on Iraq," Canberra Papers on Strategy and Defense, No. 148 (Canberra: Strategic Defense Studies Centre, Australian National University, 2003), p. 55.

7. In 1946 George F. Kennan raised the viewpoint that domestic factors determined that the Soviet Union needed a permanent external enemy and that the experience and status of Soviet leaders decided that they must describe the external world as evil, dangerous, and hostile. American professor Diane Kunz has pointed out that Kennan "is right and . . . that his description is correct not only for the Soviet Union but also for the United States." See Diane Kunz, *Butter and Guns: America's Cold War Economic Diplomacy* (New York: Free Press, 1997), p. 328. Other publications provide similar opinions. At a conference held in Harvard University in 1997, scholars raised the idea that elite Chinese, Russians, Indians, Arabs, and Africans believed that the United States was the largest threat to the world and that these people account for two-thirds of the world's population. See Robert S. McNamara and James G. Blight, *Wilson's Ghost: Reducing the Risk of Conflict, Killing, and Catastrophe in the 21st Century* (New York: PublicAffairs, 2001), p. 52.

8. Walter A. McDougall, *The Heavens and the Earth: A Political History of the Space Age* (Baltimore, MD: Johns Hopkins University Press, 1985), p. 330.

9. Gordon R. Mitchell, *Strategic Deception: Rhetoric, Science, and Politics in Missile Defense Advocacy* (London: Macmillan, 1997), p. 31.

10. Emmanual Todd, *After the Empire: The Breakdown of the American Order* (Chinese translation) (World Knowledge Press, 2003), p. 7.

11. Jonathan Pollack, *Strategic Surprise: Sino-American Relations in the 21st Century* (Annapolis, MD: U.S. Navy War College Press, 2003).

12. Colin S. Gray, *Strategy for Chaos, Revolutions in Military Affairs and the Evidence of History* (London: Frank Cass, 2002), p. 271.

13. James William Fulbright, *The Price of Empire* (New York: Pantheon, 1989), p. 232.

14. Zhang Tuosheng and Michael Swaine, eds., *Confrontation, Gaming, Cooperation: China-US Security Crisis Management Case Studies* (World Knowledge Press, 2007), preface.

15. Ashton B. Carter and William Perry, "China on the March," *National Interest,* March/April 2007.

16. Richard N. Haass, *The Opportunity: America's Moment to Alter History's Course* (PublicAffairs: New York, 2005), pp. 17, 32, 202.

17. Thomas P.M. Barnett, *The Pentagon's New Map—War and Peace in the Twenty-first Century* (New York: Penguin, 2004), p. 181.

18. See page 56.

19. Ashton B. Carter and William J. Perry, "China's Rise in American Military Strategy," in *China's March on the 21st Century: A Report of the Aspen Strategy Group,* Kurt M. Campbell and Willow Darsie, eds. (Washington, DC: The Aspen Institute, 2007), pp. 107–117; and Ashton B. Carter and William J. Perry, "China on the March," *The National Interest,* March/April 2007, pp. 16–22. See http://www.belfercenter.org/files/carterperry_nationalinterest_marapr2007.pdf.

20. See page 59.

21. Ashton B. Carter and William Perry, *China's Rise in American Military Strategy, China's March on the 21st Century: A Report of the Aspen Strategy Group* (Aspen, CO: Aspen Institute, 2007).

22. Ibid.

Chapter 5

1. Kenneth Waltz, *Theory of International Politics* (New York: McGraw-Hill, 1979); A.F.K. Organski and Jacek Kugler, *The War Ledger* (Chicago: University of Chicago Press, 1980); Robert Gilpin, *War and Change in World Politics* (Cambridge: Cambridge University Press, 1981); Robert Jervis, "Security Regimes," *International Organization* (Spring 1982), Vol. 36, No. 2, pp. 357–378.

2. John J. Mearsheimer, *The Tragedy of Great Power Politics* (New York: W. W. Norton, 2001), p. 400.

3. See John A. Vazquez, "The Realist Paradigm and Degenerative Versus Progressive Research Programs: An Appraisal of Neotraditional Research on Waltz's Balancing Proposition," *American Political Science Review* #91, 4 (December 1997); Jeffrey Legro and Andrew Moravcsik, "Is Anybody Still a Realist?" *International Security* 24, 2 (1999): 5–55; Thomas Walker and Jeffrey Morton, "Re-Assessing the 'Power of Power Politics' Thesis: Is Realism Still Dominant?" *International Studies Review* 7 (2005): 341–356; and, on China, David L. Shambaugh, "China Engages Asia: Reshaping the Regional Order," *International Security,* #29, 3 (Winter 2004–2005), pp. 64–99. In addition, more sophisticated realist theories have come to ·replace more aggressive, zero-sum, capabilities-based variants.

4. Nicholas Khoo and Michael L. R. Smith, "Correspondence: China Engages Asia? Caveat Lector," [re. Shambaugh 29:3], 30:1 (Summer 2005), pp. 196–2005. Skeptics Khoo and Smith, leaning on Organski and Kugler, and Gilpin, can argue

that there is no anomaly here, and that China today is behaving strategically so as to avoid counterbalancing by regional states.

5. Robert Jervis, "Cooperation Under the Security Dilemma," *World Politics* 30, 2 (1978): 167–214; Wang Jisi, "China's Search for Stability with America," *Foreign Affairs* 39, 5 (2005): 39–48.

6. Richard Rosecrance, *The Rise of the Trading State* (New York: Basic Books, 1986); and *The Rise of the Virtual State: Wealth and Power in the Coming Century* (New York: Basic Books, 1999).

7. Etel Solingen, *Regional Orders at Century's Dawn: Global and Domestic Influences on Grand Strategy* (Princeton, NJ: Princeton University Press, 1998); and "Pax Asiatica versus Bella Levantina: The Foundations of War and Peace in East Asia and the Middle East," *American Political Science Review* 101, 4 (2007). Here I use "autarchic" and "inward-looking" interchangeably—even though autarchy is a more extreme version of the latter—to convey a counterinternationalizing strategy.

8. See Chapter 8.

9. Susan Shirk, *China: Fragile Superpower* (New York: Oxford University Press, 2007).

10. Wang Zhengyi, "Conceptualizing Economic Security and Governance: China Confronts Globalization," *Pacific Review* 17, 4 (2004): 523–546; Stephen Frost, "Southeast Asia: Mainland Chinese Direct Investment," *Asian Labor News*, November 26, 2003, http://www.asianlabour.org/cgi-bin/mt/mt-tb.cgi/116.

11. Wang Zhengyi, "Conceptualizing Economic Security and Governance."

12. Although this is not necessarily the case for other issues, pressures on China regarding human rights and democracy are backed by various intergovernmental and nongovernmental organizations.

13. The arguments in this section are discussed more extensively in Etel Solingen, *Regional Orders at Century's Dawn: Global and Domestic Influences on Grand Strategy* (Princeton, NJ: Princeton University Press, 1998); "Southeast Asia in a New Era: Domestic Coalitions from Crisis to Recovery," *Asian Survey* 44, 2 (2004): 189–212; "ASEAN Cooperation: The Legacy of the Economic Crisis," *International Relations of the Asia-Pacific* 5, 1 (2005): 1–29; *Nuclear Logics: Contrasting Paths in East Asia and the Middle East* (Princeton, NJ: Princeton University Press, 2007); and "Pax Asiatica Versus Bella Levantina: The Foundations of War and Peace in East Asia and the Middle East," *American Political Science Review* 101, 4 (2007).

14. See Joseph S. Nye, Jr., "U.S.-Soviet Cooperation in a Nonproliferation Regime," in *U.S.-Soviet Security Cooperation: Achievements, Failures, Lessons*, eds. Alexander L. George, Philip J. Farley, and Alexander Dallin (New York: Oxford University Press, 1988), pp. 336–352.

15. For an early full exposition and critique of the "authoritarian advantage" argument, see Carlos Díaz-Alejandro, "Exchange Rate and Terms of Trade in the

Argentine Republic: 1913–76," in *Trade, Stability, Technology, and Equity in Latin America*, eds. M. Syrquin and S. Teitel (New York: Academic Press, 1983).

16. Adam Przeworski, Michael Alvarez, Jose Antonio Cheibub, and Fernando Limongi, "What Makes Democracies Endure?" *Journal of Democracy* 7, 1 (1996): 39–55.

17. The study refers to "anocracies" as regimes that exhibit an incoherent mix of democratic and nondemocratic features. By 2006 there were seventy-seven democratic countries, forty-nine anocracies, and only thirty-four autocracies worldwide. Center for International Development and Conflict Management, University of Maryland College Park, Peace and Conflict 2008, http://www.cidcm.umd.edu/pc/chapter04/graphs/figure_4_1.asp.

18. Karen Remmer, *Military Rule in Latin America* (Boston: Unwin Hyman, 1989); Jose Maria Maravall, "The Myth of the Authoritarian Advantage," in *Nationalism, Ethnic Conflict, and Democracy*, eds. Larry Diamond and Marc F. Plattner (Baltimore: Johns Hopkins University Press, 1994). Robert Barro suggests that democratization initially increases economic growth but may retard growth once a moderate level of democracy has been attained. However, these findings do not speak to the issue of democracy rendering economic reform more legitimate, and hence more stable and less reversible. See Robert J. Barro, *Determinants of Economic Growth: A Cross-Country Empirical Study* (Cambridge, MA: MIT Press, 1997).

19. Martin Lipset, "Some Social Requisites of Democracy: Economic Development and Political Legitimacy," *American Political Science Review* 53 (1959).

20. Various studies found that economic development does not invariably lead to democracy but rather that the chances for democracy to survive are greater when the country is wealthier. See Adam Przeworski, José Antonio Cheibub, and Fernando Limongi, *Journal of Democracy* 7, 1 (January 1996), pp. 39–55; Przeworski, Alvarez, Cheibub, and Limongi, "What Makes Democracies Endure?"; and Adam Przeworski, Michael Alvarez, Jose Antonio Cheibub, and Fernando Limongi, *Democracy and Development: Political Institutions and Well-Being in the World, 1950–1990* (Cambridge: Cambridge University Press, 2000). Democracy is assumed to be least reversible where annual per-capita income rises above $6,000. At lower income levels, economic growth with low/moderate inflation heightens democracy's probability of survival. Very high levels of economic development arguably make democracy immune to antidemocratic coups.

21. Mary E. Gallagher, "'Reform and Openness': Why China's Economic Reforms Have Delayed Democracy," *World Politics* 54, 3 (2002): 338–372.

22. The Chinese government reported some 87,000 disturbances of public order in 2005. Thomas J. Christensen, Deputy Assistant Secretary for East Asian and Pacific Affairs, Statement Before the House Committee on Foreign Affairs, Subcommittee on Asia, the Pacific, and the Global Environment, Washington, DC, March 27, 2007, http://china.usc.edu/ShowArticle.aspx?articleID=435. See also

Shirk, *China: Fragile Superpower*, citing the Social Blue Book produced annually by the Chinese Academy of Social Sciences.

23. Edward Mansfield and Jack Snyder, "The Sequencing Fallacy," *Journal of Democracy* (March 18, 2007).

24. Sheri Berman is skeptical that the "right" sequence can reduce violence during democratic transitions. Thomas Carothers advises gradualism, not sequencing. Mansfield and Snyder (2007) suggest that the most likely implementers of well-sequenced reforms toward democracy are not dictators but moderate groups that seek to curtail the power of the old authoritarian elite but fear rapid descent into chaos. Carothers disagrees, arguing that democracy is the result of vigorous democrats in civil society, as in Chile, South Korea, and Taiwan, among others. Sheri Berman, "How Democracies Emerge: Lessons from Europe," *Journal of Democracy* 18 (January); Thomas Carothers, "How Democracies Emerge: The Sequencing Fallacy," *Journal of Democracy* 18 (January 2007).

25. David Zweig, *Democratic Values, Political Structures, and Alternative Politics in Greater China* (Washington, DC: U.S. Institute of Peace, 2002); Shirk, China: Fragile Superpower.

26. These advantages are not necessarily shared by mixed (democratic/nondemocratic) dyads and partners. Whether or not there is an actual record of more checkered implementation of international agreements by nondemocracies, as some findings suggest, liberal democracies are strikingly mistrustful of nonliberal states (Michael Doyle, "Kant, Liberal Legacies, and Foreign Affairs," Philosophy and Public Affairs [1983], and uncertain about the latter's domestic and international commitments.

27. For an overview of these findings, see Etel Solingen, "The Global Context of Comparative Politics," in *Comparative Politics: Rationality, Culture, and Structure*, eds. Mark I. Lichbach and Alan S. Zuckerman (Cambridge: Cambridge University Press, 2008).

28. U.S. Deputy Assistant Secretary for East Asian and Pacific Affairs Thomas J. Christensen argued that "without a more open and democratic domestic system, based on the rule of law, and, therefore, a predictable political environment, it will be more difficult for China to achieve and maintain the internal stability and the trust among its neighbors necessary to achieve a smooth transition to a leading role in the international community." Christensen, Statement Before the House Committee on Foreign Affairs.

29. *Peace and Conflict* 2008.

30. Christensen, Statement Before the House Committee on Foreign Affairs, 2007.

31. Etel Solingen, "From Threat to Opportunity? ASEAN, China, and Triangulation," in *China, the United States, and Southeast Asia: Contending Perspectives on Economics, Politics, and Security*, eds. Sheldon Simon and Evelyn Goh (London:

Routledge, 2007). On China's growing commitment to multilateralism, see Alastair I. Johnston, "The Myth of the ASEAN Way? Explaining the Evolution of the ASEAN Regional Forum," in *Imperfect Unions: Security Institutions over Time and Space*, eds. Helga Haftendorn, Robert O. Keohane, and Celeste A. Wallander (New York: Oxford University Press, 1999), pp. 287–324; and Alastair I. Johnston, in *Social States: China in International Institutions: 1980–2000* (Princeton: Princeton University Press, 2007).

Chapter 6

1. Kevin Cheng, "Economic Implications of China's Demographics in the Twenty-first Century," *IMF Working Paper*, WP/03/29, 2003.

2. P. S. Hewitt, "The Geopolitics of Global Aging," *Harvard Generations Policy Journal*, 1 (Winter 2004): 103–113.

3. *China Daily*, December 18, 2007.

4. Zeng Yi, et al., "Sociodemographic and Health Profiles of Oldest Old in China," *Population and Development Review* 28, 2 (2002): 251.

5. Barbara Boyle Torrey, "Sharing Increasing Costs on Declining Income: The Visible Dilemma of the Invisible Aged," in *The Oldest Old*, eds. Richard Suzman, David P. Willis, Kenneth G. Manton. New York: Oxford University Press, 2002), pp. 381–393.

6. Athar Hussain, "Demographic Transition in China and Its Implications," *World Development* 30, 1 (2002): 1828.

7. United Nations Development Programme 2006, at http://hdr.undp.org/hdr2006/statistics/indicators/.

8. Zhang Yi, "Jingzhong: woguo nuer chusheng xingbie zai chixu shangsheng [Warning: An Imbalance of the Sex Ratio in China], in *2003 nian: Zhongguo shehui xingshe fenxi yuce* [2003: Circumstances and Analysis of China's Society], ed. Ru Xin, et al. (Beijing: shehui kexue wenxian chubanshe, 2003), pp. 66, 73.

9. Zhu Chuzhu, Li Shuzhou, Qiu Changrong, Hu Ping, and Jin Anrong, *The Dual Effects of the Family Planning Program on Chinese Women* (Xi'an: Xi'an Jiaotong University Press, 1997), p. 88.

10. *SCMP*, August 25, 2003, Internet edition.

11. Barry Naughton, *The Chinese Economy: Transitions and Growth* (Cambridge, MA: MIT Press, 2007), 129–130.

12. This figure does not include the 2.5 million military personnel who are classified neither as urban nor as rural. It compares to the urbanization rate in the United Kingdom during the 1880s, that in the United States in 1911, and in Japan in 1950.

13. For an excellent review, see Kam Wing Chan, "Misconceptions and Complexities in the Study of China's Cities: Definitions, Statistics, and Implications," *Eurasian Geography and Economics* 48, 4 (2007): 383–412.

14. Y. Zhou and L. J. C. Ma, "China's Urbanization Levels: Reconstructing a Baseline from the Fifth Population Census," *China Quarterly* 173 (2003): 177.

15. Wang Mengkui, quoted in *Financial Times*, November 27, 2003.

16. In the 1840s British total trade was over 40 percent of GDP.

17. Tony Saich, "Globalization, Governance, and the Authoritarian Westphalian State: The Case of China," in *Globalization and Governance*, ed. Joseph Nye and Robert Keohane (Washington, DC: Brookings Institute, 2000).

18. *China Daily*, October 27, 2004.

19. Dianna Farrell, Ulrich A. Gersh, and Elizabeth Stephenson, "The Value of China's Emerging Middle Class," *The McKinsey Quarterly*, June 28, 2008, accessed at http://www.mckinseyquarterly.com.

20. Michael Mann, *The Sources of Social Power, 1760–1914*, vol. 2 (Cambridge: Cambridge University Press, 1993), especially chap.16.

Chapter 7

1. "Communiqué of the Third Plenum of the 11th CCP Central Committee" (passed on December 22, 1978), in *Selected Documents Since the Third Plenum of the 11th CCP Central Committee*, vol. 1 (Beijing: People's Publishing House, 1982), p.10.

2. Deng Xiaoping, *Selected Works of Deng Xiaoping*, vol. 2 (Beijing: Foreign Languages Press, 1984), p.168.

3. "Communiqué of the Second Plenum of the 17th CCP Central Committee," *People's Daily*, February 28, 2008.

4. "Resolution on Promoting the Governance Capacity of the Party by the Central Committee of Communist Party of China" (passed by the Fourth Plenary Session of the Sixteenth Party Congress of the CCP on September 19, 2004), *People's Daily*, September 26, 2004.

5. Hu Jintao, "Hold High the Great Flag of Socialism with Chinese Characteristics, Strive for the New Victory in Developing a Xiao-Kang Society." Report to the Seventeenth Party Congress of the CCP on October 15, 2007 (Beijing: People's Publishing House, 2007).

Chapter 8

1. Interview with Charlie Rose on PBS by Deputy Secretary of State Richard Armitage. See press release of the State Department, December 10, 2004.

2. This section represents the views of Xu Shiquan.

3. For details, read Deng Xiaoping's talk with Winston Yang on June 26, 1983, *Selected Works of Deng Xiaoping*, vol. 3 (Beijing: Foreign Languages Press, 1994), p. 40.

4. For details, see *The People's Daily*, January 31, 1995.

5. For details, see *The People's Daily*, March 5, 2005.

6. This section represents the views of Ezra Vogel. For a comprehensive account of changing U.S. policy toward Taiwan, see Alan D. Romberg, *Rein in at the Brink of the Precipice: American Policy Toward Taiwan and U.S.-PRC Relations* (Washington, DC: Henry L. Stimson Center, 2003).

7. U.S.-China Communiqué, November 14, 1973.

8. There is only one China in the world. Taiwan is part of China. China's sovereignty and territorial integrity brook no division. See the speech made by former Vice Premier Qian Qichen on January 26, 1998.

9. The law was adopted at the Third Session of the Tenth National People's Congress of the People's Republic of China on March 14, 2005.

10. Statement by a responsible person from the ARATS on the publication by the Taiwan authorities of a document on the meaning of "one China" in the cross-straits talks, Xinhua News Agency, Beijing, August 27, 1992.

11. James Kelly's statement at the House International Committee's hearing on Taiwan.

12. See Note 9.

13. Direct trade, direct postal services and telecommunications, and direct shipping and aviation.

14. See Note 4.

15. See Note 9.

16. Ibid.

Chapter 9

1. U.S. Bureau of Economic Analysis, National Economic Accounts, Washington, DC, 2008.

2. This number is based on a sectoral approach calculation, excluding emissions from Hong Kong SAR and Taiwan province.

3. International Energy Agency, *CO_2 Emissions from Fossil Fuel Combustion, 1971–2005* (Paris: OECD, 2007).

4. Li Zhizhong, "Energy Demand and Supply Outlook in China for 2030 and a Northeast Asian Energy Community: The Automobile Strategy and Nuclear Power Strategy for China," Institute of Energy Economics (IEEJ), Japan, 2005.

5. Hu Xiulian, "Development of China Carbon Emission Scenarios Towards 2050," Presentation at UN Framework Convention on Climate Change Conference of Parties 11 Side Event, "Global Challenges Towards Low-Carbon Economy-Focus on Country-Specific Scenario Analysis," Montreal, Canada, December 3, 2005.

6. International Energy Agency, *CO_2 Emissions from Fossil Fuel Combustion, 1971–2005*.

7. "U.S. Interim Projections by Age, Sex, Race, and Hispanic Origin," U.S. Census Bureau, 2004, http://www.census.gov/ipc/www/usinterimproj.

8. Note that the number here is from statistics by the Chinese sources, which is different from the number given by the UN Development Program and shown in Table 9.2.

9. Normally every two urban people require at least one job position. This would mean that each year 6.5 million new jobs have to be created to accommodate the increase in urban population.

10. There is a particularly significant path dependency arising from the development strategies of buildings and urban infrastructures due to the low turnover of capital.

11. This is the ratio of output value from heavy industries (mainly metals, electricity, paper making, machinery, heavy chemicals, etc.) over that from light industries (mainly food processing, textiles, clothing, stationeries, etc.).

12. Pan Jiahua, Chen Ying, Xie Laihui, and Zheng Yan, "Embedded Energy in International Trade and Its Policy Implications," in *Climate Change in Global Regimes: Key Issues in China* (Beijing: China Environment Press/WWF China, 2007), pp. 25–44.

13. *BP Statistical Review* 2007.

14. Energy Information Administration, *Annual Energy Outlook* (Washington, DC: U.S. Department of Energy, 2007).

15. Zhou Shengxian, speech made at the National Conference on Atmospheric Pollution Control, May 30, 2006. But the national target set in 2001 for 2005 was a reduction of SO_2 emissions by 10 percent relative to the 2000 level.

16. K. S. Gallagher, "DOE Budget Authority for Energy Research, Development, and Demonstration Database," Energy Technology Innovation Policy, John F. Kennedy School of Government, Harvard University, February 2008.

17. World Health Organization, *Environmental Health Country Profile—China* (Geneva: WHO, 2004).

18. R. F. Garbaccio, M. S. Ho, and D. W. Jorgenson, "The Health Benefits of Controlling Carbon Emissions in China," Expert Workshop on Assessing the Ancillary Benefits and Costs of GHG Mitigation Policies. March 27–29, 2000, Washington, DC.

19. China General Customs Office. See *New Beijing News,* January 12, 2008, p. B1.

20. The number may vary due to carbon contents. However, coal equivalent is measured in standard terms, and this coefficient is in general applicable.

21. This bill would establish a cap-and-trade program within the United States requiring a 70 percent reduction in GHG emissions from covered sources, which represent over 80 percent of total U.S. emissions. The bill as amended also includes complementary policies, such as a low carbon fuel standard and provisions aimed

at enhancing energy efficiency. Taken together, the bill's sponsors believe these provisions will reduce overall U.S. GHG emissions roughly 63 percent by 2050.

22. The other two reasons are scientific uncertainty and high economic cost for meeting its Kyoto target.

Chapter 10

1. David Lloyd George, *War Memoirs: 1918* (Boston: Little, Brown, 1937), p. 308.

2. Ezra Vogel, "An Opportunity to Defuse the Taiwan Standoff," *Boston Globe,* April 12, 2008, p. A13.

3. Henry Kissinger, *Diplomacy* (New York: Simon & Shuster, 1994), p. 812.

4. In 1962 the Soviet Union was installing nuclear-tipped missiles in Cuba. Some worried that these weapons might fall under the control of a young hot-headed revolutionary leader named Fidel Castro. After careful consideration, President Kennedy issued an unambiguous warning to Soviet leader Nikita Khrushchev. He asserted, "It shall be the policy of this nation to regard any nuclear missile launched from Cuba against any nation in the Western Hemisphere as an attack by the Soviet Union on the United States requiring a full retaliatory response upon the Soviet Union." Khrushchev understood that meant nuclear war.

Chapter 11

1. The earliest signs of China's changing attitude toward nonproliferation were evident in the 1980s, but the dramatic changes occurred after 1990. See Evan Medeiros, *Reluctant Restraint: The Evolution of China's Nonproliferation Policies and Practices, 1980–2004* (Stanford, CA: Stanford University Press, 2007), pp. 36–44.

2. On the transformation of Chinese arms control policies in this period, see Bates Gill and Evan S. Medeiros, "Foreign and Domestic Influences on China's Arms Control and Nonproliferation Policies," *China Quarterly* (2000): 66–67.

3. For a concise overview, see Stephanie Lieggi, "A Decade of Chinese Arms Control: A Survey of Progress Ahead of Bush's Visit to China," Center for Nonproliferation Studies, Monterey Institute of International Studies, November 18, 2005.

4. For a very useful overview of China's domestic legislation pertaining to WMD-related exports, see Jing-dong Yuan, "China's Proliferation and the Impact of Trade Policy on the Defense Industries in the United States and China," Testimony before the U.S.-China Economic and Security Commission, July 12, 2007, especially pp. 11–12.

5. Yuan, "China's Proliferation," pp. 1, 8.

6. There is a debate among U.S. analysts about the sources and genuineness of China's conversion to the cause of nonproliferation. For an overview of the debate and an argument that China is truly converted to nonproliferation for reasons of

self-interest, see Jeffrey Lewis, *The Minimum Means of Reprisal: China's Search for Security in the Nuclear Age* (Cambridge, MA: MIT Press, 2007), pp. 109–140.

7. Both quotes in this paragraph are from "The White House: The National Security Strategy of the United States of America, September 2002."

8. This formula is employed by Yoichi Funabashi, *The Peninsula Question: A Chronicle of the Second Korean Nuclear Crisis* (Washington, DC: Brookings Institute, 2007), especially pp. 305–307.

9. Ibid., p. 305.

10. In December 2007, for example, as sanctions negotiations were at an intense phase, China signed a $2 billion energy deal with Iran. The United States proclaimed itself "deeply disappointed." See "China Signs $2 Billion Iran Oil Deal," http://www.aljazeera.net, December 11, 2007. From among countless examples, see illustratively Neil King Jr., "China-Iran Trade Surge Vexes U.S.," *Wall Street Journal* (Online Edition), July 27, 2007; and Kaveh Afrasiabi, "China Rocks the Geopolitical Boat with Iran Oil Deal," *Asia Times*, December 2, 2004.

11. Iran was a difficult issue in U.S.-China relations in the 1990s as well. See Gill and Medeiros, "Foreign and Domestic Influences on China's Arms Control and Disarmament Policies," pp. 74–82.

Chapter 12

1. Zheng Bijian, "China's 'Peaceful Rise' to Great-Power Status," *Foreign Affairs* 84, 5 (September/October 2005): 18–24. Zheng had offered this view of China as early as 2003. See "New Path for China's Peaceful Rise and the Future of Asia," speech delivered to Boao Forum for Asia Annual Conference, November 3, 2003.

2. G. John Ikenberry, "The Rise of China and the Future of the West: Can the Liberal System Survive?" *Foreign Affairs* 87, 1 (January/February 2008): 23.

3. Alastair Iain Johnson, "Is China a Status Quo Power?" *International Security* 27, 4 (2003): 5.

4. Party leader Hu Jintao reiterated that "China will unswervingly follow the path of peaceful development. This is a strategic choice the Chinese government and people have made in light of the development trend of the times and their own fundamental interests," in his *Report to the Seventeenth National Congress of the Communist Party of China* on October 15, 2007.

5. Wang Jisi, "China's Search for Stability with America," *Foreign Affairs* 85, 5 (September/October 2005): 43.

6. Peter J. Katzenstein, *A World of Regions: Asia and Europe in the American Imperium* (Ithaca, NY: Cornell University Press, 2005), p. 1.

7. David M. Lampton, "China's Rise in Asia Need not Be at America's Expense," in *Power Shift: China and Asia's New Dynamics*, ed. David Shambaugh (Berkeley: University of California Press, 2005), p. 306.

8. Zhang Yunling and Tang Shiping, "China's Regional Strategy," in Shambaugh, *Power Shift: China and Asia's New Dynamics,* p. 52.

9. Zhang Yunling, with his colleague Tang Shiping, suggested that China in the short term could not expect to have global influence but needed to exert its political influence in the regional context. They believe China would have a global voice only if it could successfully exert regional political influence. And to establish such a recognized regional influence China needed to become a responsible (regional) power. However, the position we identify here is slightly nuanced and built on a two-way model of global and regional governance.

10. Chu Shulong, "China and the U.S.-Japan and U.S.-Korea Alliances in a Changing Northeast Asia," (Stanford, CA: Walter H. Shorenstein Asia-Pacific Research Center/Shorenstein APARC Publications, June 1999), 6.

11. Richard Rosecrance, "A Grand Coalition and International Governance," in *Can the World Be Governed? Possibilities for Effective Multilateralism,* ed. Alan S. Alexandroff (Waterloo, Ont.: Wilfrid Laurier University Press/CIGI, 2008).

12. http://www.hno.harvard.edu/gazette/2003/12.11/10-wenspeech.html.

13. Robert Zoellick, "Statement in Conclusion of the Second U.S.-China Senior Dialogue," December 8, 2005.

14. Yang Wenchang (former vice minister of Ministry of Foreign Affairs), "Three Misreadings of China by the West," *Foreign Affairs Journal* 85 (Autumn 2007): 7.

15. Lawrence Summers, "Sovereign Funds Shake the Logic of Capitalism," *Financial Times,* July 30, 2007.

16. Chu Shulong, "China, Asia, and Issues of Sovereignty and Intervention," *Pugwash Occasional Papers* 2, 1 (January 2001).

17. See Paul Evans, "Constructing Multilateralism in an Anti-Region: From Six-Party Talks to a Regional Security Framework in Northeast Asia?" in *Cross Currents: Regionalism and Nationalism in Northeast Asia,* eds. Gi-Wook Shin and Daniel C. Sneider (Stanford, CA: Walter H. Shorenstein Asia-Pacific Research Center Books, 2007), pp. 99–116.

18. C. Fred Bergsten, presentation at the "Dialogue on Globalization and Shared Prosperity," Merida, Mexico, May 26, 2002.

19. S. Eaton, and R. Stubbs, "Is ASEAN Powerful? Neo-realist Versus Constructivist Approaches to Power in Southeast Asia," *Pacific Review* 19, 2 (June 2006): 135–155.

20. For an insight into the Chinese decision to offer a free trade arrangement, see Gregory T. Chin and Richard Stubbs, "The Political Economy of the ASEAN-China Free Trade Agreement and East Asian Regionalism." Paper prepared for the International Studies Association Conference, San Francisco, March 26–29, 2008.

21. Currently there are five ASEAN+1 FTAs (ASEAN-China, ROK, Japan, Australia-New Zealand [CER], and India) that have either been concluded or are under negotiation.

22. Kawai Masahiko, "Evolving Economic Architecture in East Asia," *ADB Institute Discussion Paper* No. 84 (2007).

23. The group was composed of twenty-six experts from APT countries. The report was presented in 2001 at an ASEAN+3 leaders' meeting in Brunei.

24. Robert Sutter, "China's Regional Strategy and Why It May Be not Good for America," in Shambaugh, *Power Shift: China and Asia's New Dynamics*, p. 292.

25. David Shambaugh, "Return of the Middle Kingdom? China and Asia in the Early Twenty-First Century," in Shambaugh, *Power Shift: China and Asia's New Dynamics,* pp. 41–42.

26. Yeo Yong Boon George, "Will China Be Able to Emerge Peacefully?" report presented at the Forum on Future Development of China, 2007, Hong Kong Peihua Education Foundation.

27. "Conference Discussing the New Security Concept Held in Beijing," *Renmin Ribao,* December 26, 1997, p. 4. For a review of the New Security Concept, see Chu, "China and the U.S.-Japan and U.S.-Korea Alliances in a Changing Northeast Asia."

28. Chu, "China and the U.S.-Japan and U.S.-Korea Alliances in a Changing Northeast Asia," p. 10.

29. *China's National Defense in 2000* (Beijing: Information Office of the People's Republic of China, 2000), p. 48.

30. Zhang and Tang, "China's Regional Strategy," p. 58.

31. Chu, "China and the U.S.-Japan and U.S.-Korea Alliances in a Changing Northeast Asia," p. 10.

32. Robert Zoellick, remarks at ASEAN Regional Forum, July 29, 2005, Vientiane, Laos.

33. Chairman's statement, Fourteenth ASEAN Regional Forum, August 2007, Manila, Philippines.

34. What drives SCO forward? http://www.scosummit2006.org.

35. Commentary, "A New Model for Peace," *China Daily*, July 4, 1998, p. 4.

ABOUT THE CONTRIBUTORS

Alan S. Alexandroff is the research director of the Program on Conflict Management and Negotiation (PCMN) at the Munk Centre for International Studies, University of Toronto. He has published a number of other articles on China as well as on the WTO. He is currently examining corporate governance practices in China and globally. In 2006 he was appointed a Senior Fellow at the Centre for International Governance and Innovation (CIGI). He currently is involved and leads the Global Institutional Reform Workshop and is the community facilitator for the Large Developing Economies Project.

Graham Allison is director of the Belfer Center for Science and International Affairs and Douglas Dillon Professor of Government at Harvard's John F. Kennedy School of Government. He has served as special advisor to the Secretary of Defense under President Reagan and as Assistant Secretary of Defense for Policy and Plans under President Clinton, where he coordinated Defense Department strategy and policy toward Russia, Ukraine, and the other states of the former Soviet Union. His first book, *Essence of Decision: Explaining the Cuban Missile Crisis* (1971, updated and revised second edition, 1999), ranks among the bestsellers in twentieth-century political science. His latest book, *Nuclear Terrorism: The Ultimate Preventable Catastrophe,* published in 2004, is now in its third printing and was selected by the *New York Times* as one of the "100 most notable books of 2004."

Ashton B. Carter is Ford Foundation Professor of Science and International Affairs; chair of the International Relations, Security, and Science faculty; and codirector, with former Secretary of Defense William J. Perry, of the Preventive Defense Project. From 1993 to 1996 he served as Assistant Secretary of Defense for International Security Policy, where he was responsible for national security policy on arms control in the states of the former Soviet Union, for countering weapons of mass destruction worldwide, and for overseeing the U.S. nuclear arsenal and missile defense programs.

Chen Zhiya entered the Beijing University of Foreign Studies in 1973 and graduated in 1978. He served in the Chinese Embassy in Washington, D.C., from 1979 to 1983. After this he was an associate research fellow, and then research fellow, at the Beijing Institute of International Strategic Studies. In 1986 he began a master's degree program at the Kennedy School of Government, specializing in public administration. He established the China Foundation for International and Strategic Studies (CFISS) in 1989 and is now its secretary general.

Victor Fung is group chair of the Li & Fung group of companies, and chair of the Greater Pearl River Delta Business Council and the Hong Kong University Council. He is also the chairman of the International Chamber of Commerce and chair of the Hong Kong-Japan Business Co-operation Committee. On the mainland of China, he is a member of the Chinese People's Political Consultative Conference, the International Business Leaders Advisory Council for the Mayor of Beijing, and an economic advisor to the People's Government of Nanjing. He also is a vice president of the China General Chamber of Commerce, a member of the advisory board of the School of Economics and Management of Tsinghua University, an honorary professor of Renmin University, and an honorary trustee of Peking University.

Kelly Sims Gallagher is director of the Energy Technology Innovation Project (ETIP) of the Belfer Center for Science and International Affairs at Harvard University's Kennedy School of Government and an adjunct lecturer in public policy. She has a law degree and a PhD in international affairs from the Fletcher School of Law and Diplomacy at Tufts University. Her book, *China Shifts Gears: Automakers, Oil, Pollution, and Development*, was published by MIT Press in 2006.

Gu Guoliang is senior research fellow and the deputy director of the Institute of the Chinese Academy of Social Sciences. He received a master's degree in international public policy from the School of Advanced International Studies of Johns Hopkins University in Washington, D.C. From 1990 to 1995 he worked as counselor of the Chinese delegation to the UN Conference on Disarmament in Geneva. He joined the Institute of American Studies of the Chinese Academy of Social Sciences in 1997 as the deputy director. He established the Center for Arms Control and Nonproliferation Studies in 1998 and has acted as the director of the Center since. He is also a council member of the Chinese Association of Arms Control and Disarmament.

Jia Qingguo is professor and associate dean of the School of International Studies of Peking University. He received his PhD from Cornell University in

1988. He was a research fellow at the Brookings Institution and has taught at the University of Vermont, Cornell University, University of California at San Diego, University of Sydney in Australia, and Peking University. He has published extensively on U.S.-China relations, relations between the Chinese mainland and Taiwan, and Chinese foreign policy, as well as Chinese politics. He is a member of the editorial board of *Journal of Contemporary China* (USA), *Political Science* (New Zealand), *International Relations of the Asia-Pacific* (Japan), and *China Review* (Hong Kong). He is vice president of the China Association for Asia-Pacific Studies, a board member of the China Association of American Studies, and a board member of the National Taiwan Studies Association.

Lawrence Lau is vice chancellor (president) of the Chinese University of Hong Kong. He joined the faculty of the Department of Economics at Stanford University in 1966, becoming professor of economics in 1976 and the first Kwoh-Ting Li Professor in Economic Development at Stanford University in 1992. From 1992 to 1996 he served as a codirector of the Asia-Pacific Research Center at Stanford University, and from 1997 to 1999 he was director of the Stanford Institute for Economic Policy Research. He became Kwoh-Ting Li Professor in Economic Development, Emeritus, at Stanford University in 2006. Professor Lau is concurrently Ralph and Claire Landau Professor of Economics at the Chinese University of Hong Kong.

Ernest R. May is Charles Warren Professor of American History in the Faculty of Arts and Sciences at Harvard. He has been a consultant at various times to the Office of the Secretary of Defense, the National Security Council, and other agencies. He is currently a member of the DNI's Intelligence Science Board and of the Board of Visitors of the National Defense Intelligence College. He has been dean of Harvard College, associate dean of the Faculty of Arts and Sciences, director of the Institute of Politics, and chair of the Department of History. His publications include *Thinking in Time: The Uses of History for Decision-Makers* (with Richard Neustadt); *The Kennedy Tapes: Inside the White House During the Cuban Missile Crisis* (with Philip D. Zelikow); *Strange Victory: Hitler's Conquest of France;* and *Dealing with Dictators: Dilemmas of U.S. Diplomacy and Intelligence Analysis, 1948–1990* (with Philip D. Zelikow). At the Kennedy School, he is a member of the board of directors of the Belfer Center for Science and International Affairs. From 2003 to 2004 he was senior advisor to the 9/11 Commission.

Steven E. Miller has spent twenty-five years at Harvard University's Kennedy School of Government. He currently serves as director of the International Security Program, editor in chief of the journal *International Security,* and coeditor of the International Security Program's book series, Belfer Center Studies in International Security (published by the MIT Press). Previously he was a senior research fellow at the Stockholm International Peace Research Institute and taught defense and arms control studies in the Department of Political Science at the Massachusetts Institute of Technology. He is a fellow of the American Academy of Arts and Sciences, where he has long been a member of the Committee on International Security Studies. He is among the leaders of the Pugwash Conferences on Science and World Affairs, an international scholarly association based in Rome. Miller has written extensively on nuclear weapons issues, U.S. security policy, and U.S. foreign policy. He has coauthored several books: *Soviet Nuclear Fission: Control of the Nuclear Arsenal in a Disintegrating Soviet Union* (1991); *Avoiding Nuclear Anarchy: Containing the Threat of Loose Russian Fissile Material and Nuclear Weapons* (1996); and *War with Iraq: Costs, Consequences, Alternatives* (2002).

Joseph S. Nye, University Distinguished Service Professor, is also the Sultan of Oman Professor of International Relations and former dean of the Kennedy School of Government at Harvard. He received his bachelor's degree summa cum laude from Princeton University, did postgraduate work at Oxford University on a Rhodes scholarship, and earned a PhD in political science from Harvard. He has served as Assistant Secretary of Defense for International Security Affairs, chair of the National Intelligence Council, and Deputy Under Secretary of State for Security Assistance, Science, and Technology. He is author of *Soft Power: The Means to Success in World Politics* (2004); *Understanding International Conflict* (5th ed.); and *The Power Game: A Washington Novel.*

Pan Jiahua is deputy director of the Research Centre for Urban and Environmental Studies, Chinese Academy of Social Sciences. He received his PhD at Cambridge University in 1992. Research interests include economic and social dimensions of sustainable development, energy and development, climate policy, and economics of the environment and natural resources. He is the author of 150 papers and articles in academic journals, magazines, and newspapers.

David K. Richards, a private investor since 1991, is based in Santa Monica, California. In prior years he was a professional investment manager of mutual funds, pension funds, and endowments. From 1985 to 1991 he was managing director and vice chair of PRIMECAP Management in Pasadena, California. From 1973 to 1985 he managed part of several mutual funds of American Funds, the Capital Group, Los Angeles, where he was senior vice president of Capital Research and Management and president of Fundamental Investors Fund. He is a graduate of Harvard College, Wadham College, Oxford, and the

Harvard Business School. He serves on Harvard's Committee on University Resources, the Dean's Council of the Faculty of Arts and Sciences, the Dean's Council of the Kennedy School of Government, and the Belfer Center. He is a Foundation Fellow of Wadham College and member of the Chancellor's Court of Benefactors of Oxford University. At the RAND Corporation, he serves on the board of advisors of RAND Health and the Center for Middle East Public Policy. He initiated and funded the RAND study *Building a Successful Palestinian State,* published in 2005.

Richard Rosecrance, adjunct professor in public policy at Harvard's Kennedy School, is also a research professor of political science at the University of California and senior fellow in the Belfer Center for Science and International Affairs. He is the former director of the Burkle Center for International Relations at UCLA. He has written widely on international topics, including *The Rise of the Trading State* (translated into Chinese, Japanese, Arabic, German, and Indonesian); *The Rise of the Virtual State* (translated into Japanese, Chinese, German, and Spanish); *America's Economic Resurgence; The Costs of Conflict* (coeditor); *The Domestic Bases of Grand Strategy* (translated into Chinese); and *The New Great Power Coalition* (editor). He is editor of *No More States? Globalization, Self-Determination, and Terrorism* (2006) and is completing a book titled *Mergers Among Nations,* to be published in 2009.

Tony Saich is the Daewoo Professor of International Affairs and director of the Harvard University Asia Center. He is faculty chair of the Asia Programs and the China Public Policy Program at the Kennedy School of Government, Harvard University. He also sits on the executive committees of the Fairbank Center and the University's Asia Center. From 1994 until July 1999 he was the representative for the China Office of the Ford Foundation. Prior to this he was the director of the Sinological Institute at Leiden University, the Netherlands. He has written several books on developments in China, including *China's Science Policy in the 80s* (1989); *Revolutionary Discourse in Mao's China* (1994, with David E. Apter); *The Rise to Power of the Chinese Communist Party* (1996); and *The Governance and Politics of China* (2004). He recently finished editing a book on reform of China's financial sector and on HIV/AIDS in China. He studied political science in the U.K. and has taught at universities in England, the Netherlands, and the United States.

Etel Solingen is professor of political science at the University of California–Irvine. She has been vice president of the International Studies Association (ISA) and president of its International Political Economy Section. She was awarded a MacArthur Foundation Research and Writing Award on Peace and

International Cooperation, a Social Science Research Council–MacArthur Foundation Fellowship on Peace and Security in a Changing World, and a Social Science Research Council Abe Fellowship, among others. Her most recent book, *Nuclear Logics: Contrasting Paths in East Asia and the Middle East* (Princeton University Press, 2007), is the recipient of the 2008 Woodrow Wilson Foundation Award for the best book on government, politics, or international affairs by the American Political Science Association, and of the 2008 APSA's Robert Jervis and Paul Schroeder Award for the best book on international history and politics. She is also the author of *Regional Orders at Century's Dawn: Global and Domestic Influences on Grand Strategy* (Princeton University Press, 1998); and other books and articles on international relations theory, international political economy, comparative regionalism, institutional theory, democratization, and economic reform.

Mingchun Sun is a senior economist at Nomura International in Hong Kong. He received his PhD in 2006 in management science from Stanford University. He was a senior economist at Lehman Brothers Asia in 2006–2008, a senior analyst at Capital One Financial in 2002–2004, and an economist at the Chinese University of Hong Kong as well as at China's State Administration of Foreign Exchange from 1993–1999.

C. H. Tung is vice chairman of the National Committee of the Chinese People's Political Consultative Conference, People's Republic of China and chairman of the China-United States Exchange Foundation. Prior to the vice chairman appointment he served as chief executive of the Hong Kong Special Administrative Region, People's Republic of China, from July 1997 to March 2005. He studied in Hong Kong and the United Kingdom, graduating from the University of Liverpool in 1960 with a degree of marine engineering. He was conferred the Honorary Doctorate of Laws, University of Liverpool; and Honorary Doctorate of Social Sciences, Hong Kong University of Science and Technology.

Ezra F. Vogel is Henry Ford II Professor of Social Sciences at Harvard, honorary director of the Program on U.S.-Japan Relations, and former director of Harvard's East Asia Research (now Fairbank) Center. He was the second chair of the Council for East Asia Center, the first director of the Harvard University Asia Center, and former director of the Program on U.S.-Japan Relations at the Center for International Affairs. Vogel holds a bachelor's degree from Ohio Wesleyan, a PhD from Harvard, and honorary degrees from a number of institutions, including Chinese University in Hong Kong. His most current books include *Japan as #1: Lessons for America and Four Little Dragons: The Spread of Industrialization in East Asia,* and *One Step Ahead in China: Guangdong Under Reform.*

Wang Jisi has been dean of Peking University's School of International Studies since March 2005. He is concurrently director of the Institute of International and Strategic Studies at the Party School of the Central Committee, the Communist Party of China; a guest professor of the National Defense University of the People's Liberation Army; vice chair of the China Reform Forum; and president of the Chinese Association for American Studies. He was director and a senior researcher of the Institute of American Studies at the Chinese Academy of Social Sciences in Beijing from 1993 to 2005. He is a founding member of the Pacific Council on International Policy in Los Angeles; an International Council Member of the Asia Society in New York City; an Advisory Council Member of the Center for Northeast Asian Policy Studies of the Brookings Institution in Washington, D.C.; an advisor to the East Asian Security Program of Stanford University; an international advisor to the Institute of Global Conflict and Cooperation, University of California; and an advisor to the Asia Center, Harvard University.

Xu Shiquang currently serves as president of the Institute of Taiwan Studies of the Academy of Social Sciences of China and is vice chairman of the National Society of Taiwan Studies of China. He did postgraduate work at the Institute of International Relations and served for twenty years as diplomatic correspondent for Xinhua News Agency and *Guangming Daily,* based in Dar es Salaam, Beirut, and London, then as bureau chief of the *People's Daily* at the United Nations. He was also director of the international department of the *People's Daily.* He has edited nearly a dozen books on Taiwan.

Yang Jiemian received his BA from the Shanghai Teachers' University, masters' degrees from the Shanghai Institute for International Studies (SIIS) and the Fletcher School of Law and Diplomacy, and a PhD from the Shanghai International Studies University. Currently he is senior fellow and president of the SIIS and a member of the Shanghai Committee of People's Political Consultative Conference. He is on the boards of China's Association for International Studies, the Chinese People Institute of Foreign Affairs, the National Association of China-U.S. Friendship, the Association of American Studies, the Shanghai Association of International Relations, and the Shanghai Association of Taiwan Studies, among others. He is also a guest professor/fellow at the PLA National Defense University, Fudan University, Shanghai International Studies University, and Tongji University.

Yu Keping is professor and director of the China Center for Comparative Politics & Economics (CCCPE), and also professor and director of the Center for Chinese Government Innovations, Peking University. His major fields include political philosophy, comparative politics, globalization, civil society, governance, and politics in China. Among his many books are *Emancipation of Mind and Political Progress* (2008), *Globalization and Changes in China's Governance* (2008), *The Institutional Environment of Civil Society in China* (2006), and *Democracy and Top* (2006).

Zhang Yunling is a professor and director of the Institute of Asia Pacific Studies, Chinese Academy of Social Sciences (CASS) as well as a member of the Foreign Relations Committee in the National Committee of Chinese People's Political Consultative Conference and chair of the Academic Committee for International Studies at CASS. He served as a member of the East Asian Vision Group (2000–2001), China-ASEAN Cooperation Official Expert Group (2001), and the Task Force of ASEM (2003–2004). Educated at Shandong University and the Graduate School of CASS, Zhang has been a visiting scholar at Harvard and Johns Hopkins University, visiting professor at the European University Institute, and senior visiting professor at the Massachusetts Institute of Technology. His major publications include *China-U.S.-Japan Relations in Transition* (1997), *International Environment for China in the Coming 10–15 Years* (2003), *East Asian Cooperation: Searching for an Integrated Approach* (2004), *State and Civil Society in the Context of Transition: Understanding Non-Traditional Security in East Asia* (2005), *Emerging Urban Poverty and Social Safety Net in East Asia* (2005), and *Emerging East Asian Regionalism: Trend and Response* (2005).

Zhou Hong is a professor of European politics and modern history and director of the Institute of European Studies at the Chinese Academy of Social Sciences (CASS). She is an elected member of the Academic Divisions of CASS and the elected deputy director of the Division of International Studies. She also is chair of the Chinese Association for European Studies. Her recent publications include *Donors in China* (2007), *Whither the Welfare State?* (2006), "Asymmetries and Symmetries in China-EU Partnership" (2004), *EU and American Models Compared (*edited 2003), and *Foreign Aid and International Relations* (edited 2002).

INDEX

Acheson, Dean, 7, 9–10
African Union (AU), 138, 143, 146
American Institute in Taiwan, 112
Angell, Norman, 44, 208
APEC. *See* Asia-Pacific Economic
 Cooperation
ARF. *See* ASEAN Regional Forum
Arms control
 Biological Weapons Convention,
  165, 169
 Chemical Weapons Convention
  (CWC), 165, 169
 China-U.S. disagreements regarding,
  174–175
 Comprehensive Test Ban Treaty
  (CTBT), 165, 169
 cooperation regarding, 163–167
 factors impeding cooperation, 172–175
 factors promoting cooperation,
  167–171
 the future of cooperation regarding,
  175–178
 nuclear nonproliferation treaty
  (*see* Treaty on the Nonproliferation
  of Nuclear Weapons)
 weapons of mass destruction
  (*see* Weapons of mass destruction)
ASEAN. *See* Association of South East
 Asian Nations
ASEAN Regional Forum (ARF), 140,
 189, 191–192
Asia-Pacific Economic Cooperation
 (APEC), 147, 183, 185–187

Asia-Pacific region, governance of. *See*
 Regional governance
Association of Relations Across the
 Taiwan Straits, 114–115
Association of South East Asian Nations
 (ASEAN)
 China's "charm offensive" and, 69, 77
 disputes in the South China Sea,
  code of conduct for peacefully
  settling, 149
 as a pioneer in East Asia regionalism,
  187–189
 regional cooperation and the birth
  of the charter of, 138
 security dimensions of, 192 (*see also*
  ASEAN Regional Forum)
Australia Group, 166
Authoritarian advantage theory, 72–73

Bali Action Plan, 134
Barnett, Thomas, 55
Belarus, 159
Bergsten, Fred, 186
Biological Weapons Convention,
 165, 169
Bismarck, Otto von, 33
Britain
 comparison of relations with Germany
  and the U.S. from the 1890s to
  World War I, 4, 11–14, 44
 the U.S., relations with, 4, 13–16,
  94, 199
Buck, Pearl, 9

Burma (Myanmar), 32
Bush, George W., 49, 113, 132–134, 141, 148, 172–173

Cao Gangchuan, 198
Carnegie Endowment for International Peace, 58
Carrefour, 90
Carter, Ashton B., 55, 57
Carter, Jimmy, 7, 10, 112
Center for International Development and Conflict Management, 73
Chamberlain, Joseph, 11–12
Chan, Charlie, 6, 9
Chemical Weapons Convention (CWC), 165, 169
Chen Shui-bian, 145
Chen Zhiya, 61–66
Chiang Ching-kuo, 113
Chiang Kai-shek, 110
Chiang Mai Initiative, 188
China
    diplomacy and international relations of (*see* International relations)
    economy of (*see* Economy, the)
    energy supply and natural resources of, 125–126
    global policies and status of (*see* Global governance; Globalization)
    historical position in Asia of, 23
    the middle class and status-quo politics, 88–89, 92
    nationalism and antiforeign sentiment in, 89–90
    Olympics, host of 2008 Summer, 26, 90
    political reform, pressures for, 90–92
    population and demographic challenges facing (*see* Population challenges)
    "soft power" of (*see* Soft power)
    the U.S., relations with (*see* China-U.S. relations)
    "World Factory" title earned by, 20
China, Peoples' Republic of. *See* China
China, Republic of. *See* Taiwan
China Foundation for International and Strategic Studies (CFISS), 54, 58
China Radio International, 26
China-U.S. relations
    Americans' interest in China, 3–6
    changes in China and, 79
    cooperation, challenges and opportunities for, 69–70
    crisis management and (*see* Crisis management)
    development of over time, 197–198
    diplomatic relations, establishment of, 108
    economic (*see* Economic relations)
    the future of (*see* Future of China-U.S. relations)
    issues confronting and the necessary adjustment of interests, 207–212
    military (*see* Military relations)
    Nationalist-Communist civil war, U.S. policy of nonintervention in, 9
    North Korea's nuclear weapons program and (*see* Korea, Democratic People's Republic of)
    political (*see* Political relations)
    "Prisoners' Dilemma" incentives and cooperation in, 201–203
    regional governance in the Asia-Pacific (*see* Regional governance)
    Taiwan (*see* Taiwan)
China-U.S. Track II Dialogue, 55
Chinese Investment Corporation (CIC), 39–40
Chu Shulong, 182, 184, 190
Churchill, Winston, 156
CIC. *See* Chinese Investment Corporation
Clean Air Act (U.S.), 126
Clemenceau, Georges, 13
Cleveland, Grover, 12
Clinton, Bill, 10, 113

Close Economic Partnership
Agreement, 187
CNN (Cable News Network), 90
Committee of One Million, 6
Comprehensive Test Ban Treaty
(CTBT), 165, 169, 176
Confucianism, 23
Confucius Institutes, 26
Coolidge, Calvin, 16
Corwin, Edward, 4
Council on Security Cooperation in the
Asia-Pacific (CSCAP), 189, 192
Crisis management
bilateral, 140–141
between China and the U.S. as step
toward global, 137, 151
conceptual changes about, 143–144
concrete changes in handling,
144–146
context of relations, changes in,
142–143
effective, need for improvements to
achieve, 149–150
multilateral, 141–142
necessity of for China's economic
goals, 155–157
North Korea with nuclear weapons an
example of failed cooperation,
157–161 (*see also* Korea,
Democratic Peoples' Republic of)
opportunities, realizing, 148–149,
150–151
points of disagreement regarding, 153
shared national interests, recognition
of, 154–155
strategic cooperation/vision and,
146–148, 157–161
Taiwan as example of successful, 157
See also Arms control
Crouching Tiger, Hidden Dragon, 26
Culture
Confucianism of Chinese, 23
global popular, 26
soft power and, 23, 25–26, 28–29

Declaration on the Conduct of Parties in
the South China Sea, 77
Democracy
economic conditions and transitions
to, 72–74
economic liberalization, international
relations, and, 70–72
internationalization and transitions
to, 199–200
nationalist war as risk of transitions
to, 74–75
nuclear nonproliferation
commitments and, 71
as political value in China and the
U.S., 96–100
public participation, shared interest in
increasing, 101–102
reliability of allies and, 76
Democratic efficiency theory, 73
Democratic peace theory, 70–72,
75–76, 199
Deng Xiaoping, 36, 58, 68, 96,
108–109, 112
Deutsch, Karl, 199
Dulles, John Foster, 7

East Asia, regionalism in, 187–189
East Asian Summit, 27
East Asian Vision Group, 188
Economic relations
Beijing Consensus *vs.* Washington
Consensus, relative appeal to
developing countries of, 26–27, 29
benign security relationship as
essential for, 155–157
China and the West, divergent tracks
of development after 1750, 35
commercial banking, interest of
foreign investors in, 42
East Asia regionalism and, 187–189
financial and trade imbalances,
38–40
foreign direct investment (FDI) in
and by China, 40–42, 44, 69, 73

Economic relations *(continued)*
  global governance and, collaboration
    regarding, 183
  interdependency of economies, 36,
    84–85, 197
  reciprocity in the longer term, 42–43
Economy, the
  changes in the international, 19–20
  China, excess liquidity built up in, 39
  China's place in a globalized
    production world, 36–37, 68–70
  Chinese demographic trends and,
    80–84
  Chinese performance over long-range
    history, 23, 35
  Chinese performance over recent
    decades, 23, 29, 36
  climate protection and, compatibility
    of, 127–132
  democratic transitions and, 73–74
  employment growth in China, 84
  globalization of *(see* Globalization;
    Internationalization)
  growth in energy consumption and
    greenhouse gas emissions,
    119–121, 124–125 *(see also*
    Energy; Global warming)
  growth rates and change in China,
    characteristics and concerns
    regarding, 84–88
  U.S. government deficit spending and
    monetary policy, 39
Einstein, Albert, 53
Eisenhower, Dwight D., 7
Energy
  China's demand for, benign security
    relationship required to meet,
    156–157
  consumption of and greenhouse gas
    emissions, 119–121 *(See also*
    Global warming)
  diversification, potential benefits of,
    130–131
  renewable, potential for, 129–130
  security, 127–129, 131

Energy Independence and Security Act
    of 2007 (U.S.), 131–132
Environment, the
  collaboration regarding, opportunity
    for, 194
  convergence of problems
    regarding, 201
  ecological governance, shared interest
    in, 102
  global warming *(see* Global warming)
  policies of China and the U.S.
    compared, 126
European Union (EU)
  arms embargo imposed on China,
    27–28
  crisis management as a concern
    of, 143
  greenhouse gas emissions, reduction
    in, 121
  steady expansion of, 19–20
  Taiwanese provocation, opposition
    to, 145

Family-planning policy, demographic
    distortions from China's,
    80–82
FDI. *See* Foreign direct investment
Ferdinand, Archduke Franz, 210
Fissile Material Cutoff Treaty
    (FMCT), 176
Foreign direct investment (FDI),
    40–42, 44, 69, 73
Foreign policy
  China honors commitments of,
    48–49
  Chinese multilateral diplomacy and
    promotion of international
    cooperation, 26–27
  definition of "policy" and examples
    of U.S., 8–9
  diplomacy through soft power, 32
    (see also Soft power)
  domestic politics and, 12, 14, 17
  politics of national defense spending
    and, 18

special relationships in (*see* Special
   relationships)
Taiwan as key issue in (*see* Taiwan)
"Transformational diplomacy," 30
U.S. struggle to formulate and pursue
   coherent China policy, 3–4, 6–11
See also International power
   realignments; International
   relations
Four Nos, 110, 190, 195
France, 90
Franklin, Benjamin, 4, 6
Funabashi, Yoichi, 170
Future of China-U.S. relations
   arms control, cooperation regarding,
      175–178
   capital mobility and economic
      openness in the global economy,
      42–43
   changes in the world environment
      relevant for, 19–21
   past international realignments as
      precedent for, 17–19
   peace and democracy, possibilities of,
      199–200
   possible scenarios of, 92–94, 203–205
   shared vision of the future, as resting
      on, 212
   Taiwan, hypothetical circumstances
      under which direct conflict could
      occur over, 116–117

G8, 139
Gallagher, Mary, 73
General Agreement on Tariffs and Trade
   (GATT), 19, 138
George, Yeo Yong Boon, 189
Germany
   Britain, relations with from the 1890s
      to World War I, 4, 11–14, 44
   the middle class in late
      nineteenth-century, 92
Global Alliance Against Nuclear
   Terrorism, 159–160
Global governance

China's position in, regional
   governance and, 180–182
collaboration of China and the U.S.
   on, 182–185, 194–195
Global warming
   climate protection and energy
      security/development goals,
      compatibility of, 127–132
   common concerns, differing paths
      regarding, 135–136
   economic characteristics and,
      124–125
   environmental policy and,
      comparison of, 126
   global governance collaboration
      regarding, potential for, 183
   greenhouse gas emissions, current and
      future levels of, 120–121
   greenhouse gas emissions and energy
      consumption, factors driving,
      121–127
   greenhouse gas emissions in
      China and the U.S., basic data
      and policy challenges regarding,
      119–120
   greenhouse gases, shared goal of
      reducing, 21
   joint action on climate change,
      cooperation on, 134–135
   joint action on climate change,
      disagreements regarding, 132–134
   natural resource endowments and,
      125–126
   population dynamics and, 122–124
   technological innovation and, 127
   See also Energy; Environment, the
Globalization
   China's commitment to, 68–69, 75
   crisis management and, 141 (*see also*
      Crisis management)
   government reform and innovation
      as part of a shared agenda for,
      100–101
   organization of the world economy,
      China and, 36–37

Globalization *(continued)*
    peaceful transition to, 138–139
    "trading states" and, 68–70
    See also Internationalization
Great power relationships, 11–18,
    211–212
Greenfield investments, 40–41
Greenhouse gases. *See* Global warming
Grey, Sir Edward, 13
Griswold, A. Whitney, 8–9
Guo Shuqing, 83

Haass, Richard, 55
Hara Kei, 16
Harding, Warren G., 14
Harte, Bret, 6
Hu Jintao, 28, 32, 97, 109–110,
    161, 190
Hu Xiulian, 121
Hughes, Charles Evans, 14–16
Human rights, 90–91, 95–96,
    98–99, 184
Hussain, Athar, 81

Ikenberry, G. John, 179
Immigrants, Chinese, 5–7
India, 148–149, 171
Institute of Energy Economics, Japan, 121
Intergovernmental Panel on Climate
    Change, 131
International Atomic Energy Agency
    (IAEA), 165, 169, 176
International Energy Agency, 121
International law, Chinese national
    law and, 48
International Monetary Fund (IMF),
    19, 138
International power realignments
    American-Chinese relationship and
        the possibilities for, 17–18
    Britain, Germany, and the U.S.
        at the end of the nineteenth
        century, 11–14
    crisis management as alternative to
        wars for (*see* Crisis management)

    learning from historical precedents,
        potential for, 11
    the U.S., Britain, and Japan in the
        1920s, 14–17
International relations
    arms control (*see* Arms control;
        Nuclear weapons; Weapons of mass
        destruction)
    authoritarian advantage theory,
        72–73
    balance between China and the U.S.
        in, 198–199
    benign security relationship with the
        U.S., Chinese need for, 155–157
    border dispute between China and
        the former Soviet Union, resolution
        of, 49
    China's New Security Concept,
        189–190, 195
    Chinese diplomacy, trends in, 26–27,
        77–78, 173–174
    Concert of Great Powers, potential
        for, 200–201
    crisis management (*see* Crisis
        management)
    democratic peace theory, 70–72,
        75–76, 199
    diplomatic relations established, 108
    East China Sea, territorial disputes
        in, 149
    force and sanctions, disagreements
        about use of, 173–174
    global governance (*see* Global
        governance)
    globalization and economic
        liberalization (*see* Globalization;
        Internationalization)
    hegemonic transition, 12–14
    new institutions and norms of, 19–21
    peaceful transition of the
        contemporary system, 137–139
    regional governance (*see* Regional
        governance)
    rise of China, relations with the U.S.
        and, 179–182

transitions to markets and
democracies, timing of and, 72–74
two approaches to understanding
the behavior of Great Powers in,
67–69
U.S. accommodation of China's
interests and growth, need for,
87–88, 89
war and peace, China and U.S.
perspectives on, 139–140
Internationalization
in China, political uncertainties of, 75
democratic peace and, 70–72
transitions to markets,
democratization and, 72–74
See also Globalization
Iran, 164, 171–174
Iraq War
criticism of the U.S. regarding,
138, 148
decline in America's soft power due to,
25–27
democracies and war, as outlier from
norms regarding, 76
dependency on purchase of U.S.
securities by other nations, 200

Japan
East Asian economic partnership
agreement proposed by, 188
East China Sea, territorial disputes
in, 149
economic ills of the 1990s in, 38
Taiwanese provocation, opposition
to, 145
U.S. relations during the 1920s,
14–16
U.S. support for China against, 8–9
Jiang Zemin, 88, 109, 184, 189
Joffe, Josef, 25
Johnson, Lyndon, 10
Joint Declaration on the Strategic
Partnership for Peace and
Prosperity, 77
Judd, Walter, 9–10

Kato Tomosaburo, 16
Katzenstein, Peter, 181
Kazakhstan, 159
Keating, Timothy, 198
Kelly, James, 115, 159
Kennan, George, 8
Kennedy, John F., 160
Keynes, John Maynard, 42
Khadafi, Moammar, 174
Khrushchev, Nikita, 210
Kim Jong Il, 158–160
Kindleberger, Charles, 6
Kissinger, Henry, 5, 10, 158, 204
Knowland, William F., 5
Korea, Democratic Peoples' Republic of
(North Korea)
differing Chinese and U.S.
relationships with, 164
nuclear weapons program of, 32,
76–77, 157–161, 170, 185
(*See also* Six-Party Talks)
Korea, Republic of (South Korea),
sterilization efforts and capital
flight in, 39
Kyoto Protocol, 119, 132–133

Lampton, David, 181
Lee Kuan Yew, 155
Lee Teng-hui, 107, 113
Lenovo, 40
Li Gun, 158
Li Zhizhong, 121
Liberalization of the economy.
See Internationalization
Lipset, Seymour Martin, 73
Lloyd George, David, 154
Lodge, Henry Cabot, 12

Machiavelli, Niccolo, 25
Manchurian Incident of 1931, 8
Mansfield, Edward, 74
Mansfield, Mike, 10
Mao Zedong, 46–47, 204
Marshall, George, 8–10
Masahiko, Kawai, 188

McDougall, Walter, 50
McKinley, William, 12
Mercosur, 138
Military relations
 Chinese perspective on American
  principles, 49–51
 Chinese perspective on Chinese
  principles, 46–49
 constructive cooperation and
  expanding, 58–60, 64–66, 198
 empathy as critical for, 51–54
 incidents in, 50–51
 the New Security Concept and,
  189–191
 power-based theories of international
  relations and, 67–68
 prudent hedging in, 61–63
 revolution in military affairs and,
  52–54
 shaping of, 54–58, 62
 significance of, 45–46, 55–56
 Taiwan as issue in, 56–57, 60, 63–64
  (*see also* Taiwan)
 war and peace, China and U.S.
  perspectives on, 139–140
 as weakest link/most dangerous aspect
  of current U.S.-China relationship,
  18, 56, 61
Missile Technology Control Regime
 (MTCR), 166, 177
Mitchell, Gordon, 50
Morgenthau, Hans, 25
Mundell-Fleming conditions, 42
Mutual Assured Destruction (MAD),
 nuclear deterrent concept, 211
Mutual Assured Destruction of
 Economy (MADE), economic
 deterrent concept, 210
Myers, Richard, 198

Nationalism, in China, 89–90
Natural resources, energy policy and,
 125–126
New Security Concept, 189–190, 195
Nixon, Richard, 10, 111, 140, 204

North Korea. *See* Korea, Democratic
 People's Republic of
Northeast Asia Peace and Security
 Mechanism, 77
NPT. *See* Treaty on the Nonproliferation
 of Nuclear Weapons
Nuclear Suppliers Group, 165–166, 169
Nuclear weapons
 Chinese cooperation with
  nonproliferation after the early
  1990s, 163–166
 Chinese noncooperation with
  nonproliferation before the early
  1990s, 163, 165
 the future of China-U.S. cooperation
  regarding, 175–178
 Iran and, concerns regarding, 164,
  171–174
 nonproliferation treaty (*see* Treaty on
  the Nonproliferation of Nuclear
  Weapons)
 North Korea and (*see* Korea,
  Democratic Peoples' Republic of)
 nuclear-weapons-free-zones, 71, 77
 terrorism and, 158–160
Nye, Joseph, 29

Olympics, summer 2008, 26, 90
One China principle/policy, 107–111,
 113–115, 117
"Open door" trade policy towards
 China, 7, 15

Pace, Peter, 198
Pakistan, 148–149, 171
Peoples' Republic of China.
 See China
Perry, William J., 55, 61–63
Plan of Action to Implement the
 Declaration on the Strategic
 Partnership for Peace and
 Prosperity, 77
Polanyi, Karl, 19
Policy, definition of, 8
Political relations

conflict over core values, significance
of, 91–92, 95–96

divergence of core values, 91, 97–100

regional governance, cooperation in
(*see* Regional governance)

shared core values, 96–97

shared interests, 100–103

Taiwan and (*see* Taiwan)

See also Democracy; International
relations

Population challenges

aging, dependency ratios and, 80–81

employment growth to match
population growth, 84

energy consumption, population
growth and, 119, 122–124

male-female ratio distortion by family
planning policy, 81–82

urban middle class, 88–89, 92

urbanization, 82–84, 123–124

Power

Chinese effort to combine hard and
soft, 33

definition and components of, 23–24

power as Herrschaft, 20

power as Macht, 20

power as Gewalt, 20

"smart," 33

soft (*see* Soft power)

See also Military relations

Prisoners' Dilemma, 201–203

Przeworski, Adam, 72

Qian Qichen, 189

Qualified Domestic Institutional
Investors (QDIIs), 40

Reagan, Ronald, 10, 113

Regional governance

the Asia-Pacific Economic
Cooperation, 147, 183, 185–187

the China-U.S. relationship and,
179–182, 185, 188–189,
191, 193–196

East Asia regionalism, 187–189

organizations and institutions in the
Asia-Pacific, impact of, 185

regional organizations in the
Asia-Pacific, 186

responsible power in, China as,
181–182

security and the ASEAN Regional
Forum, 191–192

security and the New Security
Concept, 189–191, 195

security and the Shanghai
Cooperation Organization,
192–194

Renewable Energy Law (China), 130

Revolution in military affairs (RMA),
52–54

Rice, Condoleeza, 30

RMA. *See* Revolution in military affairs

Roosevelt, Franklin Delano, 5, 9

Roosevelt, Theodore, 12–13, 17,
160–161

Rosecrance, Richard, 68, 182

Rudd, Kevin, 201

Rusk, Dean, 5

SCO. *See* Shanghai Cooperation
Organization

Shambaugh, David, 188

Shanghai Communiqué of 1972,
111, 113

Shanghai Cooperation Organization
(SCO), 138, 140, 143, 153, 182,
191, 192–194, 193

Singapore, 87

Six-Party Talks, 77, 142–143, 146, 157,
170, 185, 190, 195–196, 198

Snyder, Jack, 74

Soft power

Chinese, 23, 26–28, 33–34

Chinese and U.S., benefits in a non-
zero-sum game between, 33–34

Chinese and U.S., interactions
between, 30–33

Chinese discourse and views of their
own, 28–30

Soft power *(continued)*
 cultural *vs.* political factors as
  elements of, 29
 culture in, role of, 23, 25–26, 28–29
 description of, 24
 resources of, 24–26
 U.S., 25–27
South Africa, 159
South Korea. *See* Korea, Republic of
Southeast Asia Nuclear Weapons Free
  Zone Treaty, 77
Special relationships
 U.S.-Britain, 4, 13, 94
 U.S.-China, Americans' presumption
  of, 3
Straits Exchange Foundation, 114–115
Subsidiarity, 20
Sudan, 32
Summers, Lawrence, 183

Taft, William Howard, 7
Taiwan
 China-U.S. military relations and,
  56–57, 60, 63–64
 comparison of Chinese and American
  policies regarding, 114–117
 crisis management, as example of
  successful, 157
 Deng's Six Points, 108–109
 evolution of China's policy, 108–110
 evolution of U.S. policy, 110–114
 future of, 116–117
 Hu's Four Points or "4 Nevers," 110
 Jiang's Eight-Point Proposal, 109
 policies and interests regarding,
  significance of, 107–108
 secessionists in, Chinese military
  preparedness against, 47, 56
 separatists, China-U.S. cooperation in
  response to, 198
 Shanghai Communiqué, 111
 U.S. arms sales to, 112–113, 175
Taiwan Relations Act, 7, 64, 112, 114
Tang Shiping, 181, 191

Terrorism
 nuclear, 158–160
 as opportunity for collaboration
  in regional and global
  governance, 184
 shared opposition to the threat
  of, 21
 trends that will maintain the danger
  of, 65
Tibet, 8
Todd, Emmanual, 50
Torrey, Barbara, 81
Trading states, 68–70
"Transformational diplomacy," 30
Treaty of Amity and Cooperation, 77
Treaty on the Nonproliferation of
  Nuclear Weapons (NPT), 71, 158,
  163, 165, 169, 171, 175–176
Truman, Harry, 7, 111, 114
Twain, Mark (Samuel Clemens), 11

Ukraine, 159
United Nations (UN)
 arms transparency mechanism,
  Chinese participation in, 47
 Charter of as basic precondition in
  international affairs for China, 59
 creation of, 19
 Framework Convention on Climate
  Change, 119, 133
 High-Level Panel on Threat,
  Challenges, and Change, 158
 nonproliferation efforts of, 169
 peacekeeping operations of, China
  and U.S. contributions to, 27,
  45–46, 184
 Security Council, China and U.S. as
  permanent members of, 96
 Security Council as a platform for
  crisis management, 141
United States
 anti-Chinese discrimination in, 5–7
 Britain, relationship with, 4, 12–14,
  13, 94, 199